THE COMPLETE
BOOK OF
TAILORING

By Adele P. Margolis

HOW TO DESIGN YOUR OWN DRESS PATTERNS

PATTERN WISE

THE COMPLETE BOOK OF TAILORING

THE DRESSMAKING BOOK

HOW TO MAKE CLOTHES THAT FIT AND FLATTER

DESIGN YOUR OWN DRESS PATTERNS

FASHION SEWING FOR EVERYONE

THE COMPLETE BOOK OF TAILORING

Revised Edition

ADELE P. MARGOLIS

Illustrated by Judy Skoogfors

Doubleday & Company, Inc.
Garden City, New York   1978

Library of Congress Cataloging in Publication Data

Margolis, Adele P
  The complete book of tailoring.

  First ed. published in 1964 under title: The
complete book of tailoring for women who like to sew.
  1. Tailoring (Women's) I. Title.
TT519.5.M36   646.4'04
ISBN: 0-385-11106-1
Library of Congress Catalog Card Number 77–82959

Copyright © 1964, 1978 by Adele P. Margolis
All Rights Reserved
Printed in the United States of America

To my grandsons
JOHN and PETER FERNBERGER
to whom the first *Complete Book of Tailoring* was dedicated
and who "suit" me even better with every passing year

Suit Yourself

Fashions come and fashions go, but tailoring goes on forever. However you break it down into separates of every kind and description, or however you put it together in suits, coats, or ensembles, it's still tailoring.

Since "tailored" is a term applied to style as well as construction, the tailored style runs the gamut from the practically instant, one-layer, fusible-interfacing job to the REAL tailoring with its sculptured, many-layered, built-in shaping and its network of tiny hand stitches, all of which take time . . . time . . . time.

The former is great for achieving an effect with a minimum of work. It is a method for those who prefer speedy machine-made products to the admittedly slower hand finishing of fine craftsmanship. True, it produces a here-today, gone-tomorrow (not literally, of course) tailored garment. Since in the making one doesn't have time to develop an attachment for the garment, it is no great heartbreak to dispose of it after short-term wearing. It has its virtues! Not the least of these is that it is a relief to have something that doesn't take forever (though it only seems that way) to make.

A REAL tailored garment becomes a way of life in the making. The tailoring process builds so steadily, and the results are often so spectacular each step of the way, that one develops a real affection for the project in production. It has the long life expectancy of any work of art. This is the tailoring for those who still love well-constructed, expensive-looking, timeless clothes. Lots of work, but worth it!

a

Fig. 1

These, then, are the two parallel concepts of tailoring that today exist side by side: the contemporary and the classic.

Classic tailoring (Fig. 1a) starts with the fashion fabric and works in toward the figure with an understructure consisting of interfacings, underlinings, interlinings, linings, paddings, and weights. Considering what goes on underneath, its characteristic trimness is a miracle of construction.

Contemporary tailoring (Fig. 1b) starts with the figure and works out toward the outermost layer of clothing. Its casual, relaxed no-

b

shape results from the piling on of layer upon layer upon layer of single-thickness garments: cape over coat, jacket over sweater over blouse over skirt—as many layers as fashion dictates, the weather permits, or the wearer desires. Contemporary tailoring achieves its effect by abolishing the linings, facings, inner structure, often even the seam allowances and the hem. Such little shaping as it has depends on the shape of the wearer.

There are times when one wants the fun and freedom of the new tailoring and times when the occasion and the mood call for the classic.

A sewer has to be ready for both. Hence the dual tailoring techniques in the new COMPLETE BOOK OF TAILORING.

Take your choice—and enjoy, enjoy.

Philadelphia, Pennsylvania   ADELE POLLOCK MARGOLIS

Directions for Using This Book

This book may be used in large or small doses, in its entirety or in bits and pieces.

If you are new at tailoring, it would be wise to start at the beginning and proceed with your tailoring project step by step as you study the appropriate passage.

However, this procedure would be rough on the sewer who is impatient to get on with a garment that may be under way and who feels that all she needs is just a little help with a specific technique. Almost all confirmed sewers are in this class. There is always something "in the works." All one needs is a bit of information to complete that jacket or suit or coat that has been kicking around for some time. If this is your need, just turn to the relevant passage. Perhaps eventually you will be lured to read the parts that are not your immediate concern.

Here, then, is what is included in this book and where you will find the information you seek.

Contents

Suit Yourself   vii

PART I   TIPS FOR TAILORS

Chapter 1   Pick a Pattern   3
Choice of pattern—taking your measure—sizing yourself up
for tailoring

Chapter 2   Find the Fabric   13
Wool: the classic fabric for tailoring—other natural and
synthetic fibers used for tailoring—a few do's and don'ts in
choosing fabrics

Chapter 3   Pattern and Fabric Co-ordinated   20
Dart control: the system for shaping clothing—design built
into the pattern—design built into and applied to the
fabric—what happens when pattern design and fabric design
come together—meticulous matching

Chapter 4   Sewing Materials   47
All one needs to get started—pattern, fabric, trimmings,
findings

Chapter 5   Tools—a Tip-off on Technique   52
Equipment and tools for stitching, layout, measuring, cutting,
trimming, marking, and hand stitching—assorted helps—
pressing equipment—miscellaneous items

Chapter 6   Made to Measure   62
The flawless fit of tailoring—your measurements—the pattern
measurements—how to adjust the pattern for figure needs

Chapter 7   Testing, Testing! The Trial Muslin   89
What a trial muslin can do—materials for the test—putting
the muslin together—what to look for in the fitting—muslin to
pattern

PART II   CONVERTING CLOTH TO CLOTHING

*Chapter 8   The Character of Cloth and How to Utilize It in
Tailoring*   119
Fabrics hang with the grain—what to do about fabric when it
is cut, finished or printed off-grain—knit goods have grain,
too—how to prevent shrinkage: treating woolens, cottons,
linens, silks, synthetics

Chapter 9   Prepare the Pattern   130
Readying the pattern for cutting—duplicate pattern pieces can
be helpful—double thicknesses and the seams that join
them—allowances for turnbacks of collar, cuffs, lapels—seam
and hem allowances

Chapter 10   Layout Logic   136
The layout that comes with the pattern—how to work out
your own layout—standard pattern arrangements—special
fabrics, special layouts—matching stripes, plaids, checks, and
design motifs—trial layout

Chapter 11   Pinning, Cutting, Marking   157
Pinning the pattern to the fabric—a few words of advice about
the cutting—markings that need to be transferred to the
fabric—marking materials—pattern removal and fabric
protection—stay stitching

Chapter 12   The Shape of Fashion   170
Classic (structured tailoring) vs. contemporary (unstructured) tailoring—interfacings for "soft" tailoring—interfacings
for "hard" tailoring—interfacing the unlined jacket or coat—
total support: the underlining or backing—shaping and foundation fabrics—the interlining—the lining—shoulder rein-
forcements and pads—underlining, interfacing, and weighting
a hem

PART III   TAILORING TECHNIQUES

Chapter 13   And Sew a Fine Seam   207
How to stitch darts and seams in fashion fabric, in the
interfacing, in underlined garments—seams and darts in the
no-lining jacket or coat—how to join matching cross seams,
plaids, stripes, checks—variations on a seam—how to release
straining, eliminate rippling and bulk

Chapter 14   Special Fabrics—Special Handling   249
Knit or not: stitching fabrics with stretch—stitching short-pile
and deep-pile fabrics—stitching the phony furs and the pseudo
suedes—a hidden-construction method for two-faced fabrics

Chapter 15   Pressing Problems   260
How to press worsted, hard-surfaced, or firmly woven
woolens—how to press silks, cottons, linens, man-made
fibers—how to press naps, piles, fake furs, and simulated
suedes—contour pressing: tools and techniques used in
pressing for shape—other pressing problems: cuffs, welts,
flaps, bound buttonholes, bound pockets, pleats, fullness,
hems, zippered areas—pressing a skirt or pants—the final
pressing: before and after the lining insertion—right-side
touch-up

Chapter 16   Tricky Trio—Buttonhole, Pocket, Zipper   290
The standard zipper closing: regulation or slot-seam installation—how to set and stitch an exposed zipper and a separating zipper—the hidden-zipper closing—the fly-front zipper installation—the one-strip and two-strip methods of making bound buttonholes—hand-worked and machine-made buttonholes—precision closing: correct location and proper sewing on of buttons, snaps, hooks and eyes—patch pocket construction—the pocket set in a seam or slash, the bound pocket, the welt pocket, the flap pocket—fake flaps and would-be welts

PART IV   PUTTING IT ALL TOGETHER

Chapter 17   Sew the Shell   355
The first fitting—a plan for action: the unit method—how to join the fashion fabric and the understructure—the second fitting—stitching the construction seams

Chapter 18   Portrait Area—Set of Collar, Set of Sleeves   373
The collar and lapel: a unit—making the collar fit—collar contour: pad stitching, blocking—preparing the lapel—how to attach the collar to the garment—sleeve setting and stitching—propping up the sleeve cap

Chapter 19   Hemming Ways   406
Measuring and marking the hem—removing any fullness at the hem edge—the interfaced hem—the tailor's hem—the hem in an underlined garment—weighting the hem

Chapter 20   Classic Tailoring Is a Many-layered Thing   418
Lining, the last of the layers—made by machine, inserted by hand—how to handle the lining hem: the attached hem, the free-hanging hem—how to make and insert an interlining

Chapter 21   The Stripped-down, Unstructured, Unlined Tailoring   430
Some general suggestions on patterns and construction—the inside as decorative as the outside: decorative seams and darts—the fusible interfacings—short cuts

Chapter 22   Skirts and Slacks: A Snap   436
The anatomy of a waistband—correct placement vital—how to determine the length and width of the band—the stiffened-to-stand band—an easy way to attach the waistband: standard method, topstitched method—the inside waistband—suggested sequence for fitting skirts and pants—hints on pants construction

And Sew On   451
The artist signs the work

Index   453

Part I
TIPS FOR TAILORS

Chapter 1

Pick a Pattern

Which comes first—the pattern or the fabric? This is like that ancient question about which comes first, the chicken or the egg. The arguments are endless.

You have a hoarder's drawerful of beautiful, unusual, never-to-be-found-again (you think) fabrics. What sewer hasn't? This could be the year to make up one of those lengths. You start with the fabric.

A new fashion magazine arrives. You postpone whatever chores seemed pressing a moment ago and settle yourself for the search. Somewhere there must be a pattern for that perfectly handsome suit —or coat. The choice of fabric can come later.

Sometimes your ideas are built around a particular design; sometimes around a special fabric; sometimes (happy day!) both simultaneously. *That* jacket in *that* fabric.

Not because of bias in any direction but simply for purposes of discussion, let us start with the pattern.

PATTERN POSSIBILITIES

Unless you are a professional (but even some professionals wouldn't dream of doing this) or a genius, it's foolhardy to put scissors to cloth without using a pattern for any but the most shapeless of styles. Of course, there's the folklore of somebody's mother or aunt or little dressmaker around the corner (do they still exist?) who never used a pattern. But, by and large, the clothes looked it. It's conceivable that some gifted individuals could cut from mind's-eye patterns, yet one wonders if they would have used this cut-now, work-it-out-later system if there had been available to them then, as there are to us now, the variety and perfection of high-style commercial patterns.

With the large number of home sewers in this country, patterns have become big business. Since the competition is keen, all the pattern companies offer a large selection of styles designed to cover the many levels of sewing experience and a wide range of figure types and sizes.

All the pattern companies claim their patterns are easy to follow. For beginners, each has its special easy-to-make patterns. The advertising copy lures the beginning or impatient sewer with the prospect of having the garment practically make itself in no time at all.

There is much to be said for reaching a little beyond your experience, but you'll have less frustration and less struggle if you grade yourself as a sewer and choose the degree of pattern difficulty you can comfortably handle.

If tailoring is new to you, don't multiply your tailoring problems by choosing a complicated pattern. A safe rule to follow is this: the fewer the pattern pieces, the fewer the problems. A pattern that has thirty-two pieces is obviously going to be more difficult to put together than one that has twelve. Remember that the loveliest clothes are most often of simple design, beautiful fabric, fine fit, and exquisite workmanship.

Get the pattern you like even if it does cost a little more. The cost of the pattern is a very small item in the total cost of the garment. An extra dollar or two may make the difference between an ordinary design and a superb one. If you were buying your coat or suit, would an extra dollar or two discourage you from buying an original design or even a very good copy?

CHOOSING A PATTERN SIZE

Patterns must be sold in standard sizes, simply because this is the only practical way to deal with the problem of size for the millions of buyers. There's the rub! For practically no one is a true standard size. *Standard* describes a mythical figure. It is a statistic made up by averaging the measurements of groups of people, few or none of whom conform to standard in all measurements.

To accommodate the many variations within standard sizes, patterns and clothes are now cut for figure types as well. There is on the market a whole array of designs for Misses, Women's, Half-sizes, talls, shorts, full-bosomed, flat-chested, long-waisted, short-waisted, Juniors, Petites, and gradations in between. With luck, if one chooses the correct size and figure type, one will come close to one's personal measurements.

Of course, there are not all styles in all sizes and figure types. Each style is designed for specific sizes. What might look smashing on a size 8 could be a disaster in a size 14½.

One cannot assume that a ready-to-wear size is the size one should choose for a pattern. It is too variable. A size is anything a manufacturer and his staff decide it is from their experience and their success. While a set of commercial standards for ready-to-wear is issued by the Office of Commodity Standards, National Bureau of Standards, U. S. Department of Commerce, in practice the clothing industry never has adopted a uniform system of sizing. Who can blame it? Americans are great name buyers. A manufacturer who makes his fortune on a unique set of measurements that departs somewhat from the standard is hardly inclined to share the secrets of his success with his competitors.

There is this, too. An expensive size 8 may equal an inexpensive size 10 or even 12. The higher-priced firms sell flattery as well as merchandise. After all, you have to get a little something extra for all that money.

Home sewers, there is some comfort. The pattern industry *has adopted* a uniform system of sizing. Once you've determined your size and type, you can be fairly certain *that* size will fit regardless of whose pattern you are buying.

TAKE YOUR MEASURE

Some figure measurements are necessary to determine your figure type, your size, and the alterations you may initially want to make in the pattern. These are length and width measurements. The shaping had best wait for the trial muslin fitting.

You will need a tape measure, enough string to encircle your waist, and a little help from a friend. The best measurements are taken over a slip and/or bra and girdle. (if you wear them). Length measurements for figure type are taken without shoes. Pants length is best determined with shoes.

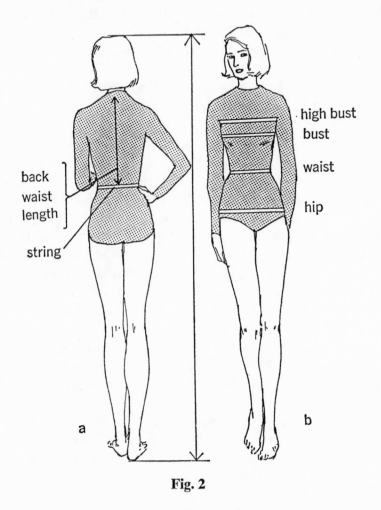

Fig. 2

Length Measurements

1. Measure your over-all height from the top of your head (not your hairdo) to the floor (Fig. 2a).

2. Tie a length of string around your waist.

3. Have someone measure your back waist length from socket bone to waistline string (Fig. 2a). (To locate your socket bone, bend your head forward. The socket bone is the prominent bone on which your head is hinged.)

Circumference Measurements

All circumference measurements are snug but not tight measurements (Fig. 2b).

1. Measure the high bust. Bring the tape around the body directly under the arms.

2. Measure the bust. Bring the tape measure around the body across the fullest part of the bust, slightly raised in back (Fig. 2b).

3. Measure the waist (in the hollow of the waist or where you would like the waistline to be—slightly above or slightly below the natural waistline).

4. Measure the hips around the fullest part.

Pants Measurements

Use the same waist and hip measurements. You will need some additional measurements.

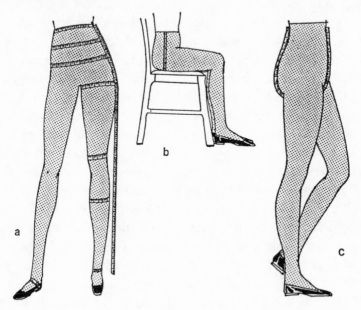

Fig. 3

1. Measure the *length* of the leg on the side seam from the waist-line to the top of the shoe heel (Fig. 3a).

2. The thigh measurement is taken at the fullest part of the upper leg (Fig. 3a). Note how far below the waistline you are taking this measurement.

3. For fitted styles, you may need the measurements for knee, calf, ankle, and instep (Fig. 3a).

4. To measure the crotch depth, sit on a hard chair. Measure the distance from the waistline to the chair (Fig. 3b).

5. Measure the full crotch length (not too tightly) from back waistline between the legs to front waistline (Fig. 3c).

SIZING YOURSELF UP

Armed with the set of your measurements, consult the Standard Measurement Chart that is found in all complete pattern catalogues. Study it until you locate a set of measurements most nearly like your own. If you are a rarity, you may match all four measurements (bust, waist, hips, back waist length) needed to determine your figure type and the size of all garments except pants. (Pants sizes are generally determined by hip measurement.) If you are lucky, perhaps you will match three of the four. If you are a borderline size—that is, somewhere between two sizes—choose the smaller and grade it up.

It is generally more advisable to make a pattern larger than smaller. Should the discrepancy between bodice and skirt measurements be very great—say, a difference of more than one size—it may be better to buy two patterns, one for your top and one for your bottom, altering both so they merge at the waistline. This would be particularly desirable if the design had considerable or intricate detail.

The crucial fitting area of any garment is the neck-shoulder-chest area. If a garment doesn't fit right here, it doesn't matter how perfectly it fits elsewhere. Waist and hips are comparatively easy to adjust. Therefore, for most women's figures, the upper figure measurements are the best guide for size—the bust, the shoulders, the chest.

SIZES FOR TAILORED GARMENTS

Buy the same size pattern for a jacket, a coat, a suit, or any garment designed to be worn over another that you would for a dress. All the necessary allowances are built right into the pattern.

Here are *two other ways* to help you determine your size. They are both advocated by experienced pattern salespeople.

METHOD I

If you are 5 feet 5 inches or under, choose a pattern one size smaller than your bust measurement would indicate. If you are tall or large-bosomed, choose the size indicated by the bust measurement. Always take into account your shoulder width. If you are broad-shouldered or square-shouldered, use the size indicated. If you are narrow-shouldered, you may do well with a smaller size.

METHOD II

If the difference between the high bust and the bust measurement is more than 2 inches, then use the high bust measurement *as if* it were the bust measurement and determine the pattern size from that. The high bust better reflects build than the bust measurement, which deals with a fleshy area. Make a bust alteration to fit.

Having gone to such trouble to determine it, insist on the correct pattern size. Stores that carry patterns stock only a few in each size. (A complete line in all sizes would take considerable storage space.) If your size is not on hand, order it.

It is frustrating to get all set to sew in an unexpected bit of free time only to discover that the pattern of your choice in your size is not available. The temptation is to take the pattern on hand and try to alter it. This is inviting trouble. It is not just a case of taking it in a little here or letting it out a pinch or two there. Every pattern piece needs corresponding grading[1] to keep the design in scale.

[1] Grading is the process of increasing or decreasing pattern size. The change is *gradual* rather than in one place, hence the term "grading." If you are a size 6 and the patterns you love generally start with size 8, or if you're size 16 and the patterns stop at size 14, you may want to investigate the system of pattern grading. Instructions for grading patterns will be found in *How to Make Clothes That Fit and Flatter* by Adele P. Margolis (Garden City, N.Y.: Doubleday & Company, 1969).

THAT EXTRA ADDED SOMETHING—EASE

Have you ever noticed that the clothes you most often reach for are those that are "easy" to wear? They let you do all the things one normally does in clothes without putting too much of a strain on you or them.

Sometimes it's the style that makes for the comfort (some fullness rather than tight fitting). Sometimes it's the fabric (like the movability of knits). In truth, most fabrics don't have sufficient "give" to permit body movements if fitted strictly in accordance with body measurements.

Next best to *moving with* a flexible fabric is *moving inside* an inflexible one. This room to move about in is called *ease*. The question of ease is a puzzling one to many sewers—understandably so, since it is a variable factor depending on the following:

1. *The fabric*
The more elastic the fabric, the less ease is necessary. The more rigid the fabric, the more ease is necessary.

Some fibers have more stretch than others. Except when used in knits, synthetic fibers tend to have less stretch than natural fibers. Some weaves have a tendency to make any fiber stiffer. For instance, firmly woven fabrics, like men's-wear suiting, have less give than loosely woven fabrics. The structure of the fabric makes a difference, too: knit fabrics have considerable more elasticity than woven fabrics.

2. *The function of the garment*
Active sportswear requires more ease than spectator clothes. Styles for relaxed moments can have as much ease as one may require for the relaxing, while show-off clothes can be fitted as tightly as the figure can stand the showing.

3. *The design of the garment*
Since fullness, or the lack of it, is so much a matter of style, it is the designer who determines the amount of it any given garment is to have over and above the basic amount of ease in the master pattern.

4. *You, yourself*

Some folk aren't comfortable unless they are wearing clothes at least two sizes larger than they really need, while others are never happy unless their clothes look as if they were two sizes too small for them.

Here is an easy way to tell how much ease you like in your clothes. Try on a favorite dress or skirt or jacket. Pinch out the excess fabric until the garment fits tight at chest, bust, waist, hips. Measure the amount of the "pinch." Add this amount to your body measurements.

5. *The pattern company*

The "staple" or block that most pattern companies use as a basis for all pattern-making is based on a set of standard body measurements issued by the Bureau of Standards. Even though they start with the same measurements, pattern companies have different policies in regard to ease. Some add a little more, some less. The amount is what the pattern producers considered appropriate for the size. (Some pattern companies will tell you what their policy is in regard to ease. That can be very helpful, since there are different amounts of ease provided for different sizes and different styles.)

The difference in the amount of ease added to body measurements accounts for the difference in the fit of patterns produced by the various pattern companies. This may explain why you prefer one above the others.

6. *The designer*

Then there is the amount of fullness the designer thinks right for the style.

What neither the designer nor the pattern company can possibly know is the material from which you've chosen to make your garment. Here *you* become the designer. (They do make good suggestions, which you will find on the back of the envelope.) And, of course, neither of them knows how you like to wear your clothes.

7. *Whether the garment is to be worn under or over another garment*

When it comes to jackets, capes, coats, and ensembles, it is difficult to predict the exact amount of ease. That depends on what the garment is to be worn over. For instance, if a jacket is meant to be worn over one layer (a blouse or a non-bulky sweater) it will have less ease than if it is to be worn over two layers (say, a blouse and sweater or a blouse and vest). When a coat is designed to be worn over a blouse and jacket, it will have more ease than one designed to be worn over a dress alone. If, in wearing, you depart from the planned co-ordinates, the outer garment will fit with more or less ease.

Compare the total amount of your body measurements plus ease with the measurements of your pattern, which already include the ease. Sometimes, even if your measurements differ slightly from the standard, the style and the ease will accommodate the difference. That is why you can often wear a smaller-size pattern than actual body measurements plus ease call for.

Should you decide that you want a little more or less ease than the pattern provides, you can add or subtract the amount you choose.

As you can see, size, style, and ease are so integrated that it sometimes takes a little experimenting to arrive at just the correct balance of the three. Your trial muslin will help you decide that.

Chapter 2

Find the Fabric

Any fabric can be tailored: not only the traditional woolens and worsteds, but the whole gamut of materials from the practical to the glamour fabrics!

WOOL: THE CLASSIC FABRIC FOR TAILORING

Of all the many fabrics currently available, wool is still *the* classic fabric for tailoring. Hard or soft, lightweight or heavy, smooth or rough, nothing beats it for holding a tailored shape. It is a versatile insulator, protecting against heat, cold, and dampness. The wool fibers are alive and resilient. The cores of the fibers have a great affinity for dyes, so that wool can be produced in many colors. Its strength and wearing quality are legendary.

As for the sewing, wool is perhaps the easiest fabric to handle. It doesn't slide or slither. It is easy to stitch. (Even the old sewing machines that have trouble stitching some of the new synthetics work like magic on wool.) It can be both eased and stretched. It can be pressed, pounded, steamed, and blocked to shape effectively.

There are two types of woolens: those called woolens and those called worsteds. These are classified one or the other according to the kind of fibers and the process of making them into yarns.

Woolens are woven from yarns of short, fuzzy, uncombed fibers that are twisted together loosely. They cross and intermingle, leaving protruding ends, making a bulky yarn with a soft, fuzzy, fluffy surface. The "country tweeds," fleece, flannel, chinchilla, bouclé, and mohair (among others) are made from such yarns. Since these are supple cloths, they are best used for styles with soft, easy lines.

Worsteds are woven from long fibers combed parallel before spinning, tightly twisted together to give a smooth, dense, compact, firm, hard surface. The weaves are distinctly visible in worsteds. In this group are the gabardines, serges, twills, sharkskins, coverts, Glen plaids, hound's-tooth checks, and other men's-wear fabrics. These are the fabrics of which the traditional tailored suits and coats are made.

Consider the relative merits of each with regard to your ability to handle the fabric.

	Woolens	*Worsteds*
1.	Look best when made up in easy, relaxed lines.	Make stunning strictly tailored suits.
2.	Show wear more readily than worsteds.	Can stand hard wear, though they have a tendency to get shiny.
3.	Porous surface makes them good insulators.	Firm, hard surface reduces their insulating quality.
4.	Stitching, both machine and hand, is hidden in the fuzzy surface.	Machine and hand stitching is clearly visible on the smooth surface.
5.	Press well generally; nap or pile woolens require special handling.	Respond well to pressing but require force for flattening seams and edges.
6.	Suitable for unpressed pleats and soft effects.	Hold sharp pleats and creases well.
7.	Comparatively easy to shrink out or ease in fullness.	More difficult to shrink out or ease in fullness.
8.	Can be shaped well but do not hold their shape without the assistance of interfacings and underlinings.	Can be shaped well and hold their shape with less interfacing.
9.	Muss easily.	Resist wrinkling.

OTHER NATURAL FIBERS USED FOR TAILORING

LINEN AND COTTON

Displaced for a while by the ubiquitous synthetic fibers, both linen and cotton are making a comeback as warm-weather favorites. The heavier weights of both make handsome suiting materials.

RAW SILK

A handsome, textured fabric that comes in both light and heavy weights, the latter best for tailoring.

SYNTHETIC FIBERS

There are so many fabrics of man-made fibers and so many new ones continually being developed that even people in the field have trouble keeping up with them. There is no doubt that chemically developed fibers have revolutionized the textile industry. These new fibers do things formerly only dreamed about. Chief among their virtues: they are wash-and-wear and crush-resistant (a boon to travelers). Desirable as they are, there is this to be considered: because of their non-breathability, they have poor insulating qualities, being warm in the summer and cold in the winter. Some of the synthetic fibers present problems in machine stitching, particularly in the older-model sewing machines.

When it comes to tailoring, fabrics of synthetic fibers cannot be pressed or blocked to shape as the natural fibers can, thereby losing some of the quality expected of a tailored garment. But they can be and are tailored to produce interesting jackets, skirts, and pants. Adapt the tailoring techniques to suit your fabric.

A FEW DO'S AND DON'TS IN CHOOSING FABRICS

There are sensible ways to choose fabrics, if you are sensible—or fainthearted. For instance, the following fabrics are easy to handle:

solid colors, medium weights, plain weaves, firmly woven, allover surface designs, two-way-design units, cottons, linens, and most woolens.

Somehow, despite their known difficulties, the hard-to-handle fabrics always seem the most appealing: stripes, plaids, checks, blocks; some woolens and many synthetic fibers; raised surfaces: looped, napped, fuzzy, furry; very stretchy, very loosely woven, very sheer, very heavy, *very* anything.

The first category (easy-to-handle fabrics) will present fewer problems. If, however, you have sufficient eagerness, determination, and patience to carry you over the rough spots, then DO choose a fabric from the second category (hard-to-handle fabrics) and learn to master it.

In either case, DO choose a fabric you love, to carry you through the hours of work and the discipline of sewing. There is this, too: if you don't enjoy the color and feel of the fabric while you are working on it, chances are you won't wear it when you have finished it—assuming you do.

DON'T compromise on the quality of the fabric. The same effort and labor go into inferior fabric as into good fabric. Most tailored garments require comparatively small yardages of fabric, so the saving is not that much. A few extra dollars per yard of fabric will reward you with a truly expensive-looking and long-lasting suit or coat or cape.

DON'T skimp. Get the yardage you need. A few extra inches may save you hours of time and effort in laying out and cutting your pattern. Not enough fabric may force you to change a design you love to something that doesn't have quite the flair of the original. Allow sufficient yardage for straightening the grain; sponging the fabric; altering the pattern; placing, spacing, and matching surface-design units, stripes, checks, plaids; and for the directional placement of naps, piles, design motifs, or bias cuts.

DON'T succumb to novelty fabrics unless: you can afford to indulge yourself in time as well as labor and money; they present a challenge to you; you will have a lot of fun making them up; or you must get the "whimsy" out of your system even if you have to give the garment away afterward!

There was a time when one would really have to search for handsome fabric. Now the chief problem is which of the many enticing yardages to choose and when to stop buying. Inexpensive as well as expensive lines offer a vast array of exciting colors, textures, and designs. It is almost impossible to make a bad choice. What one must aim for is an inspired choice.

SELECT A LINING

Another major fabric consideration is the lining. Perhaps you've always thought of a lining as a mere cover-up for the considerable internal workings of a tailored garment. Linings are like eyeglasses in the following respect: if they have to be, why not make them beautiful? Let them be seen and enjoyed. Why not add a splash of color, a dash of pattern, or a toasty-warm texture (Fig. 4)?

If the outer fabric is a solid color or has a solid-color effect, you have unlimited choice—colors that match, colors that blend, colors that contrast, prints, stripes, plaids, and weaves. If the outer fabric is elaborate in weave or has a printed surface, then your lining is best limited to a solid color.

If you are making a coat, consider the color of the dresses or suits over which it will be worn. (Remember that one coat can't go over everything.) Choose a color for the lining that picks up the color of the outer fabric and yet blends with the clothing over which it will be worn.

A coat with lining and dress that match or a suit with lining and blouse that match can make a costume out of what might otherwise be just another wardrobe item.

Lining is best when of some soft fabric that facilitates slipping the garment on and off. It is usually lighter in weight than the outer fabric. Soft or lightweight satin, satin-backed crepe, crepe, soft taffeta or peau de soie, surah, China silk, soft cottons—these all make fine linings. When stiff, heavy, quilted, or fur linings are used, the sleeve lining is usually made of some soft lining fabric.

With the perversity of all fashion, linings sometimes defy the rules. A silk coat with a wool lining can be useful as well as startling. Wool with a contrasting wool lining makes a snug as well as a beautiful coat.

Fig. 4

The lining should be opaque, so that it really covers the inner construction.

If the lining will show through a loosely woven outer fabric, choose one that matches in color. Or back the coat fabric with an opaque underlining; this will leave you free to choose any contrasting or figured lining.

Whatever you do about the lining, don't be timid about it. Let it, too, make a fashion statement.

Chapter 3

Pattern and Fabric Co-ordinated

It is not enough to choose a beautiful pattern and a beautiful fabric. They must be beautiful together. To co-ordinate the two, one must understand something about the built-in design of each.

The pattern is a blueprint that tells how the garment is to be laid out, cut, stitched, and assembled in order to create the design. It is a flat length of paper, as the fabric is a flat length of cloth.

By a shaping system called "dart control," the pattern indicates how that flat length of cloth is to be manipulated to fit a figure that has depth, height, and width, as well as a series of curves within its roughly cylindrical shape. Dart control is the basic structure of all flat patterns, whatever the design. It applies equally to women's, men's, girls', boys', and children's clothing. It applies to any kind of garment —to jackets, skirts, blouses, pants, capes, coats, dresses: whatever— and even to parts of a garment like sleeves, collars, and pockets. This is how it works.

DART CONTROL: THE SYSTEM FOR SHAPING

Say your hips measure 36 inches and your waist measures 26 inches. The skirt must fit at both waist and hips, despite the difference in measurements. You need some way of handling that 10-inch differential. One way is to shape the garment by darts (Fig. 5a). But dart control need not be a dart. It may be a seam as in the skirt illustration (Fig. 5b), pressed pleats (skirt of Fig. 5c), unpressed pleats

Fig. 5

(skirt of Fig. 5d), gathering (Fig. 5e)—even smocking (not likely in tailoring, but an alternative method). Any device is acceptable just so it provides enough cloth where the figure is larger and "takes it in" where the figure is smaller.

Wherever on the body there is a difference between two adjoining measurements (hips and waist, bust and waist, lower shoulder blades and waist, upper shoulder blades and shoulders) or wherever movement creates a bulge (as at the elbow), some form of shaping is necessary. This form of shaping is called dart control.

Dart control always represents a relationship. It is the difference between a larger measurement and a smaller adjoining one. The greater the difference, the greater the need for control and the larger the amount of control. The smaller the difference, the less need for control and the less amount of control. A figure that has 35½-inch hips and a 23½-inch waist (a 12-inch difference) needs more shaping (more control) than one with 34-inch hips and a 24½-inch waist (a 9½-inch difference). It is not whether a figure is short or tall, heavy or slim, that determines the amount of shaping it needs. It is the relationship between two adjoining measurements.

Columnar figures, however heavy, slim, short, or tall, *need less shaping* because there is less difference between adjoining measurements (Fig. 6a).

Hourglass figures, however heavy, slim, short, or tall, *need more shaping* because there is more difference between adjoining measurements (Fig. 6b).

Dart Control Is Placed Just Where It Is Needed

In the bodice, since the bust area needs the most shaping, the largest amount of control is placed in front. In the skirt, since the buttocks area needs more shaping, the largest amount of control is placed in the back. Note that shaping is also found on the side seams

Fig. 6

to conform with the tapering of the bodice and skirt toward the waistline (Fig. 7).

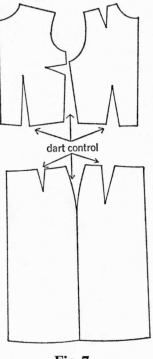

Fig. 7

Dart Control Can Be Divided

One large dart produces one large bulge. One small dart produces
one small bulge. To avoid or minimize a large bulge, the dart control
can be divided. The division may be on different seam lines (Fig.
8a), or on the same seam line, as in the pants illustration (Fig. 8b).

No Control

The relaxed, nonrestrictive, loosened shapes of contemporary design have dispensed with some or all of the shaping provided by dart

Fig. 8

control (Fig. 9): a boon for the flat young who really don't need it
and for the not-so-flat, not-so-young who are better off without it.
Wear the wrong bra or girdle and that painstakingly fitted shaping is
displaced!

Fig. 9

Pinwheel Patterns

The fascinating thing about dart control is that while the amount of
control remains constant, it may be shifted or divided so that it appears anywhere on bodice, skirt, or sleeve. There is only one rule: the
darts (and shaping seams) must originate at an outside seam and end
up at or pass over the crest of a figure curve. It's as if the high point

of the curve were the pivot of a pinwheel from which the control can be swung in any direction (Fig. 10).

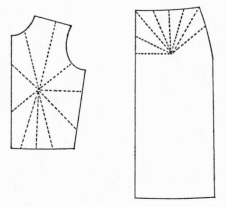

Fig. 10

DESIGN BUILT INTO THE PATTERN

A different position for a dart means a new design for a garment (Fig. 11).

The shaping is in no way altered by the position of the control. It doesn't make any difference whether the darts come from the center, sides, top, or bottom, or whether the pattern is for a dress, jacket, coat, skirt, or pants. The same rules apply; the same shaping results.

The easiest way to shape a garment is by darts and many fine patterns achieve their control on this simple level. To many a designer, however, a dart is an incomplete line going nowhere, which is very frustrating. For the designer uses *line* to express his ideas just as a painter uses color, or a musician the notes of a scale, or a writer words. So the artist-designer prefers lines for dividing the garment space into interesting shapes. Some designers are very clever at incor-

Fig. 11

porating the control in these interesting style lines, so clever that you may find it difficult to discern just where the shaping does occur (Fig. 12).[1]

Here is how you can tell. Place the pattern sections side by side, with the grain lines parallel to each other.

Do you see the darts that form on the seam line? They are the control (Fig. 13a). When the sections of the garment are joined, the control is hidden in the seam.

[1] Those interested in pursuing the subject of design by dart control will find a full discussion of the subject in *Design Your Own Dress Patterns* by Adele P. Margolis (Garden City, N.Y.: Doubleday & Company, 1971).

Fig. 12

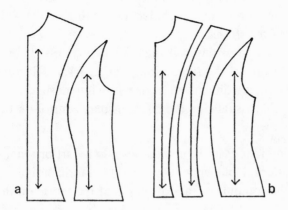

Fig. 13

Not all seam lines are control lines. Some are style lines just there for decorative effect (Fig. 13b). You can always tell which seam is a shaping seam by making the above test.

WHAT HAPPENS WHEN PATTERN DESIGN AND FABRIC DESIGN COME TOGETHER

When concentrating on design, the designer cannot at this stage complicate his or her work by considering what will happen to the fabric when the darts and seam lines are stitched up. That comes later when the fabric is chosen.

The sewer picks up the problem when she buys the fabric and the pattern. Now she is confronted not only by a *pattern that has a design* but by a *fabric that has its own design as well*. It's when these two separate design entities are put together that problems may develop.

Note what happens to a simple vertical waistline dart in various figured materials.

In Fig. 14a, the vertical dart is perfectly acceptable, for in no way does it disturb the plain-weave, solid-color fabric.

In Fig. 14b, the waistline dart cuts right into the design unit. What a pity! You bought the material because of that beautiful flower. Why destroy it?

Horizontal stripes are easily matched and balanced on the vertical dart (Fig. 14c).

Vertically striped material produces a chevron shape (Fig. 14d). This may or may not be objectionable, depending on the width, color, and location of the stripes.

A vertical dart in a diagonal material is hopeless. It produces an unsightly distortion of the fabric design (Fig. 14e). Diagonals, either woven or printed, are difficult to incorporate into design.

Having trouble visualizing the effect of dart control on fabric? Try one of the following:

1. In buying fabric, fold the material into a dart or seam similar to that of the pattern. Note what happens to the fabric design.

2. Trace the prominent lines or motifs of the fabric on the pattern. (Don't try to copy the whole design.) Pin the darts or seams closed. Note what happens to the fabric design.

Fig. 14

DESIGN BUILT INTO THE FABRIC

Alas! You cannot avoid the problem by sticking to solid-color materials. The design of such fabric may be in the way it is woven or knitted. While, in some cases, not nearly so obvious as with a printed surface, the problem remains. Here again, one must study the effect of the pattern design on the *built-in design of the weave or knit*.

THE BASIC WEAVES

A set of lengthwise yarns (warp) is placed side by side in a loom. A set of crosswise yarns (filler, weft, woof) is threaded over and under the warp yarns. In principle, weaving is the same today as when humans first began to weave cloth. The advances are mainly in the manner of lifting and separating groups of yarns so the filling yarn can be shot through with one motion of a shuttle. What was once a slow hand operation on a small loom is now mechanically and speedily done on a huge loom.

Since the warp yarns must bear the stress of lifting and lowering, they are pulled taut when set in the loom. Because they must bear the weight of the filler yarns, they are often of tougher and stronger yarn.

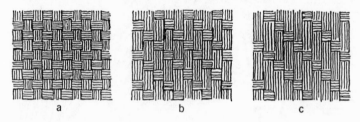

a   b   c

Fig. 15

The Plain Weave (Often Called the Linen Weave)

The simplest weave is the plain weave (Fig. 15a). Its most elementary form is an under-one, over-one design. It is *nondirectional* (two-way) and has no right or wrong side unless the fabric is finished in a special way. In a solid color it is the easiest weave to use. All style lines show to advantage. Pattern pieces may be locked into position like a giant jigsaw puzzle without any concern for which is up and which is down. Because it does not divert attention from any design applied to it, it is the weave most often used for printed fabrics.

In coating materials, variations in the plain weave are produced by using two or more adjacent warp yarns as one unit and an equal number of adjacent filling yarns as one unit, producing a thicker fabric.

The Twill Weave

In the twill weave (Fig. 15b) either the warp or the filler threads are interlaced in such a way that they progress one or more spaces to the right or to the left, up or down. The diagonal lines (wales) give an interesting design and texture to the surface.

Twill weaves are directional (one-way). They *do* have a right and wrong side. When the diagonal lines proceed from upper left to lower right on the right side, they will go from upper right to lower left on the wrong side. Twill weaves have no up and down except when they are napped.

Many suit and coat materials are made in the twill weave: gabardine, serge, covert, flannel, sharkskin, tweeds, herringbones. When the fabric is napped, the twill weave may not be visible but it is there just the same. Broadcloth, suede cloth, fleece, and velour are a few such fabrics.

When a twill weave is comparatively inconspicuous (as in some flannels) there is little problem in pattern selection, layout, and cutting. When the diagonal wales are obvious, the choice of pattern is limited; and layout and cutting, more complicated. In fact, many patterns are labeled "Not suitable for obvious diagonals." Better heed that advice or you may end up with wales mismatched at the seams and going in opposite directions at center front or center back of a collar. One could safely say that twill weaves present too many problems for beginning tailors.

The Satin Weave

The satin weave (Fig. 15c) is similar to the twill weave. The yarns interlace in a progression, too, but the intervals are longer. The ratio is anywhere from 4 to 1 to 7 to 1. Sometimes, in an attempt to avoid a twill effect, the yarns are held down in different places in each row.

Because the interlacing is minimal, yarns *float* on the surface of the cloth. Woolens woven in this weave produce a dramatic effect. The lengthwise floats of silk yarns produce a beautiful luster, as in satin cloth. In cotton fabrics, the crosswise floats produce a smooth cloth with lesser sheen: for example, polished cotton and sateen.

Whether wool, silk, or cotton, the long floats of satin-weave fabrics bruise easily. The floats may catch and break. Pressing is perilous. In the silks and cottons, pins and needles leave holes when they are removed, making corrections and alterations almost impossible.

For satin-weave fabrics, a directional (one-way) layout of pattern pieces is essential for uniform color throughout the garment. This is because the direction of the light affects the color of the satin weave. It is one color going up, another going down.

Unless you are pretty sure of yourself as a sewer, don't attempt the satin weaves.

VARIATIONS ON A THEME

From these three basic schemes for producing cloth it is possible to achieve an endless variety by using:

1. Different kinds of yarns—strong as in coatings, fragile as in chiffon, random thick-and-thin as in raw silk, crinkled as in worsted, looped as in bouclé, slubbed as in shantung, and so on.

2. Heavy yarns in one direction, lightweight yarns in the other. This produces a ribbed effect, either lengthwise, crosswise, or diagonally, as in grosgrain, faille, bengaline, ottoman.

3. Paired or multiple threads for a loosely woven, soft fabric like basket weave, monk's cloth, or hop sacking.

4. Combinations of fibers like silk and wool, linen and wool, wool and synthetics, and other blends.

5. Different colors for warp and filler yarns, either random or organized, as in tweeds.

6. Yarns woven at right angles to the surface of the cloth to produce a pile, as in velvet and velveteen, or to join double thicknesses, as in a two-faced reversible fabric.

7. Novelty processes. Crepe and seersuckers are examples of this. Tightly twisted and/or plain yarns are shrunk to produce a crinkled effect.

These are but a few of the many variations—limitless, it seems—that create the fabrics we love.

MORE COMPLEX WEAVES

The variations in the simple weaves may produce a complex effect, but there are several weaves that really are more complex by virtue of their structure.

The *leno weave* produces lacy fabrics. In this weave, the warp yarns are twisted around the filling yarns, often in a figure eight (Fig. 16a).

The *Jacquard weave* produces some of the most intricate and most beautiful fabrics—the brocades, the damasks, and the tapestries (Fig. 16b). Such cloth is woven on a loom that has a computerized control of each yarn (these may be in the hundreds).

Dobby weaves are produced on a loom similar to the Jacquard but far less complicated. Bird's-eye piqué is an example of this weave (Fig. 16c).

KNITS FOR TAILORING

They started as sweaters and graduated into dresses. Now they achieve new stature as suits and coats. Whether unstructured (to preserve their movability and shape-without-stitching) or as fully structured as any woven fabric (for a classic appearance), they lend themselves well to the tailoring process.

Whereas woven cloth is made by interlacing horizontal and vertical

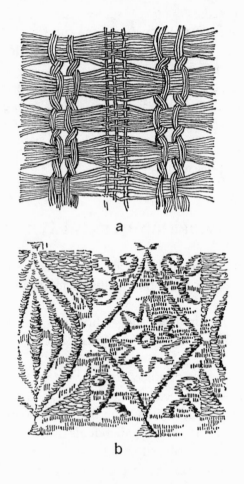

a

b

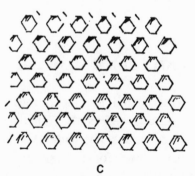

c

Fig. 16

yarns, knitted fabric is made by intermeshing a series of continuous rows of loops in such a way that each loop interlocks with the preceding loop. A vertical series of loops is called a *wale;* a horizontal series of loops is called a *course.*

The fact that loops can straighten out when stretched and return to loops when released gives knits their great elasticity and flexibility.

Two stitches, *knit* (Fig. 17a) and *purl* (Fig. 17b), are the basis of knit construction. Of course you recognize them from all the sweaters you've ever worn or made.

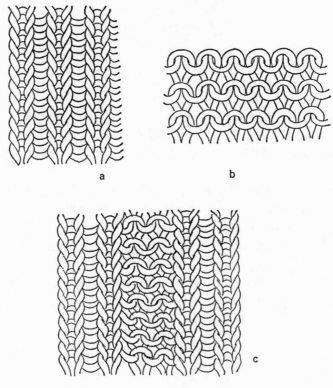

Fig. 17

Alternating knit and purl stitches in the same row can produce a ribbed effect (Fig. 17c) that provides an excellent, snug fit. An intriguing variety of designs can be created from just these two stitches.

Filling Knits

In knitting, when the yarn runs horizontally across the fabric in a series of loops (Fig. 18a), it is called a filling knit (Fig. 18b).

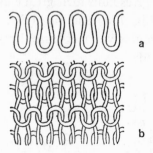

Fig. 18

The crosswise yarns are interlocked in a chain of stitches. When a link (loop) in the chain breaks, the fabric "runs" or "ladders." This is what happens to filling-knit stockings. Care is required in cutting filling knits.

Filling knits are usually made on circular machines, producing a tubular cloth. Jersey is a well-known, much-worn filling knit.

Double knits are filling knits made on a rib knitting machine. Because of their body, the double knits are the best knits to use for tailoring.

Two sets of needles cast off stitches in opposite directions so they interlock. This produces a heavier cloth that looks alike on both sides. It is knitted flat, like woven cloth.

Warp Knits

When the loops run vertically, the fabric is a warp knit. In warp knits, the yarn follows a zigzag path and forms a loop at each change of direction (Fig. 19a). These loops interlock with other loops formed by adjoining warp yarns following a similar zigzag path (Fig. 19b).

Fabrics of warp knits aren't as sheer as the filling knits but they are much stronger (mesh stockings are an example of a warp knit). Because they don't run or snag, they are easier to cut.

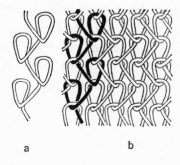

a   b

Fig. 19

Tricot is a warp knit often used in lingerie and as a backing for laminated fabrics. You'll recognize it by the crosswise rib on the wrong side.

Raschel knits are warp knits that have a lacy appearance. They resemble the leno weave in that a yarn (in this case a chain or series of loops) holds the openwork in place.

Sliver Knitting

Fake furs are made by the sliver knitting process. This is a knit-pile construction, just as velvet is a woven-pile construction.

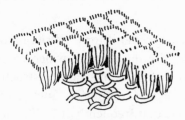

Fig. 20

Sliver knitting produces both the plain jersey backing and the pile at the same time. Bunches of loose fibers are locked in place by the looping action of the backing yarn over the knitting needle (Fig. 20).

Like woven materials, knitted fabrics are produced in great variety. This is achieved by using different fibers, different yarns, a variety of patterns, a variety of colors, ingenious and intricate methods of interlocking, and combinations of any of these.

Most knits are used on the vertical grain since they stretch more in a crosswise or diagonal direction. For this reason, it is a good idea to avoid crosswise or diagonal seams and flared or circular skirts. A good rule for the selection of a pattern for a knit is: the fewer the seams the better, and those preferably on the vertical grain.

DESIGN APPLIED TO FABRIC

Long ago some primitive fabric designer discovered that if one repeated a single motif over and over again in a planned, formal, regular pattern, one could cover a large area in a rhythmic and harmonious design. Fabric designers have been doing this ever since.

In every fabric with an over-all design, whether woven or knitted or superimposed by printing, there is a place where the single design motif starts all over again. This is known as a *repeat*.

METICULOUS MATCHING

When an artist creates a motif for a fabric, he or she must also devise some way to disguise the point at which each repeat begins and ends. The trick is to make the mechanical structure indiscernible so that the flow of the design is continuous. Some textile designers are so clever and so ingenious that frequently it is difficult to find the joining or to tell where the repeat begins and ends. But discover this you must, for the repeats must be matched in order to preserve the continuity of the fabric design in your garment. The only exception to this would be a fabric of very small motifs in an over-all coverage (Fig. 21) where the disturbance caused by the darts and seams is minimal.

Watch for the movement of the fabric design. Turn the fabric around to determine whether there is a difference in direction up and down or from side to side.

Fig. 21

Directional fabrics require more yardage, since all the pattern pieces must be placed so that they go in one direction. Nondirectional fabrics are more economical, since the pattern pieces can be dovetailed in any direction.

The ultimate in careful and sensitive cutting are the illustrations in Fig. 22.

Fig. 22

The flowers on the right and left fronts of Fig. 22a are so matched that, when buttoned, the entire front forms the complete floral unit.

The flower motifs of Fig. 22b are so placed that there is no break in the over-all design despite the fact that part of a flower falls on the closing extension and the other part on the left front, or part on a flap and part on the jacket. The sleeves have been so cut that the spacing of flower motifs has been observed.

Whether printed, woven, or knit, all stripes, plaids, blocks, and checks must be matched.

Fig. 23

The matching of blocks is not only horizontal at the construction seams but vertical as well. The blocks on the pants begin where the jacket leaves off. The vertical line of the block follows from shoulder to ankle. Note how the patch pocket and flap have been so carefully positioned that they continue the fabric design both horizontally and vertically (Fig. 23a).

In a two-piece ensemble, the matching must be both top to toe and under and over (Fig. 23b).

Sometimes, in an effort to dodge the intricate matching, part of a garment is cut on the bias. The collar and sleeve band of this design have been so cut. Happily, the bias cut, with its change of direction of stripes, also contributes to the design interest (Fig. 23c).

Every part of a garment that joins or overlaps another part must match or complete the unit. This rule applies to the major sections and to the smaller parts: the undercollar must match the upper collar; the facing must match the edges to be faced; the pockets, buttonholes, and belts must match the areas in which they are located.

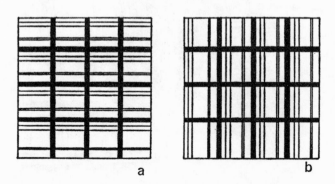

a   b

Fig. 24

There is work enough in matching the units of a nondirectional design, be it stripes, plaids, or other motifs. Matching a directional design is a bit more complex. The one-way movement of the design may be up and down (Fig. 24a) or right and left (Fig. 24b).

MISMATCH OR MISHMASH

One of the hallmarks of fine custom-made clothing or of expensive ready-to-wear is this meticulous matching of stripes, plaids, or motifs.

However, with the charming perversity that makes fashion so intriguing, along comes a vogue for mismatching (Fig. 25).

Fig. 25

If the theme of the style or the fabric design is playful, syncopated, then not only can a mismatch be consistent with the design intent, it can actually enhance it.

If the theme of the style or fabric is orderly, then mismatching only produces a mishmash.

Whatever else it looks, mismatching must look as if it was done on purpose with design a forethought—never as if one didn't know any better.

MORE YARDAGE NEEDED

It's elementary! To match design units you need more material than when a fabric is a solid color. How much more depends on the size of the repeat, the movement of line and color, and the number of pattern sections that need matching.

If the repeats are small, less material is needed than if they are large. If the fabric design is directional (one-way), more material is needed than if it is nondirectional (two-way). If only two lengths need matching, less material is needed than if half a dozen lengths need matching.

This has been but a brief discussion of pattern and fabric construction. *Construction can be an important clue to use.*

Chapter 4

Sewing Materials

The time has come to assemble everything you will need—pattern, material, findings, equipment—to produce your tailored garment.

THINGS TO THINK ABOUT BEFORE YOU BUY YOUR PATTERN

1. Choose simple patterns in the beginning. The designer patterns are for more advanced sewers.

2. The fewer the pattern pieces, the fewer the problems.

3. Choose an incoming style rather than one that has already seen the peak of its popularity. This should give you years of fashionable wear—a legitimate expectation for a tailored garment.

4. The shaping of your garment is accomplished by the darts and seams. From the standpoint of fit, a control seam or a combination of darts is better than a single dart.

5. The darts and seams should be consistent with the fabric used. Solid colors in medium-weight fabrics with a smooth surface make the choice of pattern limitless. All seams, darts, and details are clearly visible, with no distortion of the surface design of the fabric. They may be curved, vertical, horizontal, or diagonal.

6. Style lines and darts are lost in rough-textured, napped, or nubby fabrics. Painstaking work and intricate seaming won't even show. Save yourself the time. Choose a pattern with simple lines.

7. When plaids, checks, or stripes are used, choose straight rather than curved style lines; choose a design with either horizontal or vertical darts that can be balanced on the straight lines of the fabric design.

8. If you are big-hipped, don't select styles that have sleeves, jackets, belts, or other details that end at the hipline.

9. If you have a thick rib cage, a thickening waistline, or a protruding abdomen, hide them under an overblouse. Don't expose them with a tuck-in blouse.

10. Kimono sleeves or dropped-shoulder styles are by nature bulky. They appear even bulkier in wool, especially heavy wool. This can be a disastrous choice, particularly in a jacket, when the wearer's figure is short and heavy.

THINGS TO THINK ABOUT BEFORE
YOU BUY YOUR FABRIC

1. Solid colors permit unlimited pattern selection.

2. Light, bright colors; shiny and raised surfaces; hard and stiff fabrics; elaborately figured fabrics; bulky, nubby, looped fabrics—all make your figure appear heavier.

3. Contrasting colors for jacket and skirt make your figure appear shorter.

4. For beginners, woolens are easier to handle than worsteds.

5. Fabric that is too anything—too sheer, too heavy, too bulky— is harder to handle than medium-weight wool.

6. Plaids, stripes, checks, and some design motifs require matching. Be sure to buy sufficient yardage, depending on the size and direction of the repeat and how many seams have to be matched.

7. Naps, piles, and one-way-design motifs require pattern layout with all pattern pieces going in the same direction (neck to hem). Buy sufficient fabric.

8. Allow enough fabric to take care of straightening the grain, sponging or shrinking when necessary, alterations to the pattern, matching, and directional cutting.

9. Sharp pleats require firm, close weaves; unpressed pleats are better in soft fabrics.

10. Soft, limp, or stretchy fabrics must be completely underlined for strictly tailored garments.

11. It is easier to set the sleeve cap in soft, loosely woven wool than in hard, stiff, or closely woven materials.

12. Hard-to-stitch fabrics include ribbed fabrics like ottoman; heavy coatings; nap or fleece fabrics; corduroy or velveteen, which "creep" in stitching; and some of the new synthetics, like polyesters and Qiana, unless you have one of the newer model machines that are built to take the new fabrics.

13. If the garment is to be *structured,* the choice of fabric is almost limitless, since the understructure can supply what the material lacks by way of firmness. If the garment is to be *unstructured,* then the fabric itself must have enough body to sustain the lines of the design.

MORE THINGS TO THINK ABOUT

Over and above the special findings for a particular design (zippers, snaps, hooks and eyes, binding, grosgrain ribbon, tailor's tape, and so on, you will also need to give some preliminary thought to the items both visible and invisible that are so essential to the success of the garment.

What You Do See: What you see right off along with the fashion fabric are the BUTTONS. There they sit right out front. They can make or break a design. They should not be treated as an afterthought or a necessary evil. They must be planned for, co-ordinated with the fabric, and carefully selected for size. While *there is no rule as to the kind of button to use, there is a rule as to the correct button size.*

When a garment is buttoned, its two sides must overlap each other for a secure closing. The overlap is an extension of the material beyond the closing line toward the outer edge. There is a rule governing this width: the width of the extension equals the width of the button to be used (Fig. 26a). When the garment is buttoned, there should be half a button's width between the rim of the button and the finished edge of the garment (Fig. 26b). In addition to a good overlap, this bit of mathematics ensures a proper setting for the button.

You may use a slightly smaller button in the same space, but rarely a larger one. Should you be tempted to do so, make sure that the rim of the button never comes closer than ½ inch to the finished edge of the garment (Fig. 26c).

This rule applies wherever buttons are used on the garment—sleeves, collars, cuffs, pockets, skirt bands, and so forth.

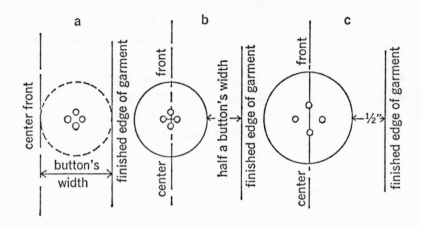

Fig. 26

For most home sewers, it is better to use the size of button indicated on the pattern than to attempt to make pattern changes on the opening extension (unless, of course, you know pattern making). Such changes may involve the width of the lapel, the size of the collar in relation to it, and/or other style details.

Gone are the days of standard bone buttons for strictly tailored coats or jackets. Use what pleases your fancy or carries out the design idea you have in mind: wood or metal buttons, pearl or rhinestone buttons, jeweled buttons, self-covered buttons. Whether you use new buttons or old, modest ones or conspicuous, just remember they are a prominent and important feature (often the only one) of the design. Caution: When it comes to color, "near 'ems don't count." It is better to have a contrasting color or texture than one that doesn't quite match.

What You Don't See: When it comes to making a tailored garment, what you don't see can hurt you. If the *understructure* and the *thread* are not right for the style and the fabric, the lines of the design may collapse and the stitching that holds all together may come apart.

In a classic tailored garment, the understructure is so vital a part of the construction that the subject is dealt with at length in Chapter 12. Read the whole "inside story" before you decide which shaping materials will be best for your purpose.

HANGING BY A THREAD

Because your garment is literally held together by a thread, it is very important that it be the right thread for the fabric. Ideally, the thread should be of the same fiber as the fabric so that it has the same tensile strength and elasticity. Use cotton thread for cotton fabrics; they are both vegetable fibers. Use synthetic thread for synthetic fibers; they are both artificial fibers. Use silk thread for silk or wool fabrics; they are both animal fibers.

In tailoring wool, use silk thread for all construction seams; it provides the necessary strength to hold the seams together for the life of the garment. Use mercerized cotton thread for all handwork. Its dull finish blends with the dull, dry finish of most woolens, particularly in places where the stitching may be visible.

If silk thread in a matching color is hard to find (it grows increasingly more so), use a good grade of mercerized cotton thread instead. In fact, you are safer with cotton thread for all sewing, since the synthetic fibers do not work well (skip stitches) on many home sewing machines.

Because thread works up a bit lighter than it appears on the spool, it is generally better to select a color which is just a shade darker than the fabric. However, if light striking the fabric produces a sheen and makes the color appear lighter (as in satin fabrics), select a color of thread a shade lighter than the fabric.

Chapter 5

Tools — a Tip-off on Technique

Most home sewers are in awe of the tailored perfection of professional custom-made clothing. However does it get that way? Well, one of the ways it gets that way is by the use of specially designed equipment for every operation that goes into producing that tailored look.

Fortunately for home sewers, custom tailoring came before mass production and the tools still used by fine tailors the world over are available for home sewers, too. Factory machinery is not necessary. It is true that factories can get some effects that home sewers can't—particularly when it comes to pressing. Home tailoring equipment can nevertheless produce a reasonable facsimile.

Somewhere in that vast pile of fabrics, trimmings, supplies, gadgets, and dressmaking equipment that all sewers seem to accumulate is a good deal that can also be used for tailoring. There are, however, some tools used specifically for tailoring that may be new to you. These can be purchased at a tailoring or dressmaker's supply store, a department store, or one of the numerous fabric chain stores or mail order houses.

Some of the tools can be made by you or by any willing friend or relative to the dimensions provided in Fig. 28.

Whether the tailoring is classic or contemporary, the following equipment is essential.

FOR STITCHING

Tailoring requires only a simple, *straight-stitching sewing machine in good working order*. It need not be the newest or most complicated model. That is not to say the newer machines are not fun to have. From the standpoint of tailoring, it's not the fancy stitches that make them so appealing. (The only really useful one is the zigzag stitch.) It's their more powerful motors that make it possible to stitch all types of fabrics more effectively.

FOR LAYOUT

A *good cutting surface* that is flat, firm, and large enough to take the wide woolen fabric is needed. A dining room table (protected, of course), a folding table, a cutting board—any of these will do. If you have no other suitable surface, a floor will do. (A bed will not do; it is not firm enough.)

FOR MEASURING

A *tape measure* of the sturdy, nonstretchable type.

A *yardstick;* a 12-inch or 18-inch *ruler;* a *gauge.*

A *skirt marker:* the most accurate is an adjustable ruler mounted on a stand and one that uses pins rather than chalk for the marking.

A *tailor's square* (L square) can also double as a skirt hem marker, though its chief use is for determining grain and for making pattern alterations.

Pins: No. 16 Dressmakers' pins are an all-around good size. For heavier materials, use Nos. 17 or 20. For very heavy materials use T pins (upholsterer's pins).

FOR CUTTING AND TRIMMING

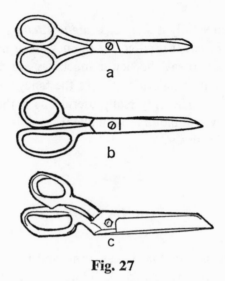

Fig. 27

A pair of *trimming scissors* for the considerable slashing, snipping, grading, and trimming (Fig. 27a).

A pair of *7-inch shears* for general use (Fig. 27b).

For cutting woolens, use a pair of *bent-handled tailor's shears* (Fig. 27c). The bottom blade of such shears slides along the cutting surface so that the material is not lifted for the strike, thereby ensuring more accurate cutting.

A pair of *scissors* specially reserved for the cutting and patching of paper patterns.

Very helpful are the new *saw-toothed scissors and shears* designed to cut fabrics of synthetic fibers.

Needless to say, points and edges of all scissors and shears are kept sharp and ready for action. Be selfish! Keep them with your sewing equipment. Don't permit them to get absorbed into general household usage that may blunt the cutting edges.

FOR MARKING

Marking materials are used for transferring the pattern markings or needed adjustments to the fabric.

Tailor's chalk in assorted colors: the chalky kind is preferable to the waxy kind since it can be used on all fabrics, including synthetics. Be sure to get chalk that can be brushed off or ironed out.

Dressmaker's carbon paper (a carbon designed especially for fabrics that comes in assorted sizes and colors) and a *tracing wheel* make excellent markings on fabrics that can take them.

Basting thread in assorted colors can be used for right-side markings and for fabrics on which other marking devices will not show. Use prewaxed cotton thread or silk thread—the latter a luxury, to be sure, but excellent on fabrics that may be marred by heavier thread.

FOR HAND STITCHING

Needles: Though Sharps and Betweens are the regulation needles used for tailoring, crewel (embroidery) needles are perhaps easier to use. Crewel needles are like the Sharps in length but have the added virtue of long eyes for easy threading. No. 8 Crewel needles, with their sharp points, are fine for the considerable hand sewing in tailoring. The larger No. 7 Crewel needle is used for heavier fabrics. The smaller No. 10 is excellent for finer fabrics, the silks, and other lining materials.

Thimble: You may get away with not using a thimble for your dressmaking projects, but the firmer, heavier fabrics used in tailoring require the use of a thimble. The traditional tailor's thimble is metal and open-topped. The needle is pushed through the layers of cloth from the fingernail side, using the whole arm for the motion rather than just the middle finger or the hand. If you prefer, use your familiar *dressmaking or embroidery thimble,* but do use one.

Stitch ripper: It often takes more time to rip out stitching than it took to do it in the first place. The time can be considerably reduced with the use of a stitch ripper. Not only is this a time saver, but its sharp prong point can reach easily into delicate and difficult areas with more precision and safety than scissors.

ASSORTED HELPS

A *bodkin:* a long, blunt needle with a large eye used for turning casings, tubings, and cordings and for rounding out the eyelets of hand-worked buttonholes.

Wooden cuticle sticks: very handy for getting into the corners of collars, lapels, welts, and so on.

PRESSING EQUIPMENT

A great part of your permanent equipment is used for pressing. As you are introduced to the following tools, you will get a preview of some of the pressing problems and how to handle them. Because pressing is such a vital part of the tailoring process, the subject is discussed at length in Chapter 15.

While very useful for some fabrics, a *steam iron* tends to leave the round imprints of the steam openings when the requisite pressure is applied to certain woolens. On such fabrics, a five- or six-pound *flat iron* is preferable. Professional tailors use heavier irons, but they are impractical for home sewers (even assuming you could find one, could afford it, and had the strength to use it).

A well-padded, sturdy *ironing board* of good working height.

A *table-top ironing board* (Fig. 28a) for pressing small areas.

A *sleeve board* (Fig. 28b) or a *sleeve roll* (Fig. 28c): used for pressing the sleeve seams and for blocking the sleeve cap. Buy or make the sleeve roll to the dimensions given in the illustration. Use the same materials as for the tailor's ham (see page 58).

A *clapper or pounding block* (Fig. 28d): used for pounding seams flat and edges crisp in firmly woven, hard-surfaced woolens. It is a heavy block of nonresinous hardwood sanded smooth so that it will not snag any fabric.

A *press block* (Fig. 28e): used in conjunction with the pounding block. Like it, the press block is smooth and of nonresinous hard-

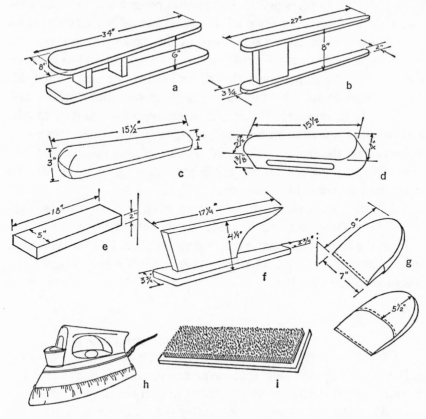

Fig. 28

wood. A new, clean breadboard, cheeseboard, or chopping block will do. (Needless to say, they don't travel back and forth between sewing room and kitchen.) An extra clapper to be used as a press block is a wonderful convenience. It is just right for pressing sleeve seams in fabrics that need pounding.

An *edge and point presser* (Fig. 28f): great for getting into and for pressing the points of collars, cuffs, lapels, welts, flaps, and so on. It is also used to prevent seam imprints on the right side of the fabric when the seams are pressed open over its long surface.

A *press mitt* (Fig. 28g): a "handy" piece of equipment for getting into and under hard-to-reach places. It is also good for shaping small areas and for patting flat those materials one dare not pound with the block.

Press cloths: In pressing, the iron should never come in direct contact with the fabric; a press cloth is always placed between the cloth and the iron. Since only a small area of the garment is pressed at a time, the press cloths can be fairly short, narrow strips—4 to 6 inches wide by 8 to 10 inches long. Buy or make them of unsized muslin, drill, or linen. Wash them thoroughly to make sure that all sizing and lint have been removed. Old, worn sheets, pillowcases, dish towels, and napkins, though unprofessional, are effective for this purpose.

To protect the surface of napped, nubby, or any other raised surfaces, use strips of self fabric. There generally appear to be suitable scraps that fall away in the cutting.

In lieu of a press cloth, try a *slip cover* (Fig. 28h) or a *plate cover* for the iron. The former can be made and the latter bought.

A *needle board* (sometimes called a velvet board) (Fig. 28i): used for pressing pile fabrics. The board has a flexible base from which protrude spaced "needles."

Assorted Rolls and Press Pads

Blocking in the contours that have been so painstakingly fitted and stitched into the garment is an extremely important part of classic tailoring. Indeed, it is one of its distinguishing features. To accomplish this, a great variety of press pads or cushions that fit practically every curve of the body have been devised. You really don't need all of them, nice as they are to have. Where there is a duplication of function, choose the press pad easiest for you to come by or to use.

The most all-purpose shaping device is the *tailor's ham,* so called because it is shaped like a ham. Somewhere on its rounded surface there is a curve that will match most shaped sections of a garment.

To make the tailor's ham, cut two bias egg-shaped pieces of heavy, firmly woven material—silesia, duck, drill, unbleached muslin, or wool—to the dimensions in Fig. 29a. For an especially useful ham, cut one side of smooth material, the other of nubby or napped material. Dart the broader end for even more shaping. Machine-stitch the two thicknesses, leaving the narrower end open. *Pack very tightly* with hardwood sawdust until the ham is quite hard. It cannot hold its shape unless it is. Some sewers use old nylon stockings for the

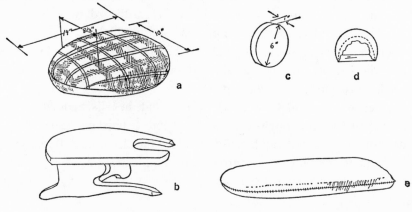

Fig. 29

stuffing. The commercial hams are stuffed with cotton waste or wool scraps.

A *tailor's board* (Fig. 29b): desirable but not essential. It may be used with or without a padded cover. It has a number of shaped surfaces for pressing various contour seams.

Have you noticed that most of the pressing equipment is made of wood? That's because most woolen fabric requires more steam than that produced by an ordinary steam iron. This added moisture becomes a problem on the usual well-padded ironing board, which tends to reflect moisture rather than absorb it. Wood, on the other hand, does absorb moisture quickly and effectively. This shorter, natural drying time is important in the pressing and shaping of wool.

The following tailor's cushions and pads, varying in size and shape, are designed for specific areas of the garment. Some can be bought. Others can be made of the materials used for the tailor's ham.

Collar press pad No. 1 (Fig. 29c): Cut two circles of the material 6 inches in diameter and one 1-inch bias strip to join them. Stitch the circles to the bias strip, leaving an opening for the stuffing. Pack tightly with sawdust. Close the opening with hand stitches.

Collar press pad No. 2 (Fig. 29d): Cut a bias strip 6 inches wide by 12 inches long. Fold this rectangle lengthwise and stitch the long side. Stuff tightly to within 2 inches of each end and hand-stitch across the pad. Overlap the unstuffed ends and stitch them securely to each other. These 2-inch ends can be stiffened with cardboard or buckram, which makes it easier to hold the press pad. If you wish, the ends may be tacked to a heavy piece of cardboard or plywood 2 inches by 4½ inches, so that the pad can sit upright.

For shaping the sleeve cap: Use either of the above collar press pads, the narrow end of the tailor's ham, the broad end of a sleeve board, a press mitt, or a sleeve pad.

A *sleeve press pad* (Fig. 29e): a long, flat, heavily padded tailor's cushion just wide enough to be inserted into a finished sleeve. It has one rounded end that can be slipped under the sleeve cap. Buy one or make one to the dimensions provided in the illustration. This is a very useful pad for pressing sleeve seams open and for blocking the sleeve cap.

Miscellaneous Helpful Items

Small basin of water: Pressing is done with moist heat. Steam can be produced by use of a damp press cloth and a hot, dry iron. Keep a basin handy for dampening the press cloths.

A *sponge* for dampening the press cloth or the fabric.

Brown wrapping paper used as a cushion to prevent imprints caused by the seam allowances, pleats, flaps, welts, and so on, when pressed. Cut strips of wrapping paper to a suitable length and a little more than three times as wide as the area you wish to protect. Fold in thirds lengthwise.

This is a lengthy list, to be sure. But one must admit it's easier to do any job well if you have the proper tools with which to work. Aside from the cost of a sewing machine, which presumably you already have, even were you to splurge and buy everything you need, you would not be spending very much. You can more than make up the entire cost in the amount saved by making your first tailored project. If you can resist buying that one extra length of enticing fabric that you may not sew up for years anyway, you'll have the money needed for most of the tailoring tools.

"I'VE GOT THEM ON THE LIST"

If you can't afford to rush right out and buy all the equipment immediately, why not make up a suggested gift list and display it prominently? Everyone will be so pleased that you are an enthusiastic sewer and so grateful for the suggestions (it's hard to know what gift to buy!) you'll have all the equipment you need in practically no time at all.

Chapter 6

Made to Measure

In and out of fashion come the no-shape garments. They have their considerable merits, but, after a while, most of us tire of the anonymity of clothes labeled small, medium, large, and one-size-fits-all. We long for the individuality of clothing contours that bear some reasonable relation to the figure. Even just enough shape to suggest there is a person inside will do—as is the case with most tailored garments.

The ultimate in flawless fit is a fine tailored garment. "Made-to-measure" is that magic phrase long associated with the best in custom tailoring.

In practice, home sewing bears a closer relation to custom work than it does to factory production. This means that the home sewer has as many opportunities for achieving a personalized fit as does the professional tailor. Once one has experienced that kind of individualized dressing, one can never be satisfied with a production-line job.

HOW TO ADJUST THE PATTERN TO MEET YOUR MEASUREMENTS

After a garment has been cut, it is too late to make any major changes. The best one can hope for then is to make minor changes in the seam allowances and perhaps even sneak a little off the darts. The size, the ease, the shaping, the placement of the silhouette seams, the leeway for more flattering fit—all the criteria by which good fit can be judged—have already been fixed in the cut-out pattern. Doesn't it make sense, then, to start your fitting by adjusting the pattern as close to your figure requirements as measurements and mathematics can make it?

Armed with your personal measurements (page 6), a tape measure, the pattern, and the following information, you should be able to bring the pattern fairly close to your needs.

MEASURE THE PARTS THAT MAKE THE WHOLE

1. Assemble all the parts of the pattern that make each completed front, back, and sleeve of a coat or jacket; all the parts that make the front and back of the skirt or pants. Set aside all applied pieces (like pockets) and all double thicknesses (like facings).

2. Place the front and back patterns with center front and center back parallel to each other and waistlines of front and back in line with each other (Figs. 30a, 30b, and 30c). Place the upper and

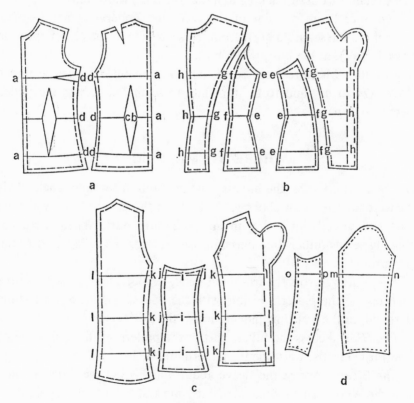

Fig. 30

under sleeves with grain lines parallel to each other and elbow positions in line with each other (Fig. 30d).

3. Measure the part of the pattern that will appear on the surface of the finished garment. *Measure from seam line to seam line.* Do not include anything that will end up in a seam or a dart. Use your tape measure like an adding machine.

4. Measure only to the line on which the garment will close. Do not include any section (like an extension) that overlaps a part of the garment already measured.

FOR EXAMPLE:

Fig. 30a: Measure from the center front and back to the dart (*a* to *b*), from the dart to the side seam (*c* to *d*), at the waist, or from the center front and back to the side seam (*a* to *d*).

Fig. 30b: Measure from seam line to seam line (*e* to *f*), from seam line to center front or back (*g* to *h*), at the bust, waist, hips.

Fig. 30c: From a point in line with the underarm marking (*i*) measure to the seam line (*j*), from the seam line to the center front or back (*k* to *l*), at the bust, waist, hips.

Fig. 30d: Measure from seam line to seam line across the upper sleeve (*m* to *n*), and from seam line to seam line across the under sleeve (*o* to *p*).

WHERE TO MEASURE

The Bust: Across the fullest part of both front and back. This measurement is taken about ½ inch above the point of any waistline dart and directly in line with any underarm dart. When there are shaping seams rather than darts, measure across the fullest part of the pattern.

The Waist: Across the front and back, as indicated by the waistline marking on the pattern, in line with the widest part of any waistline dart and/or the waistline indentation at the side seam.

The Hips: Across the fullest part of the pattern at the hipline. Note how far below the waistline the pattern hipline is.

The Biceps: Across the sleeve about midway between the shoulder and the elbow. In tailored garments, most standard sleeves fit most arms, since the styling provides sufficient fullness to accommodate

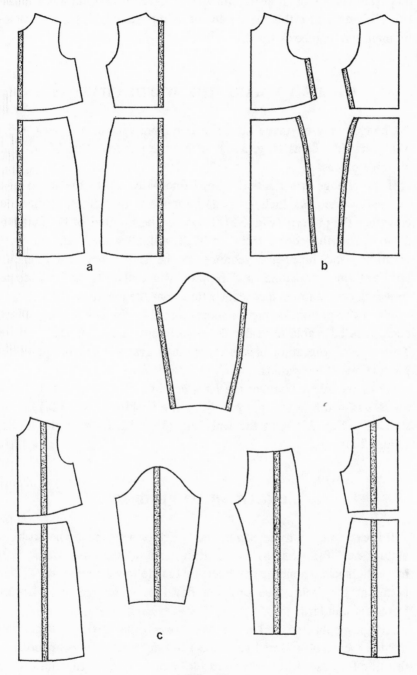

Fig. 31

moderate variations in girth. Unless you have an unusual figure problem (in which case this measurement is important), this is one measurement that can be skipped.

WHERE TO MAKE THE WIDTH CHANGES

Changes may be made at the center front and center back (Fig. 31a), the side seams (Fig. 31b), within the pattern (Fig. 31c), or in all three places.

If the change is a relatively small one—say, up to the width of a seam allowance (⅝ inch)—it can be made at the center, at the side, or within the pattern (Fig. 31). However, be mindful of the fact that a change at the center front or back will alter the neckline, bust, waistline, and hipline. A change at the side seam will alter the armhole, bust, waistline, and hipline. Remember to make a corresponding correction in any section that joins the key piece.

When the pattern change is more than the width of a seam allowance, it is advisable to make the adjustment in two or three places. This type of alteration makes the change gradual and preserves the proportions of the pattern.

All of the above changes are *balanced* or *even* changes. It is possible to add width in *one place only:* at the neckline (Fig. 32a), at the shoulder (Fig. 32b), at the waistline (Fig. 32c), or at the hipline (Fig. 32d).

LENGTH MEASUREMENTS

It is easy enough to determine the length of a garment when it has a natural neckline: that is, a line fitting around the base of the neck from the socket bone at the back to the hollow between the collarbones at the front. The problem develops when the style departs from this standard.

All garments designed to be worn over other articles of clothing (which means all tailored garments) are automatically dropped from this line for ease. In the standard block or basic pattern, that drop is ⅛ inch in jackets, ¼ inch in coats.

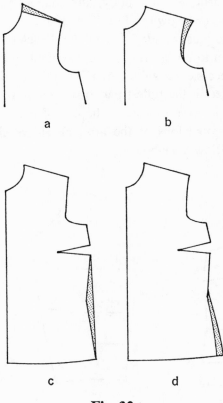

a   b

c   d

Fig. 32

Many garments, tailored or not, are dropped even more for design purposes. How much depends on the designer. One never knows. Sometimes the artist's drawing on the pattern can be misleading. The pattern description on the back of the envelope merely notes that it is a dropped neckline but does not tell how much the drop is. So you can see how difficult this makes it to determine exactly the length from neck to waist or to hem. You can see, too, why a muslin fitting could be of vital importance in this respect (see Chapter 7).

Where to Make the Length Measurements

In the figure, the great divide is the waistline. It determines the proportion of bodice above to body below.

The waistline of the pattern is designed to fit the waistline of the body. To preserve this waistline shaping of the pattern, while provid-

ing for the proportions of the body, any changes in length must be
made either above or below this line (Fig. 33a).

In the arm, the great divide is the elbow. It determines the proportion of upper arm to lower arm. The corresponding point on the pattern of a one-piece sleeve is the dart (Fig. 33b) or the elbow easing;
in a two-piece sleeve, the fullest part of the curve of the sleeve seam
(Fig. 33c). To preserve the sleeve shaping of the pattern while providing for the proportions of the arm, all sleeve changes must be
made above or below the elbow.

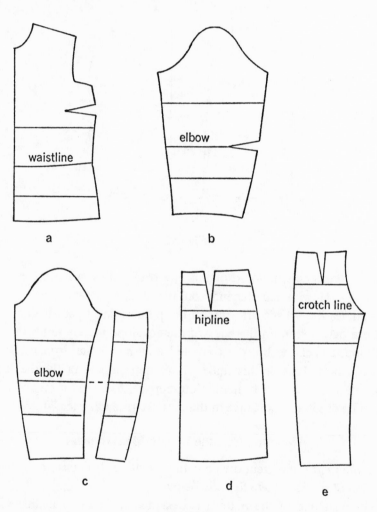

Fig. 33

The dividing line *in a skirt* is the hipline. Changes may be made above or below the hip (Fig. 33d).

In pants fitting, the divide is the line of the crotch. Make any length changes above or below the crotch line (Fig. 33e).

NOW MEASURE THE PATTERN

1. Measure the center-back length of the pattern from neck to waist and from waist to hem, from seam line to seam line (Fig. 34a). (The front pattern can be adjusted accordingly.)

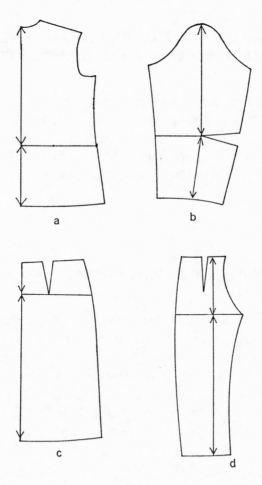

a   b

c   d

Fig. 34

2. Measure the length of the sleeve pattern from shoulder to elbow and from elbow to wrist (Fig. 34b). When the sleeve is less than full length, this presents the same problem in determining length as the dropped neckline. The trial muslin will help to determine a suitable length from elbow to wrist.

3. Measure the center-front length of the skirt pattern from waist to hipline and from hipline to hem (Fig. 34c).

4. Measure the center-front length of slacks from waist to crotch and from crotch to hem (Fig. 34d).

COMPARE THE PATTERN MEASUREMENTS WITH YOUR PERSONAL MEASUREMENTS

Remember that your width measurements are whole measurements, while the pattern measurements are only half. Halve your personal width measurements to correspond to those of the pattern.

Also remember that you must add ease to your body measurements, while the pattern already includes all the ease necessary for the size and style.

YOUR PORTRAIT IN PAPER—THE BASIC PATTERN

Unless you particularly enjoy going through all this arithmetical rigmarole of measuring and altering every pattern you plan to use (often with its indeterminate and hard-to-judge measurements), there is no need to—if you have a basic pattern. A basic pattern is your portrait in paper. It is made to your measurements and fitted to your figure. It includes all the necessary ease. It is both a cutting and a fitting guide. It saves hours of guesswork and complicated calculations.[1]

[1] Complete directions for making and using a basic pattern can be found in *How to Make Clothes That Fit and Flatter* by Adele P. Margolis (Garden City, N.Y.: Doubleday & Company, 1969).

A CHANGE FOR THE BETTER

Decide what needs changing and how much. Very small changes —¼ inch or less—can always be made in the seam allowances, particularly in the trial muslin. If you have to make too many changes or consistent changes of 2 inches or more, get the next size pattern. There is a 2-inch difference between pattern sizes. If most of the pattern fits but some 2-inch changes are indicated, work with the pattern you now have. Pattern changes are very specific. Make them only *where* and *if* you need them.

When there is to be more than one change, make each separately, one at a time. It is generally easier to make the lengthwise changes first, then the width adjustments.

Make all changes right on the pattern. Write notes to yourself, slash the pattern, spread, insert tissue, tuck or overlap, patch, pin, do anything that will make the change clear to you. When you have finished making the alterations, the pattern should be ready for use without any further ado. These changes should be understandable when you pick up the pattern again later, without having to puzzle out its messages or decode any of its cryptic symbols.

When you make a change in one pattern piece, remember to make a corresponding change on all pieces that join it. For instance, if you lengthen the front, you must lengthen the front facing to match. If you change the neckline, you must change the neckline facing and/or the collar and its facing. A change in a sleeve cap means a change in the armhole. And so on.

You will need some tools with which to make the changes: a ruler; a yardstick; a tailor's square or a 45-degree triangle; sharp-pointed pencils; Scotch tape; paper-cutting scissors; any tissue paper, shelf paper, or other unlined paper.

All changes in patterns should be at right angles to the grain, either vertical or horizontal. Use a 45-degree triangle or a tailor's square to determine the right angle.

Changes on Seam Lines

The pattern may be altered on any outside seam line (Fig. 35a), any inside seam line (Fig. 35b), or within the pattern section (Fig. 35c).

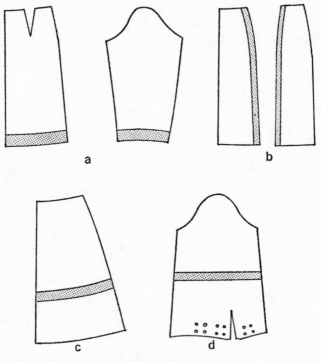

a   b

c   d

Fig. 35

When a pattern has straight lines, it is easy enough to add or subtract length at the hem (Fig. 35a). When a pattern is shaped (Fig. 35c) or styled (Fig. 35d), make the changes within the pattern to preserve the style line and details. Most patterns show where this change can be made.

Changes Within the Pattern

Changes within the pattern are made on the principle of slash and spread or its reverse, slash and overlap or tuck.

Patterns are made larger or smaller in one of two ways. The

changes may be equal or balanced across the entire length or width (Figs. 36a and 36b) or in one place only (Figs. 36c and 36d).

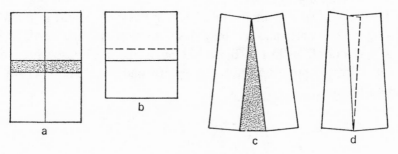

Fig. 36

To Make a Pattern Larger

1. Draw a slash line at right angles to the grain line where the change is to be made.

2. Slash and spread to the desired amount: equally across the width or length (Fig. 36a) or in one place only (Fig. 36c).

3. Insert lightweight paper or tissue paper in the spread area. (Old patterns are fine for this purpose.) Fasten with pins or Scotch tape.

To Make a Pattern Smaller

1. Draw a line at right angles to the grain line where the change is to be made.

2. Slash and overlap or tuck to the desired amount: equally for a balanced change (Fig. 36b) or in one place only (Fig. 36d).

3. Pin or Scotch-tape to position.

To make it easier to line up the spread sections of an equal or balanced change, draw a guide line parallel to the grain for a vertical change (Fig. 36a), at right angles to it for a horizontal change. (Turn the illustration around to get the effect.)

PATTERN CORRECTIONS FOR FIGURE NEEDS

There are as many fitting problems as there are sewers. Who's perfect? We cannot in a tailoring book deal in depth with all the problems of fitting. That deserves a study in itself.[2] However, here are some of the most frequent adjustments necessary. You may recognize your needs among them.

There are several methods for achieving the same result. In the following figures, note that you may slash the pattern and spread, as in Fig. a; or cut off, as in Fig. b; or add, as in Fig. c. Choose whichever method seems appropriate for the pattern and whichever method is easiest for you.

Corrections For

Thick Neck
Slash and spread; correct the armhole and neckline (Fig. 37a).
Drop the neckline (Fig. 37b).

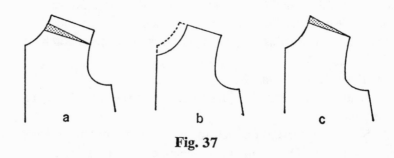

Fig. 37

Add to the shoulder seam (Fig. 37c).

Thin Neck
Reverse the procedure.

Not Enough Length at Back Neckline (garment slides back)
Add a seam allowance (or necessary length) to the back shoulder (Fig. 38).

---

[2] For a serious study of fitting and pattern alterations, see *How to Make Clothes That Fit and Flatter*, previously referred to.

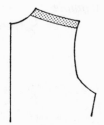

Fig. 38

Short Upper Back or Front (indicated by wrinkling across the chest
or back)

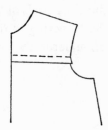

Fig. 39

Too Much Length?
Tuck the pattern (Fig. 39).

Round Shoulders
Slash and spread (Fig. 40); correct the center-back seam, neck,
and armhole.

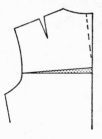

Fig. 40

Erect Back
Reverse the procedure.

Too Much Fullness at the Armhole

Tuck the armhole tapering to center front or back (Fig. 41). Correct the seam line.

Fig. 41

Longer Sleeve Cap (when there are folds at either side of the cap)

Add height at the shoulder, tapering to the notches (Fig. 42a), or narrow the cap from the shoulder to the notches (Fig. 42b).

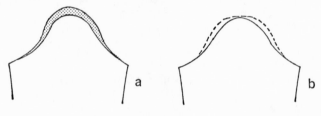

Fig. 42

Shorter Sleeve Cap

Reverse the procedure.

Broad Shoulders

Slash and spread; correct the shoulder line and the side seam (Fig. 43a). Add at the armhole (Fig. 43b).

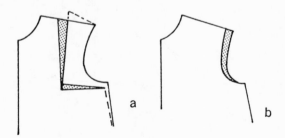

Fig. 43

Narrow Shoulders
   Reverse the procedure.

Square Shoulders
   Slash and spread at the armhole; correct the neckline and the armhole (Fig. 44).

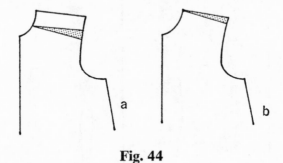

Fig. 44

Large-bosomed Figure
   Slash and spread in length as well as in width. Correct seam lines
   and any existing shaping (Fig. 45).

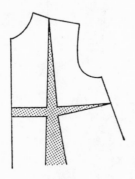

Fig. 45

Flat-chested Figure
   Reverse the procedure.

Thick Waist

Use less dart (Figs. 46 a and c), or add at the side seam (Figs. 46 b and d).

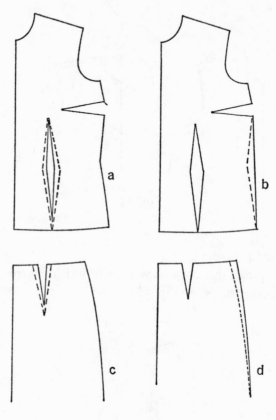

Fig. 46

Small Waist

Reverse the procedure.

Broad Back

Add at any or all places as indicated (Fig. 47).

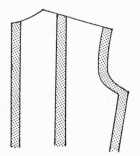

Fig. 47

Narrow Back

Reverse the procedure.

Heavy Arm

One-piece sleeve: Add at the side seams and/or slash and spread through the center (Fig. 48a).

Two-piece sleeve: Add at the seam lines and, if necessary, through the overarm section (Fig. 48b).

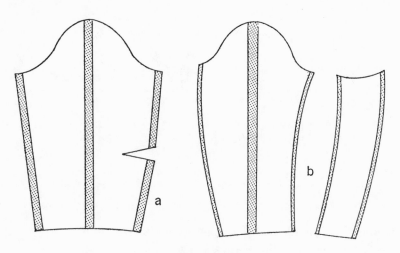

Fig. 48

Slim Arm

Reverse the procedure.

Sleeve Strains Across the Upper Arm

Add at the armhole for ease. Slash and spread the bodice for width (Fig. 49a).

Slash and spread the cap for width and length. Correct the line of the cap (Fig. 49b).

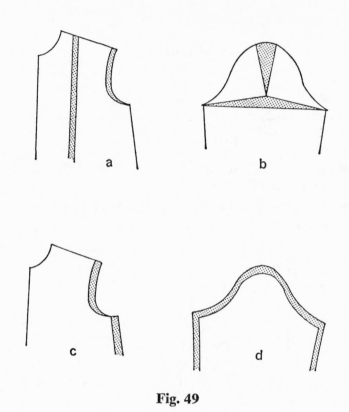

Fig. 49

OR

Add at the armhole and side seam (Fig. 49c).

Add at the cap and underarm seam (Fig. 49d).

Big-hipped Figure

Add the necessary width to the hip at the side seam. Carry the correction to the hem and taper to the waist (Fig. 50a).

Slash and spread; carry the correction to the hem (Fig. 50b).

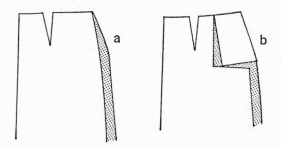

Fig. 50

Slim-hipped Figure
   Reverse the procedure.

Sway-backed Figure
   Drop the waistline at the center back and taper to the side seam (Fig. 51).

Fig. 51

Prominent Seat or Abdomen
   Slash and spread. Create a new waistline dart (Fig. 52).

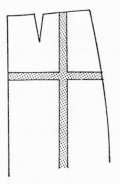

Fig. 52

Flat Rear or Flat Abdomen
  Reverse the procedure.

Skirt Cupping Under the Buttocks
  Slash and spread at the center back. Taper to the side seam.
  Correct the center-back line (Fig. 53a).
  Add at the side seam (Fig. 53b).

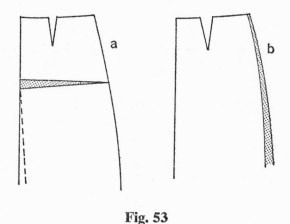

Fig. 53

Pants Changes
  Many of the skirt changes are applicable to pants changes as well.
  For instance, see the correction for sway-backed figures (Fig. 51).

Longer Crotch Length
  Slash and spread. Correct the seam lines (Fig. 54).

Shorter Crotch Length
  Tuck the pattern.

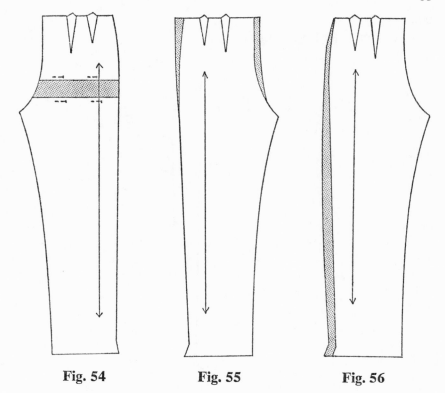

Fig. 54   **Fig. 55**   **Fig. 56**

Larger Waistline
  Add to waistline at the side and crotch seams and taper to the hip
  and crotch (Fig. 55).

Smaller Waistline
  Reverse the procedure.

Wide Hips
  Add to the side seam; taper to the waist and the hem (Fig. 56).

Narrow Hips
  Reverse the procedure.

Heavy Thighs

Add to the inner leg seam (Fig. 57).

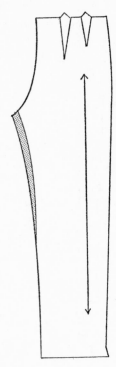

Fig. 57

Slim Thighs

Take some off the inner leg seam.

Large Seat

Slash and spread on the back crotch seam; taper to side seam (Fig. 58a). If necessary, add to the inner leg seam (Fig. 58b).

Flat Seat

Reverse the procedure.

Protruding or Flat Abdomen

Do the same corrections as for large or flat seat on the *front* crotch seam.

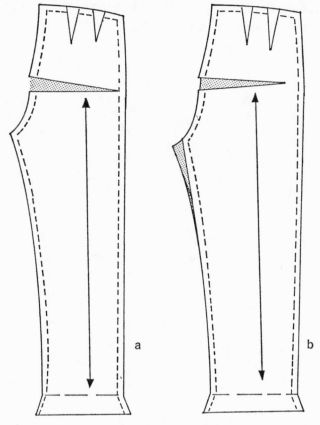

Fig. 58

PERFECT THE PATTERN

As you have undoubtedly noticed, pattern changes often produce distortions: angularity where curves are necessary, jagged lines, no lines at all, and similar aberrations. Often the grain line is thrown off by a pattern change. All of these irregularities must be corrected to make the pattern usable.

Whenever an undefined space results from a slash-and-spread, new lines must be drawn to connect the ends of the broken line (Fig. 59a) or to continue the correction (Fig. 59b).

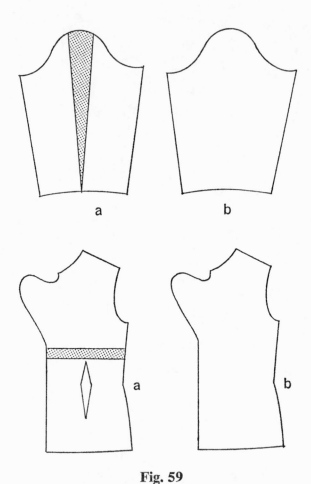

Fig. 59

Whenever a jagged line results from a slash-and-spread or overlap, a new line must be drawn to correct the protruding pattern (Fig. 60). The new line begins at the point where it originally began and goes to the point where it originally ended, cutting off all projecting edges. A *jagged grain line* is corrected in the same way.

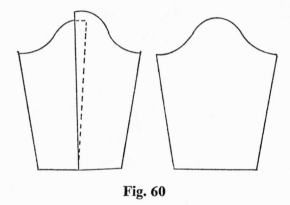

Fig. 60

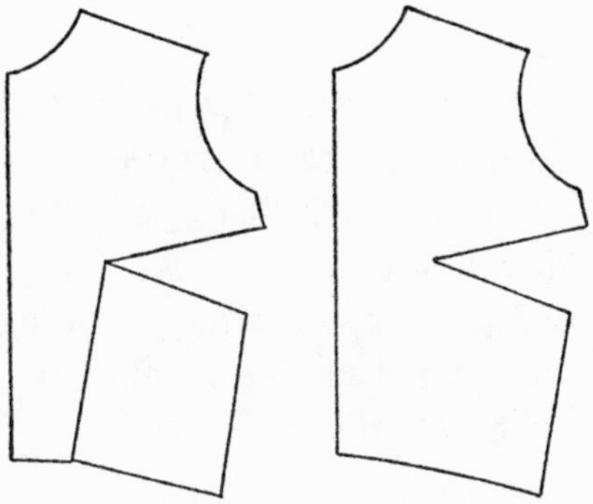

Fig. 61

When angularity results from a change where a curved line is required, correct it (Fig. 61). All circumference lines are slightly curved.

When a dart is moved from its original position, that pointed little shape at the seam line and cutting line will need to be moved, too

(Fig. 62). It represents the amount of material necessary to stitch the dart into the seam.

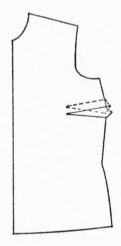

Fig. 62

All seam lines meant to join each other must be made equal in length. This may mean adding to or subtracting from the length of any given seam, as necessary. Whether you add or subtract depends on which will provide the best fit.

Make your adjusted pattern so perfect and so clear that, were you to lay it aside now and pick it up in a month, you would know without guesswork exactly how to use it.

Chapter 7

Testing, Testing! The Trial Muslin

How lovely and how easy it would be if mathematical calculations and pattern alterations alone would guarantee the fine fit of your garment. Alas! All arithmetic can do is provide the proper length, an approximate width, and a general idea of your shaping requirements. Theoretically, that should be enough. In actuality, it is not. For it is cloth and not paper that we must deal with eventually. So the real test for fit must come in cloth—not the expensive cloth of your project garment; that would be too risky a test, since only minor changes can be made once the garment is cut. A trial muslin can save you a lot of grief.

WITH THE TRIAL MUSLIN

You can check the size, fit, and ease.

You can judge how the garment looks and feels in movement.

You can determine what further alterations are necessary.

You will have a clearer idea of how the shaping and the style will co-ordinate with your fabric.

You can decide how and where to interface or underline the garment to sustain the lines of the design.

You can familiarize yourself with the construction details.

You can decide the most effective placement of the fabric design: where to place a motif, a plaid, a check, a stripe.

You will know which pieces go together, thereby avoiding possible errors in layout and cutting.

You will be able to observe how the grain falls in sleeves, collars, yokes, pockets, and so on.

You will get a good idea of what to expect in the direction of weaves, stripes, checks, and plaids.

If you make your trial muslin before you purchase your fabric, you will even have a truer idea of how much fabric you will need, particularly if you have made extensive alterations in style or fit.

Do you always need to make a test garment? Use your judgment. If you are sure of a particular style, know from experience how to adjust the pattern, have sufficient material to recut if necessary, have sufficient seam allowance to borrow in emergencies, then the test may not be necessary. But if you have any doubts at all about the style or the fitting, or have insufficient fabric to afford the luxury of mistakes, then *do* make a trial muslin.

TEST MATERIALS FOR TAILORING

The best test material for tailoring is *muslin—bleached or unbleached*—in a weight comparable to that of the fashion fabric. It is true that muslin hangs and moves and fits like what it is—muslin—and not your precious fashion fabric. Still, one does get a good idea of how becoming the style is and what needs to be done to make it fit your figure comfortably.

The test fabric need not be muslin. Any other solid-color material of similar weight will do as well. A plain surface will clearly show all seams, darts, and style details. All fitting adjustments will be highly visible.

If your suit or jacket or pants are to be of knit fabric, the test fabric should be a knit, too, since knits fit differently from the way a woven cloth does. Use an inexpensive knit goods, like *tricot, for the trial*.

Whatever you use for the trial, treat the test material as if it were your treasured fabric. It must be cut with as much thoroughness and care. How it hangs and how it fits depend on this.

PREPARE THE PATTERN FOR THE
TRIAL MUSLIN

1. Select the pattern pieces you will need. You will not need facings, pockets, or applied trimming unless they are essential for the completion of the pattern unit. Use the undercollar only, cut on the suggested grain. Pattern companies have slightly different pattern symbols. Make sure you understand those on your pattern.

2. Read through the instruction sheet. More than the picture on the envelope, the instructions reveal what the designer had in mind and how he (or she) hoped to get the effect. This bird's-eye view is important to your understanding of what's involved in the construction. If you merely follow the directions one step at a time, you are working blindly without a full realization of your goal.

3. Press out any wrinkles in the pattern with a warm iron.

4. Extend the grain lines to the entire length of the pattern. On many patterns this marking is too short for accurate pinning.

5. Make the necessary pattern alterations from your calculations.

PREPARE YOUR OWN LAYOUT CHART

Since you will not be cutting out the entire pattern and since there may be discrepancies in width between the muslin and the fashion fabric, the pattern suggestions for yardage and layout may be of very little help. Devise your own layout chart. See page 136 for suggestions.

Many sewers keep a supply of test fabric on hand in considerable yardage so that they need not worry about how much to get for an individual trial. Should it be necessary to buy an exact length especially for the trial, do a test layout on wrapping paper or shelf paper to determine the amount, or approximate it as best you can.

PREPARE THE MUSLIN

1. Tear the muslin at each cut end to establish the horizontal grain.

2. Fold the muslin as necessary. Pin the torn edges together; pin the selvages together. If the material does not lie perfectly flat in a rectangular shape, dampen it and press it to position. Sometimes pulling across the bias is sufficient.

3. Test all four corners of the muslin against any right angle—a tailor's square, a corner of a cutting board or table—to make sure that the material lies in a perfect rectangle.

LAY OUT THE PATTERN AND CUT THE MUSLIN

1. Following your own layout chart, place the pattern on the muslin with the grain lines parallel to the selvages.

2. Place the pins close to the cutting edge, about 2 inches apart. You may want to leave larger seam allowances to take care of possible changes.

3. Cut out the muslin, using sharp shears or scissors. Don't bother to cut out the notches beyond the cutting line. This slows up the cutting. The notches can be marked after cutting, along with all the other markings.

MARK THE MUSLIN

1. Transfer all the markings that will help in the assembling and fitting to the *right side* of the muslin. Use dressmaker's carbon paper and a tracing wheel.

2. Mark the stitching lines, the placement of buttons and buttonholes, pockets, all ■'s, ●'s, and ▲'s, the points at which the collar joins the garment, and any special placement or detail. *Be sure to mark the center front and center back.* Mark the notches with either the dressmaker's carbon or cut-out wedges. You may number them as they are numbered on the pattern if that will help you to put the pieces together. Use every bit of help that the designer and pattern-maker put there for your use. The markings indicate how this puzzle that is a pattern should go together easily. No need for you to spend an inessential amount of time trying to figure it all out.

PUT THE TRIAL MUSLIN TOGETHER

The quickest way to get the effect of the finished garment without actually stitching it is to *overlap and pin* all the stitching lines. Pinning gives the information we want. It is so much faster and easier to unpin or repin than to rip stitching and then join the muslin again.

1. Work with the marked side up.

2. Clip all curved seams—otherwise you will be fitting on the cutting edge rather than the fitting (stitching) lines.

3. Take full seam allowances. Pin too close to the edge and you will be testing a garment at least one size larger—perhaps more, depending on the number of sections that need to be joined.

4. Generally pins are placed lengthwise along the seam. If necessary, they may be placed at right angles to the seam to facilitate fitting, as at the center back of a two-piece undercollar. Use whatever direction won't stab you when trying on the garment.

5. Overlap the seams, either bringing one seam line directly over the other or turning under one seam allowance and bringing the fold to meet the other seam line. Ease or stretch where necessary to make the seam fit.

6. Pin the darts.

7. Overlap and pin the seam line of the undercollar on the neck seam line of the garment, stretching the collar to make it fit the garment. Start the pinning at the point where the collar joins the garment at the front and work toward the center back. Overlap the center-back seams, making any needed adjustments.

8. Make two rows of running stitches (or machine basting) across the cap of the sleeve. Pull up the gathers to form the sleeve cap. Overlap the seam line of the cap on the armhole seam line, either by superimposing one seam line directly on the other or by turning under the sleeve seam allowance and bringing it to meet the armhole seam line.

9. Pin up all the hems to get the general effect of the garment and to determine whether any further changes in length are necessary.

By this time you've learned a great deal about this newest addition to your wardrobe.

For one thing, you've discovered what it will really look like. That sketch on the pattern envelope may not have done it justice. Or that glamorized photography in the fashion book may have been deceiving.

For another thing, you have actually put all those puzzling pieces together as the instruction sheet directed you. You've gotten a preview of the intricacies of the construction. Any tendency to botch has been inflicted on the muslin and not on the fashion fabric.

Now let's see how the muslin fits!

Is the Style Right for You?

When you slip on your muslin, your first impression and your first concern are for style. If you were buying a suit or coat, you might very well try on a dozen or more in as many different shops before you found one that was just right for you. The trial muslin is the sewer's equivalent of that trying-on jaunt. You must make allowances for the difference between the muslin and your chosen fabric, but you can quickly tell whether the style is a good one for you. Many a sewer has been known to abandon a pattern upon seeing herself in the muslin and finding how impossible it is to make it fit with even a modest degree of flattery. Better to know it now before expending any more time, effort, and fabric. If necessary, choose another pattern. If the style could be good with a few changes, muslin is a fine fabric with which to experiment. If you need only make some minor alterations, these can easily be made. If it is just plain beautiful—lucky, lucky you!

Study the muslin for line, proportion, fullness; shoulders, neckline, collar; set of sleeves. Decide whether you will keep all the style details or eliminate some of them. Even if the style does carry a big-name designer label, some changes may be indicated to make it right for you. Monsieur Y and Madame Z would undoubtedly have made some slight changes (consistent with the design) to suit you if you were a private client. You do not have to accept every last little detail in the pattern envelope.

Is the Size Right?

Is there too much fullness for you, or too little? Would this be a question of style or one of size? Perhaps a smaller or larger size pattern in the same style would be the answer. Perhaps a little more or less fullness would do the trick.

Does It Fit Well?

That is the question! If it doesn't fit or can't be made to fit, forget it. If it can be made to fit but does nothing for you, forget it. What you don't need is one more exercise in stitching that will hang at the back of your closet until you give it away.

Fitting is fitting whether it be in muslin or in your chosen fabric. All the elements that constitute good fit for one are the same for the other.

SOME GENERAL SUGGESTIONS REGARDING FITTING

All fitting (muslin and cloth garment alike) is done *from the right side*. Were this not so, you would be fitting the garment in reverse.

Your shape and the shape of the garment should coincide. If you are one who depends on a bra and girdle for shape, wear for the fitting exactly what you plan to wear with the finished garment. A different bra and girdle will produce a different shape and all those carefully fitted darts and shaping seams will be dislocated.

In fitting a jacket, try it on over a blouse or sweater similar to one that will be worn under it. This will give a more accurate idea of the necessary ease.

In fitting a coat, try it on over the garment or garments to be worn under it.

While most fitting can be done simply with the muslin shell, some styles are absolutely dependent on understructure for support before one can attempt a fitting. In that event, test the muslin over a suitable underlining and/or interfacing (see Chapter 12).

Remember that the garment itself will get interfacing, underlining, facing, lining, and possibly an interlining. Allow a little ease for these.

When shoulder pads are to be used, set them into position for the fitting.

When a pattern calls for a stay to control any fullness, it is the stay that must fit. The fullness is so much added decoration.

Pin closed all slits, vents, and pleats. The garment should fit without relying on their released fullness for added width.

Pin the garment closed on the correct line, matching centers. While it may be tempting to give oneself a little more ease on this line or to make a single-breasted lap of a double-breasted garment, the pattern changes involved—closing extensions, collar, lapel, neckline, facings, even the position of the darts—are too difficult for anyone unacquainted with patternmaking.

When fitting or being fitted, stand in a natural position. Clothes must fit your posture as well as your measurements. If you "stand up straight" or "pull your shoulders back" or "tuck your stomach in" for a fitting (frequent admonitions), the garment may not fit when you are at ease and in your normal posture.

Remember that more fabrics won't "give" than will, particularly when they are underlined or interfaced. Allow sufficient ease to be comfortable.

Don't overfit! Contrary to popular notion, tight fitting is not slimming. It outlines the figure and focuses attention on all one's figure faults.

Be fastidious but not hypercritical of your fitting. Many a sewer worries herself through every last eighth of an inch when it really doesn't make that much difference. Quit while you are ahead.

Be mindful of the fact that even unfitted clothing must be long enough and wide enough, and must touch the body at certain crucial points.

SUGGESTED SEQUENCE FOR FITTING

Jacket or Coat

1. Try on the garment. Pin the center fronts closed.
2. Check the vertical and horizontal grains.
3. Start the fitting at the shoulders and work down.
4. Check the ease.
5. Check the shaping—either darts or shaping seams.
6. Correct the side seam.
7. Check the neckline.
8. Set the approximate length of the garment.

Sleeve

1. Set the sleeve cap, starting at the shoulder and working down, front and back to the notches.
2. Check the grain.
3. Pin in the underarm.
4. Check the elbow dart for correct position and ease.
5. Set the approximate length of the sleeve.

Skirt

1. Pin a length of grosgrain ribbon, tape, or waistband into position at the waist as a stay.
2. Pin the center front and center back of the skirt to position on the waist stay.
3. Pin the hips at the side seams, checking the correct position of the grain.
4. Fit and pin the area between the waist and hips. Check the darts and/or shaping seams.
5. Pin the side seams from hips to hem.
6. Determine the correct waistline seam and mark it.
7. Set the approximate length, and pin.

Pants

1. *Baste* the crotch seams front and back. Clip the curved seam allowance.

2. Pin the waistband or what passes for a waistband stay (ribbon or tape) into place.

3. Pin the center front and center back of the pants into position on the waistband stay.

4. Fit the area between the waist and hips. Check the darts and/or shaping seams. Check the crotch seam for shape and length.

5. Fit and pin the inner seams.

6. Fit and pin the side seams from hips to hem.

7. Determine the waistline seam and mark it.

8. Set the approximate length, and pin.

WHAT TO LOOK FOR IN THE MUSLIN FITTING

Ease

This is the quality that makes you reach for a particular garment because it is so livable.

You should be able to eat, and drink, and breathe, and laugh without wondering if you're about to split apart. You should be able to move your arms with a reasonable degree of freedom even in a fitted, set-in sleeve, though it isn't necessary to test everything as if you were swinging a golf club or a baseball bat. You should be able to swish your skirt easily around your hips when standing and be comfortable when seated.

And it should be possible for you to get into your pants without the services of an assistant stationed nearby to stuff you into your sausage-tight casing. Try sitting in your pants—and crossing your legs. Those who are addicted to wearing them always insist that it is because they are so comfortable. Well, make them that.

Ease is different from just plain too big. It is where a garment touches and how it glides over the body. It is not so much as to make the garment look sizes too big for you, or so little that you can't move in it. In the end, you are the only one who can determine just the right amount, for it is a matter of feel as well as appearance.

When more ease is necessary across the bosom or back

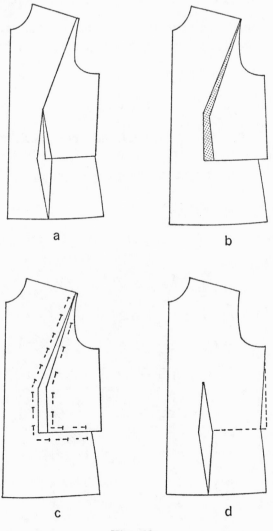

Fig. 63

1. Slash the muslin from the shoulder point to the high point of the bust or shoulder blades through any waistline dart to the waist and across to the side seam (Fig. 63a).

2. Spread the slash to the needed amount at the bust or shoulder blades (Fig. 63b).

3. Fill in the spread area with a strip of muslin, and pin (Fig. 63c).

4. Reposition the dart. Correct the side seam (Fig. 63d).

This slash-spread-insert-muslin-strip method can be used anywhere when more size or ease is indicated in the muslin fitting.

Grain

The most obvious clue to good fit is the grain. Fabric hangs with the grain and fits with it.[1]

This is how the grain should appear in your garment:

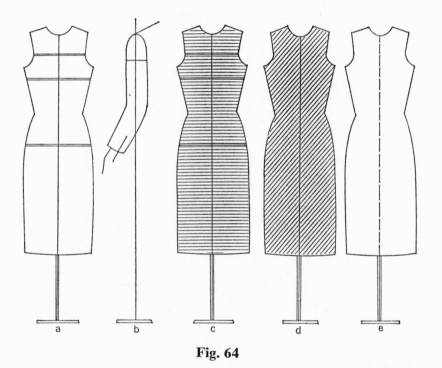

Fig. 64

[1] For a full discussion of grain, see page 119.

The center-front and center-back grain hang at right angles to the floor. This places the horizontal grain parallel to the floor. The check points are across the chest, across the bust, across the shoulder blades, across the hips (Fig. 64a).

The vertical grain of the sleeve hangs at right angles to the floor from the shoulder to the elbow. This places the horizontal grain parallel to the floor. Check across the biceps (Fig. 64b). The lower portion of the sleeve—elbow to wrist—will not follow this line, since it is shaped by the elbow darts in a one-piece sleeve or by the shaping seams in a two-piece sleeve.

Use any prominent lengthwise or crosswise yarns, stripes, plaids, or checks to locate the grain (Fig. 64c). If the garment is cut on the bias, your only guide is a line of guide basting (Fig. 64d). It is helpful to mark the vertical grain at the center front or center back with guide basting (Fig. 64e).

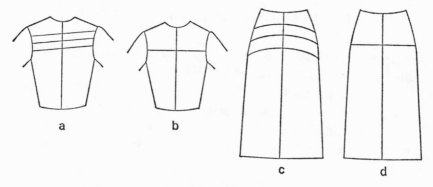

Fig. 65

Whenever the grain departs from the correct position, release the nearest seam, and lift or lower the fabric until it is in the correct position. Repin. For instance, if the grain looks like this (Figs. 65a and 65c), make it look like this (Figs. 65b and 65d).

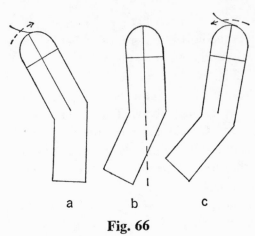

Fig. 66

If the lengthwise grain of the sleeve tilts forward (Fig. 66a) or backward (Fig. 66c), unpin the sleeve and *dial* the cap to its correct position (Fig. 66b).

THE SECRET OF SUCCESSFUL SHAPING

It's dart control that does it. The right amount of control in just the right place is the secret of successful shaping.

All darts must head toward the high point of the curve being fitted. All shaping seams must pass directly over the high point or within 1 inch of it on either side. Where there is a dart as well as a seam used for shaping, one or the other must be at or within 1 inch of the dart point.

When two darts are used, they are placed one on each side of the high point. When three darts are used, the center one is in the dart-point position, with one on each side.

AN EASY WAY TO RELOCATE A DART

1. Trace the existing dart (Fig. 67a) on another piece of paper. Cut it out (Fig. 67b).

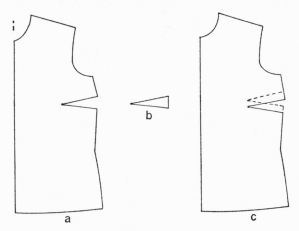

Fig. 67

2. Place the cut-out dart on your pattern in the new position and trace (Fig. 67c). (The broken line shows the position of the original dart.)

If the darts or shaping seams produce bulges above, below, or beside the high point, unpin the garment and reposition them correctly.

Bulges or *poufs* at the dart point mean that the dart is too large. Less control is needed: make a smaller dart and/or reshape the shaping seam.

Wrinkles or *folds* mean that a larger dart is needed, for more control. Push the excess material into the nearest seam or dart. Or when there is no dart or seam, create one.

LENGTH AS WELL AS WIDTH TO ENCOMPASS A CURVE

Think of any body bulge as a small hemisphere (half an orange, half a grapefruit). Note that it takes length as well as width to go over and across the half globe.

Length, width, and control are all involved in fitting.

For instance: "hiking up" or "poking out" (Figs. 68a and 68b) indicates not enough length or shaping.

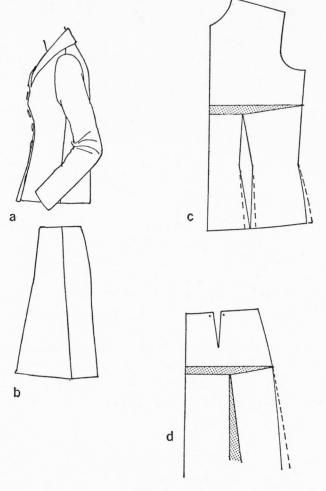

Fig. 68

To Add Length (Figs. 68c and 68d)
   1. Slash the muslin.
   2. Spread to the desired length.
   3. Fill in the spread with a strip of muslin.
   4. Correct any seams or darts that need it.

To Reshape
   1. Release the side seams or darts.
   2. Straighten the center front or back.

3. Push the excess fullness into the nearest seam or dart, or create one.

The shaping of the garment is meant to be for you. Don't be afraid to alter the amount or the position of the control darts or control seams.

Whenever a change is made in a dart (to make it either smaller or larger), the seam from which it originates is altered in length. Compensate for this by adding or subtracting as much as is necessary to make it match the seam it must join.

Each pair of dart legs must be made to match in length.

The Silhouette Seams

The neck, the shoulders, the armhole, the side seam, the sleeve hem, the waistline, and the hem outline the garment. This silhouette is dictated by fashion, function, and figure.

The neckline is anywhere either the designer or you think it should be. Wherever it is, it must fit flat against the body with no gaping or rippling.

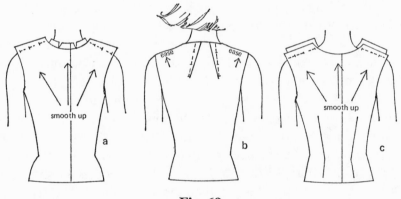

Fig. 69

Where there is gaping or rippling, unpin the shoulder seams. Starting at the center front or back, smooth the material over the body and up into the shoulder seams. Repin (Fig. 69a). Doing this may raise the neckline slightly, but it can always be scooped out a bit later. The important thing is to have a neckline that hugs the body.

A back neckline that stands away from the body can be corrected by creating a neckline dart. So that there will not be too many darts in one small area, stitch the back neckline dart as a dart but ease the amount of the original shoulder dart into the front shoulder (Fig. 69b). A good steaming over the tailor's ham should take care of this fullness.

Sometimes in correcting a gaping neckline as suggested, the front and back shoulder seams no longer match at the neckline (Fig. 69c). Trim off the neckline wherever necessary to make the neckline seams match. Should this make the neckline too deep, salvage as much as you can of the neck seam allowance.

Difficult though it is to do, the *shoulder seam* must be placed in just the right position. Thereby hangs your garment.

The shoulder seam should lie just *slightly* forward of the crest of the shoulder curve from the base of the neck to the prominent shoulder bone.

Too far forward, and the garment will look as if the back extension forms a front yoke. Too far backward, and that too-short neckline will insist on more length by pulling the garment down in back.

The overarm armhole seam curves over the top of the shoulder and continues in a slightly curved line, deeper in front, shallower in back, to the crease where arm and body join. (Notches appear on the pattern at these points.) Here ease is added across the chest and across the back. How much depends on what is to be worn under the tailored garment and how much you need for movement. Below the notches, the armhole seam swings into an underarm curve.

Shoulder widths vary with style changes. When a narrow-shouldered look is in vogue, the armhole and shoulder seams meet just at or a little beyond the shoulder point (the prominent bone on which the arm is hinged). When a broad-shouldered look is in style, the shoulder seam is extended beyond the shoulder point. When shoulder pads are used, the shoulder seam is raised and extended both front and back to accommodate the pad. The total amount added is equal to the thickness of the pad—half in front, half in back (Fig. 70). For a ½-inch pad, for instance, raise the shoulder seam ¼ inch in front and ¼ inch in back. Extend the shoulder seam at the armhole ½ inch. Draw a new armhole curve from shoulder to notch (Fig. 70).

Any fitting faults that extend to the armhole become more obvious

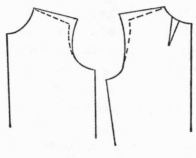

Fig. 70

when the sleeves are set in. Fit the body of a tailored garment very carefully before setting the sleeves into the armholes.

The side seam divides all circumference measurements into front and back. Correctly placed, this seam creates balance between them.

In profile, the side seam appears as a continuation of the shoulder seam (Fig. 71a).

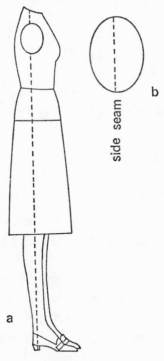

Fig. 71

At the underarm, the side seam starts ½ inch back of the middle of the total armhole (Fig. 71a) and continues in a plumb line to the floor. In doing so, the side seam divides the circumferences so that the front is larger than the back (Fig. 71b)—a variable amount at the bust, depending on the figure; about 1 inch at the waist; and 1 inch at the hips. Surprised? Did you think the skirt back would be larger? Just the opposite is true.

One good way to test for the correct position of the side seam: allow the arms to hang naturally at the sides. The middle fingers should touch the side seams of the skirt.

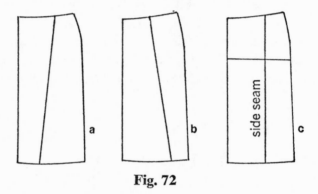

Fig. 72

If the side seam swings forward at the hem (Fig. 72a) or backward (Fig. 72b), reset the seam in the following way:

1. Release the side seams.
2. Let the fabric hang out naturally.
3. Check the grain and the dart control.
4. Repin the skirt so the side seams hang straight (Fig. 72c).

All circumference seam lines are curved to follow the natural curves of the body: neckline, bust line, waistline, hipline, and hemline.

The natural waistline is located where the indentation of the body makes the circumference smallest (Fig. 73a). If you are naturally short-waisted or heavy-bosomed, you may want to lower the waistline for a longer, slimmer look (Fig. 73b). If you are naturally long-waisted or very tall, you may look better when the waistline is raised slightly (Fig. 73c).

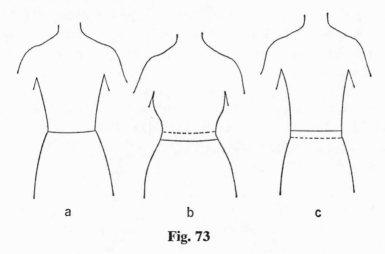

a   b   c

Fig. 73

Here is an easy way to determine your waistline. Pin a tape measure snugly around the waist. Push it so that the bottom of the tape rests at your natural waistline or in the position you would like the wastline to be. Mark the bottom line of the tape measure with pins or tailor's chalk. (See page 436 for a more complete discussion of waistline fitting.)

With arm bent, *a tailored suit sleeve* should just cover the bend of the wrist. In a man-tailored suit, the length of the sleeve exposes ½ inch of the shirt cuff. *The sleeve hem of a coat* ends just above the first thumb joint.

HEMLINES

Set the hemline of jacket, skirt, or coat as high, as low, as in-between as fashion and your figure dictate. Never mind your vow never to adopt a new fashion because you just don't like the current length. It's amazing how quickly our eyes become accustomed to a new look. Besides, you will attract a lot more attention (unfavorable) if you are out of fashion than if you expose a few inches more or less of your legs. You don't need to be the first to spring into action on a new length, but neither do you want to be the last holdout.

As previously noted, most jacket and skirt hemlines are slightly curved to follow the natural curve (circumference) of the body. The only time one would depart from this rule would be if the fabric has a horizontal line at the hem. In that case, it is more effective to follow the line of the fabric design rather than the slight curve that results from an accurate setting.

For instance, in a plaid skirt or jacket, it would be better to sacrifice the truth of the setting for an optical illusion. The straight line will make the hem look even (Fig. 74a). Were you to follow the actual curve of the body setting that goes off the straight line, the hem would look uneven (Fig. 74b).

a   b

Fig. 74

In that event, set the hipline and hemline of a skirt in a straight line, parallel to the floor, then fit the waist-to-hip area, adjusting the length here. This is the reverse of the usual procedure.

In the same way, set the hemline of a jacket or coat in a straight line parallel to the floor. Fit the bosom-to-shoulder-seam area, adjusting the length as necessary.

In each case, the hem is a firm, straight line, while the needed length is added above.

The hemline of pants should just cover the heel seam at the back crease and just touch the shoe without breaking at the front crease (Fig. 75).

Fig. 75

HIDDEN CHANGES

You have chosen a pattern because you like the design. In your overzealousness to make it fit, don't destroy or distort the style lines that attracted you. You must *fit only the part that can absorb the change in an inconspicuous way.*

Fig. 76

FOR INSTANCE:

The yoke of the skirt (Fig. 76a) is its chief design interest and must be left intact or the design will be ruined. Whatever fitting the skirt needs at the hipline (other than the side seam) can be done on the seam line of the lower skirt that joins the yoke.

On Fig. 76b, changes may be made on the seam line of the side front sections only, while the seam line of the front section remains as the designer intended it. In this way, you are both preserving the style line that intrigued you and making it fit your figure. No one will be the wiser, since you haven't tampered with the distinctive lines of the design.

FIT TO FLATTER

Believe it or not, you really can fit yourself—there is much that you can see, that you can note, and that you can reach, aided by off-again, on-again pinning. But there's no doubt about it, a little help from a friend can be a big help in fitting. Find yourself a sewing buddy, particularly one who can be objective about how your garment looks, to counter your subjectivity about how it feels.

As important as knowing when to follow the rules of fitting is knowing when not to follow them. Clothes must not only fit, they must flatter as well.

It is not a slavish reproduction of your figure that we are after, nor a slavish adherence to the lines of the design at the expense of your figure. The real trick in fitting is *to strike a balance between the lines of the design and the lines of the figure.*

The ability to do this is often more felt than learned. But give yourself a chance. Follow what rules there are. Train the eye to see and the hand to act. Most of all, develop the courage to do what needs doing. Many sewers know what is necessary but immobilize themselves by fear of moving a dart or seam.

Fitting is like sculpturing: it creates a three-dimensional form. Just as you can push clay around until you get what you want, so you can manipulate the fabric until you get the form you want.

When you are satisfied that you have done as much as you can to the trial muslin, call a halt in the fitting. Your next fitting will be in the cloth of the garment.

MUSLIN TO PATTERN

It is not the muslin one uses for the cutting out of the fashion fabric, it's a paper pattern. Muslin can too easily be forced out of size or shape or off-grain in an effort to make it fit the fabric. You can't play tricks with a paper pattern. Since it won't budge, the cutting is accurate.

1. Wherever you have made a change, mark both edges of the new seam line with colored chalk or pencil. You may add your own notches wherever they will prove helpful in reassembling the parts of the pattern. For instance, you may need a new shoulder marking on the sleeve cap if you have made any change from its original position. The repositioning of a seam or the relocation of dart control makes the original notches invalid.

2. Take the muslin apart.

3. Carefully press each section flat.

4. Draw new seam or dart lines to correct any "jumpiness" of the pin markings. Straight lines can be drawn with a ruler. Curved lines can be traced from the original pattern or drawn with an appropriate drafting instrument.

5. Study the corrected pattern.

You may find that the right and left sides are not identical. (Right and left sides of every figure vary to some extent.) If the difference is slight, it may simply mean that it has been too difficult by eye to fit both sides alike. In this case, balance the changes, center the darts, and equalize the control.

If the difference is great, both left and right sides must be considered. It will simplify matters considerably if you use the larger size for cutting so that you will always have enough material to work with. (This is because patterns generally come to you in halves to be cut in twos or on a fold.) Use the smaller side as a fitting guide.

6. Place the paper pattern over the muslin, matching key lines. Trace the corrections so they will be clearly visible. Add paper if necessary. Trim away what is unnecessary. Make your new pattern a complete record of any alterations that will make the garment fit you.

It is this corrected pattern that we will use not only for cutting out the fashion fabric but as a basis for adjusting the patterns of all inter-facings, underlinings, interlinings, and linings.

As you grow more experienced, more sensitive, more demanding in fitting, you will find yourself constantly refining, polishing, perfecting. That is as it should be. Fit where you can, fake where you must, flatter everywhere.

Part II
CONVERTING CLOTH
TO CLOTHING

Chapter 8

The Character of Cloth and How to Utilize It in Tailoring

The common ingredient of all clothing construction—be it classic or contemporary, women's, men's, or children's—is cloth. Whether you plan to put much time, effort, and money into it or whether you simply want to throw something together as quickly and as painlessly as possible matters not. Whether you are making a shift dress, a poncho, a ball gown, or a classic suit makes no difference. Fabric is no respecter of time or value or work. It goes its own merry way! This being so, one must know how to deal with its possibilities and limitations and how it can be handled to utilize its best features.

The best clues to date as to how fabric should be handled lie in the body of traditional techniques by which fine clothing has always been made. To these are added from time to time new techniques to fit the changing styles, changing fabrics, and changing needs.

You may be the one to discover previously unknown possibilities in material. You may invent new ways to apply old techniques to new situations. That is the way it is in any art: the new grows out of the tradition. So start with the available knowledge and work from there.

All fabrics, and therefore all garments, hang with the grain. (*Grain* is the name we give to a lengthwise or crosswise thread of the fabric. In patterns, this is referred to as "straight of goods.") In fact, they'll persist in hanging with the grain whether you cut them that way or not. Disregard the grain at your own peril: you may end up with an effect you hadn't anticipated and a fit you cannot rescue.

The designer utilizes the natural "hang" of the material in his or her design. The patternmaker who provides the blueprint for con-

struction designates on each pattern piece the position of the grain
that will achieve the designer's intent. You must observe these pattern
markings religiously if your finished garment is to look the way it was
planned.

As set up in the loom, the vertical and horizontal yarns are perpendicular to each other. Weaving produces a rectangular length of cloth
—grain perfect. The loom can do no less. Somewhere between the
loom and you, things may happen to the grain-perfect fabric that
makes it a problem for the sewer. The fabric may be finished off-
grain, printed off-grain, or cut off-grain.

ESTABLISHING THE TRUE GRAIN

Before one can proceed with the layout and cutting of the fabric, its
true grain must be restored. (This holds for every material that goes
inside the garment—interfacing, underlining, lining, interlining.)

If the fabric has a prominent yarn, rib, line, or stripe, you're in
luck. Simply cut along one of these.

Just as easy and just as quick is tearing the material on the horizontal grain. Many fabrics tear easily without any ill effects. Some, however, are damaged by tearing. You had better test. Close to the cut
end of the cloth, make a short snip through the selvage and into the
fabric with the points of a pair of sharp scissors. Tear a short distance. If it works, tear across the width.

When the fabric does not tear easily (as often happens in complex
weaves and firm or fuzzy fibers) or if tearing will harm it in any way,
then you must establish the grain by the following method.

Pull a crosswise thread. Make it a gentle but firm pull. Don't expect
to do the whole row at one time: there are only a few fabrics in which
this is possible. Pull a short distance. Hold the fabric up to the light so
you can see the space left by the drawn thread, and cut (Fig. 77a).
Repeat until you are clear across the width.

Sometimes the material gathers along the pulled thread. Cut following the line of the gathers (Fig. 77b), instead of the drawn thread, as
above.

In either case, you know you've been successful when you can lift
one horizontal thread across the entire width. If straightening the

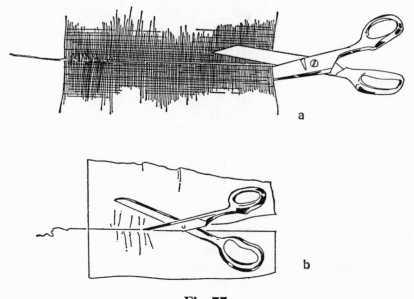

Fig. 77

grain in the ways suggested takes you forever, you're doing something wrong. Start again. It should not be too lengthy a process.

The *selvage,* as its name implies, is the self-finished edge of the material. It is the *true vertical grain* of the fabric and generally needs no further treatment. The exception would be a puckered selvage; in this case, clip every few inches to release the strain but do not cut the selvage away. If you do, you will have to establish a vertical grain as well as a horizontal one, using the same method.

FABRIC CUT OFF-GRAIN— YOUR LOSS OR THE SELLER'S?

Straightening the grain (the heavy line in Fig. 78) may reveal that the fabric was cut off-grain—unintentionally, of course. You may even discover that you have lost several inches of it by the straightening. (It's wise to buy a little extra material to take care of such contingencies.)

To prevent this, supervise the cutting of the material and insist that it be cut on-grain. This may not endear you to the one behind the

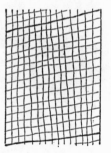

Fig. 78

counter, for it does take more time and more care. Also, the seller may lose those few inches of fabric instead of you.

Were the first length cut off the bolt on-grain, all subsequent cutting could easily be made accurate, too. Oh well, someone must start the correct cutting somewhere. Let it be with you.

OFF-GRAIN FINISH? PRESS AND PULL?

You may discover to your dismay that, far from the rectangle you were trying for in straightening the grain, you end up with this oddity (Fig. 79a). That is because the fabric was pulled off-grain in the finishing process in much the same way that you might press a handkerchief out of its rectangular shape.

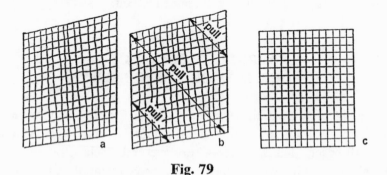

Fig. 79

Just as you can pull or press your handkerchief back into shape, so you can correct your material in the same way. Pull the grain on the

bias in the opposite direction (Fig. 79b) until the threads are restored to their original rectangular position (Fig. 79c).

If pulling dry fabric doesn't straighten the grain, dampen the cloth
or steam-press it into position on the wrong side.

CAUTION: Don't dampen silk. It water-spots. You will have to pull
and press the dry silk material into position as best you can.

Test your straightened fabric against any right angle. Use the
corner of your cutting table or cutting board, a tailor's square or a
45-degree triangle, or any other convenient squared edge, just to
make sure you have re-established the grain to its true position.

PRINTED OFF-GRAIN?
CHOOSE THE LESSER OF TWO EVILS!

You may sometimes discover after your fabric has been
straightened that it has been printed off-grain (Fig. 80).

Fig. 80

Off-grain printing doesn't happen often (there are frequent checks
at the factory), but it does happen often enough to make some yardage imperfect. When the imperfection is spotted, the factory rejects it.
That doesn't mean it isn't sold and, unfortunately, used. Such fabrics
often find their way into the mill-end stores or onto bargain counters
where they turn out to be not such bargains after all.

Off-grain printing presents a real problem for the sewer. When you
follow the print, the fabric will not hang on grain. If you follow the
grain, the printed design may march itself up hill and down dale.

What to do? Of the two evils, the lesser is to follow the printed design and hope for the best. Moral: examine fabric carefully before buying.

KNIT GOODS HAVE GRAIN, TOO

You can't assume that the fold of a tubular knit is the lengthwise grain, any more than you can assume that a straight cut across woven material is the horizontal grain.

Sometimes knits that come to you flat have been produced on a circular loom and cut at the factory or by the merchandiser. Unfortunately, the cut may not be along a lengthwise rib. Check all flat knit goods for vertical straight grain. If not on-grain, you must establish it so.

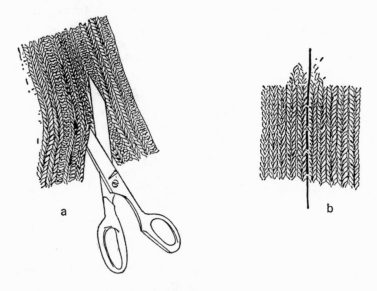

a   b

Fig. 81

Find a lengthwise rib and follow it throughout the length of the fabric. If you have sharp eyesight and a steady hand, or if the knit has a prominent rib or line, cut along it directly (Fig. 81a). When the ribs are not so easy to follow for this kind of cutting, study a few inches at a time and mark the rib with tailor's chalk or a line of guide basting (Fig. 81b). Don't worry about losing that convenient fold which you had hoped to use for the layout. One shouldn't use it anyway. The crease can never be successfully pressed out. It is better to make a new fold of fabric.

The *horizontal grain of knitted fabric* is a crosswise course. When this is a prominent line, cut along it for the crosswise grain. When it is not, establish the horizontal grain at right angles to the vertical grain. Use any convenient corner of a table or cutting board, the tailor's square, or the 45-degree triangle and a yardstick. Draw the cross grain with tailor's chalk or mark it with thread, and cut along this line.

Attention: Imperfection Ahead

When there is an imperfection in the weave or knit, the factory inspector or the fabric seller will place a loop of thread on the selvage to mark it. Whenever you see such a thread, examine the material in a line with the marking. Lay out your pattern to avoid the imperfection or to hide it in an inconspicuous spot.

HOW TO PREVENT SHRINKAGE

It's a heartbreaking experience to get a suit or dress back from the cleaner's and find it a size too small for you. To prevent such disasters, fabrics are generally treated in some way either at the factory or by you.

Treating Woolens

Woolens that have been treated at the factory are marked "Ready to sew," "Sponged," "Ready for the needle," or in some similar way. When the material is not so marked, it is wise to have it sponged by a professional service or to do it yourself. If you have any doubts at all about whether the fabric has been factory-sponged, you had better do it or have it done.

Steam pressing is not enough to do the trick. Cleaning before cutting is a good possibility, though reluctance to do this is very understandable.

Sponging is a *partial shrinking* by absorption of moisture.

A very good job of sponging can be done at home if you follow these directions:

1. Straighten the grain.

2. Fold the material in half lengthwise, with the right sides together. Pin or baste together both straightened edges and both selvages.

3. Make a sponging cloth at least 40 inches wide to accommodate the width of the folded fabric and long enough to cover it all. Old sheets will do, or a length of washable cotton bought just for this purpose. (Make sure you remove all the sizing and lint before using it.)

4. Wet one third of the sponging cloth. Starting at the wet end, roll the entire length. Let it rest until the cloth is damp (not wet), as if for ironing.

5. Spread out the sponging cloth on a large, flat surface. Place the fabric on the cloth in a perfect rectangle. Smooth out any wrinkles so that the material is absolutely flat (Fig. 82a).

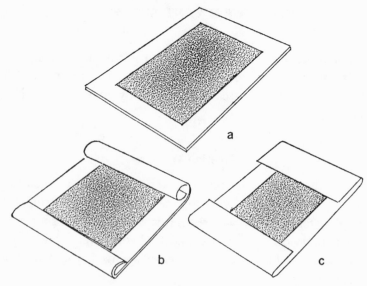

Fig. 82

6. Fold the ends of the sponging cloth over the fabric.

7. Roll the entire length of wool and sponging cloth (Fig. 82b), or fold loosely into sections from both ends to meet at the center (Fig. 82c).

8. Cover the roll or the folds completely with a Turkish towel, brown paper, or, best of all, a plastic bag. The plastic bags in which clothes are returned from the cleaner's are fine for this purpose. Covering in this way prevents the outer layers from drying while the inner layers remain damp, which would cause an uneven absorption of moisture.

9. Let stand for several hours. Most tailoring experts say three to four hours are sufficient. The Wool Bureau, Inc., recommends six to eight hours for light woolens, longer for heavier ones. Perhaps the tailoring experts are afraid that amateurs may overshrink or mat the fabric. By all means avoid overshrinking.

10. When the moisture has been absorbed, unroll the wool. Lay it out flat to dry. Smooth out any wrinkles. Make certain the grain is correct. If you don't have a large enough flat surface for drying, hang the wool over a door or shower rod well padded with Turkish towels. Turn the wool once during the drying process as if you were drying a sweater. Wool should dry naturally. Pressing fabric dry may make it stiff or push the grain out of the position we've taken such pains to set right.

11. If it is necessary to remove any wrinkling after the wool is dry, press it on the wrong side, using a press cloth. Press with the grain. Press to within 1″ of the center fold. Do not press the fold. Open the fabric and press the center section. See Chapter 15, "Pressing Problems," for the correct way to press your fabric.

One of the nice things about having the factory or a professional service do the sponging for you is that it comes back in such a beautifully finished state.

Treating Cottons or Linens

Shrinkage-resistant finishes added to cottons and linens reduce shrinking to a minimum. However, even the slightest shrinkage may affect the fit, particularly if it is a close one. Again, it is wise to treat these fabrics, too, before cutting.

Cottons and linens may be sponged in the same way as woolens, they may be dry-cleaned before cutting, or they may be rinsed in cold water. (The use of a fabric softener in the water helps preserve the finish and makes them easier to iron.) Unlike wool, these fabrics may be pressed when almost dry.

Treating Synthetics

All synthetic materials should be rinsed or soaked in cold water before cutting.

Treating Silks

All one can do with silk material is dry-clean it. It should not be subjected to water or moisture. It is not that silk can't take water but that water spots silk and may affect the dyes.

PRESHRINK EVERYTHING THAT GOES INSIDE THE GARMENT

Everything that goes inside a tailored garment (with the exception of the silk lining) should also be preshrunk.

Interfacings, unless labeled preshrunk, should be preshrunk. Set the material in a basin of hot water and let stand until it cools. Allow it to dry naturally. Press only when dry.

Interlinings of lamb's wool are treated the same as wool.

Underlinings should be rinsed or soaked in cold water and pressed when dry.

Cotton tape can be immersed in water and let stand until it has thoroughly absorbed the moisture. Allow it to dry naturally. It can be pressed to shape when used.

Some schools of thought would have you preshrink the zipper and even wrap the thread in a damp cloth for several hours. Perhaps you think this is overdoing the safety bit, but it emphasizes the point.

MORE FABRIC?

You may already have lost some fabric by straightening the grain. Now sponging or preshrinking may result in a further loss. Let me re-emphasize that, when buying fabric, it is a good policy to buy a little more than the pattern calls for. It is better to have some left over (if that should happen) rather than not quite enough.

Chapter 9

Prepare the Pattern

One might reasonably think that after all that has been done to the pattern already it would be ready for use. Not so. The corrections previously made were all for fit. Now the pattern must be readied for cutting.

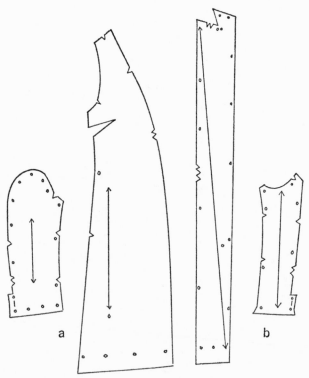

a   b

Fig. 83

Select all the pattern pieces necessary for cutting the garment. Fold the unnecessary sections and replace them in the envelope. Group the pattern pieces: those needed for the coat, jacket, or other items; those for the lining; those for the interlining; those for the interfacings. Use each group as you have need of it.

If the pattern is wrinkled, press it flat with a warm iron.

Cut off all the unnecessary margins. It is easier to cut woolens beside the pattern tissue rather than through it, particularly heavy woolens.

The grain line on many commercial patterns is inadequate (Fig. 83a). An extended grain line (Fig. 83b) ensures accuracy.

Elongate the grain lines to the entire length of the pattern (Fig. 83b). The grain line of the pattern is always placed parallel to the selvage of the material. Theoretically, measuring an equal distance in two places from a given line should establish a new line parallel to it. That may work for stable materials. Fabrics have been known to slide out of position on the cutting board between, before, and after the two anchored points. Long pattern pieces, particularly, such as pants, coats, or capes, need the added precaution of establishing the grain line parallel to the selvage in a number of places throughout their entire length. Always remember that the fabric must (and indeed will) fall with the grain however long the garment. That fall must be accurate.

When a pattern piece needs to be used more than once or reversed, it is helpful to trace and cut out an extra one: for instance, an extra sleeve or an extra pocket. This is a great advantage in a difficult layout (plaids or diagonal weaves, especially), a tight layout (just making it by a hair's breath), and when a difference in the length or width of your pattern or fabric means departing from the suggested layout.

In dealing with collars, lapels, cuffs, welts, flaps, pockets, facings, and other double thicknesses, there are the following important considerations:

1. Wherever in the garment there are two thicknesses of cloth, an upper and lower, the seam that joins them is rolled to the underside (Fig. 84a).

2. An inside curve is always shorter than an outside curve (Fig. 84b).

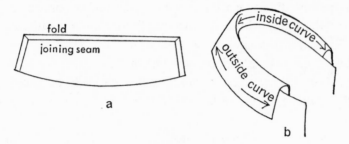

Fig. 84

To accomplish this, *an extra amount of material* is added to the length and width of the upper thickness. For instance, add to the outer edges of the upper collar, taper to the neck edge, but do not alter the edge that joins the garment (Fig. 85a).

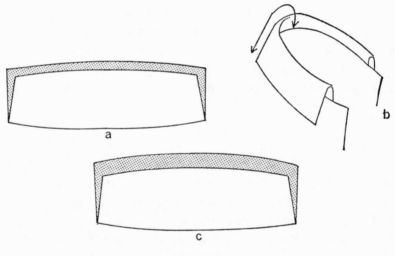

Fig. 85

This makes the upper collar somewhat larger than the undercollar.

How much length and width should one add for the seam roll? That depends on the weight and texture of the fabric. One-quarter inch makes a ⅛-inch roll for smooth, medium-weight material; ½ inch makes a ¼-inch roll for heavier weights. For very heavy or textured fabrics, add even more allowance. It is best to make a test turn to determine just how much is needed.

There is another direction in which the upper collar needs more length than the undercollar. That is the line from the *neck seam to the outside edge* (Fig. 85b). To this outside edge at the center back of the upper collar add an amount sufficient to negotiate the turn of the collar. Taper to the ends (Fig. 85c). This amount is in addition to that already added for the seam roll. This particularly is necessary for collars of heavy materials.

There are other places in the garment where one needs to make allowances for a seam roll or a turnback.

For a facing that becomes a lapel, add to the outer edge of what will eventually be the upper thickness, starting at the point where the lapel joins the collar and continuing to the break of the collar, at which point the seam roll changes direction (Fig. 86a). Below the

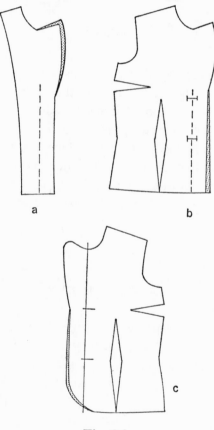

Fig. 86

break it is the front edge of the garment that needs the allowance for the seam roll (Fig. 86b).

If the lower edge of a jacket is rounded, this extra seam allowance continues around the curve (Fig. 86c).

Where there is no seam there is no problem. For instance, an upper collar–undercollar cut all in one needs no allowance on the edge to be folded under but does need it along the ends of the upper collar (Fig. 87a).

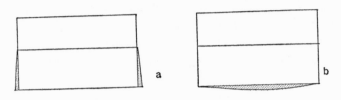

Fig. 87

When on this type of collar more length is needed from the neck seam to the outer edge, it is added to the neck edge—an exception (Fig. 87b), since there is no other feasible edge.

This principle holds for cuffs, welts, and flaps.

Why don't commercial patterns include these necessary adjustments? Sometimes they do. (It's a good idea to check your pattern before adding more.) Most often, they don't simply because the pattern company has no way of knowing the texture and weight of the material you will choose for your garment.

SEAMS AND HEMS

On most commercial patterns, seam allowances are generally ⅝ inch. Sheer fabrics need less since they are usually trimmed close to the stitching line. The same is true for many knit constructions. Heavier fabrics may need more, particularly if they have a tendency to ravel.

An extra seam allowance added to the placket on a skirt or pants will ensure an ample setting for a zipper (Fig. 88).

Fig. 88

In line with the present no-bulk theory of construction, seam allow-ances are trimmed back practically out of existence and hems are dispensed with almost entirely. This is a useful device when the cos-tume consists of many layers of single-thickness garments.

Chapter 10

Layout Logic

Breathes there a sewer with soul so dead who never to herself has said on examining a layout chart, "I can do better than that!"?

Perhaps you have on occasion sweated out the layout of a pattern on a remnant with less fabric than the pattern called for. But confess now, didn't you have to compromise on something? Didn't you have to modify the design, disregard the grain, shorten, eliminate, or supplement with some other material?

The layout chart presents the best arrangement of the pattern on a particular width of fabric with strict respect for how the garment is intended to hang from smallest to largest piece. Considerable experimenting was done before deciding on this particular layout. It will save a lot of figuring if you accept the pattern company's suggestions.

Of course variations are possible. After all, yours is a custom-made job. Your fabric may be wider, your figure requirements less. The garment may have been shortened. Perhaps you are using a contrasting collar and cuffs or facing. You may get away with less fabric in a modified layout. But even so, use the layout chart for clues to placement of pattern sections.

Should you wish to work out your own layouts, it is a good idea to keep on hand several lengths of wrapping or shelf paper cut to the standard widths of fabric—35, 39, 44, 54, and 60 inches—opened out, doubled, or folded.

Wherever possible, cutting is by twos. One cuts either two of a kind or two halves (to be joined by a seam for a whole) or a half pattern placed on a fold of fabric (to become a whole when unfolded).

Half a pattern is better than a whole pattern for large or balanced sections. It ensures that both sides of the garment are cut alike. It saves time. Folded fabric is not so unwieldy as fabric opened to full width.

Note which twos are to be cut in pairs—a right and a left, like sleeves (Fig. 89a)—and which are just duplicates, like patch pockets (Fig. 89b).

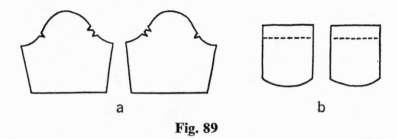

a   b

Fig. 89

Place the largest pieces first, then those that need to be on a fold. Fit in the smaller pieces. Fit shapes against each other, locking them wherever possible. *Be sure to observe the grain line* in placement.

If the fabric you are planning to use has nap, pile, or a directional weave or print, arrange all the pattern pieces so they go in the same direction—neck to hem. The repeat of design units on prints, weaves, plaids, or stripes must match.

When you are satisfied with the layout, make a little working chart. Incidentally, this is also a good way to estimate the yardage for a particular design.

WHEN YOU USE THE LAYOUT CHART THAT COMES WITH THE PATTERN

Identify each pattern piece. Since each pattern company uses different markings, different identifications, different pattern symbols, it is well to study the chart that accompanies the pattern. Sometimes the pattern pieces are labeled by letter: A, B, C, D, E; sometimes by name: FRONT, BACK, SIDE FRONT, SIDE BACK; sometimes by number: 1, 2, 3, 4. Note the position of each in the layout.

When a pattern is cut by twos or on a fold, it doesn't matter

whether the printed side of the pattern is *face up or face down.* You'll
get what you need either way.

Sometimes a shaded area on the layout chart is used to indicate
that the pattern is placed face down. This is simply because the pat-

selvages

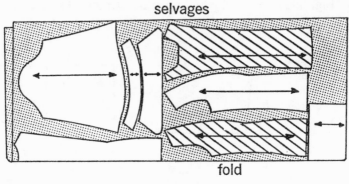

fold

Fig. 90

selvage

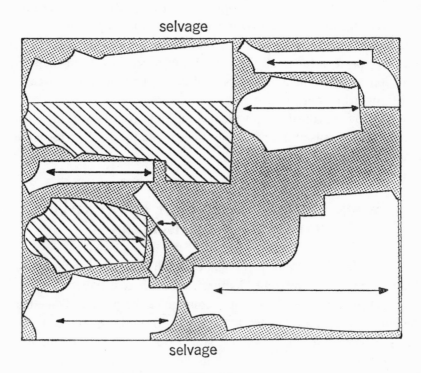

selvage

Fig. 91

tern pieces fit more compactly (like a jigsaw puzzle) if laid in a particular way (Fig. 90).

When a complete pattern is cut singly to be used on a full width of fabric, it is placed with the printed side up. This is how it will appear in the finished garment (Fig. 91).

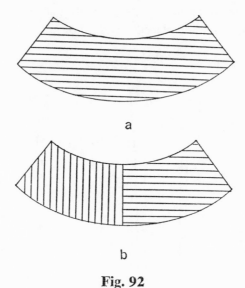

a

b

Fig. 92

When diagonally striped fabric is used, a complete collar placed on a single thickness of cloth (Fig. 92a) will avoid the mismatching that frequently results when half a collar is placed on a double thickness (Fig. 92b).

ARE ALL SEAMS NECESSARY?

There are many times when one would prefer not to cut into a beautiful fabric for a seam that has no apparent advantage. Perhaps one merely wants to avoid another seam that requires matching of stripes, checks, or plaids. Can the seam be eliminated? The answer is, "Yes, in some cases."

Two adjacent pattern pieces may be joined as one, thereby eliminating the seam, if:

1. the seam line is not essential to the design;

2. the edges are on the straight grain;

3. it is not a shaping seam;

4. the fabric is wide enough and long enough to accommodate the newly created pattern piece;

5. there is sufficient material for the necessary new layout.

Also, if the above requirements are met, a seam allowance may be ignored and the seam line placed on a fold of fabric.

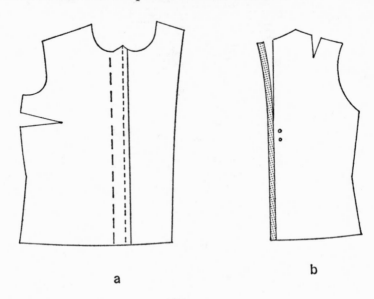

a   b

Fig. 93

FOR EXAMPLE:

(Fig. 93a) Add the facing to the front extension by overlapping the seam lines. Scotch-tape into position.

(Fig. 93b) Cut away the center-back seam allowance and place the pattern on a fold of fabric.

PLAYING WITH THE PATTERN: ECONOMICAL LAYOUTS

Pattern pieces vary in size; so do fabric widths. To fit the one on the other is like playing with a giant puzzle. The game is to place the pieces in such a way as to use the length and width of the material the most economically while at the same time observing strictly the grain of the fabric.

Whenever possible, fold the fabric with the right sides inside. This both protects the fabric and simplifies the marking. (Most marking is done on the wrong side.) There are, however, exceptions to this rule.

The Exceptions

Asymmetric patterns, cut singly, are placed on the right side of the fabric in the position in which they will be worn.

Pile against pile makes for inaccurate cutting. Therefore, in cutting pile materials like velvet, it is best to fold the material with the wrong sides together and the pile on the outside.

It is easier to match stripes, plaids, checks, or floral or geometric motifs when the right side of the fabric is up—particularly when the design is directional or when a print does not come through clearly to the wrong side.

STANDARD PATTERN ARRANGEMENTS

Here are the standard pattern arrangements used.

Lengthwise Fold

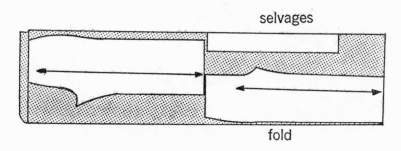

selvages

fold

Fig. 94

With right sides inside, fold the fabric in half lengthwise, matching the selvages and the straightened ends (Fig. 94).

Crosswise Fold

This is used for pattern pieces too wide to fit half the width of the fabric.

selvages

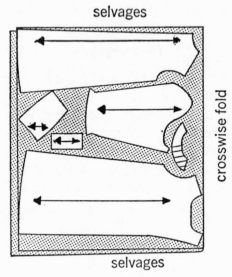

selvages

Fig. 95

With the fabric opened to its full width, fold it in half crosswise, right sides inside (Fig. 95). Match the selvages and the straightened ends.

Obviously, were the fabric to have a one-way nap, pile, or directional design, this type of fold would be ruinous—half the garment would be going up and the other half down. For such fabrics, use the open double layout.

Open Double

Mark the direction of the fabric design or nap with chalked arrows along the selvage (Fig. 96a). Measure the amount of fabric needed for the complete one-way layout. (This calls for a trial layout.) Cut at the determined length along the crosswise straight of goods. Swing the fabric around so both layers are going in the same direction. (The arrows will indicate this.) Place the two thicknesses together open full width, right sides inside (Fig. 96b).

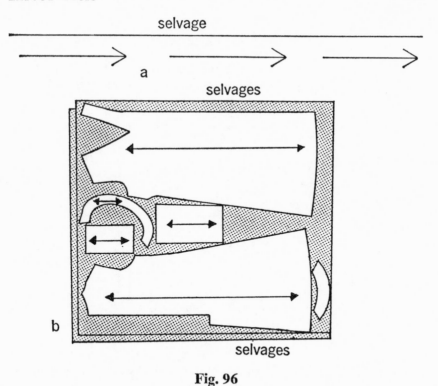

Fig. 96

Open Single, Full Width—for Asymmetric and Bias Designs

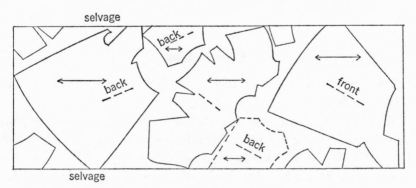

Fig. 97

Open the fabric to its full width, right side up, single thickness (Fig. 97). Place the pattern on the fabric with the printed side up.

A Double Fold

Sometimes each of several pattern pieces needs to be on a fold: for instance, the center front and center back of a skirt (Fig. 98).

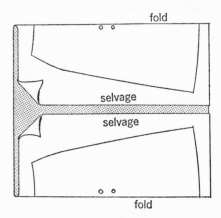

Fig. 98

Measure the widest part of the pattern. Mark this measurement in from the selvage in a sufficient number of places to provide an accurate fold line. Use pins or a line of guide basting for the marking.

If the fabric has a visible stripe, you won't need to measure. Simply fold along it.

Combinations

One part of the garment is laid on one type of fold, another part on a different fold.

You can fold fabric only one way at a time. Pin the pattern piece on the fabric in one layout. Cut it out. Then pin and cut out another (Fig. 99). Repeat as many times as necessary.

When you have decided which layout to use for your size, the view of the design you are making (there are often several options in a pattern), and the width of the fabric, circle the chart with colored pencil. In this way you will have no trouble remembering which layout you are using should you be diverted from your work (Fig. 100).

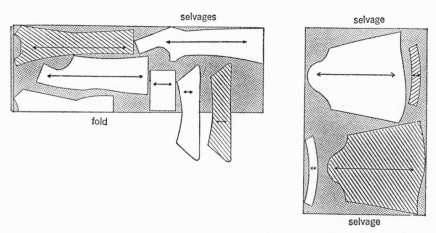

Fig. 99

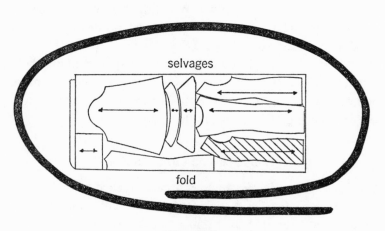

Fig. 100

SPECIAL FABRICS, SPECIAL LAYOUTS

Never mind that firm resolve never again to be trapped by a fabric that calls for engineering skills for the layout. You know your best intentions will dissolve into nothingness at the next beautiful, though complicated, material that comes along. You had better learn instead how to cope with those special layouts for special fabrics.

Short Naps and Pile Fabrics

Because pile reflects light, pile fabrics are one color when the nap runs down, another when it runs up. This makes it imperative that all pattern pieces be placed in the same direction—neck to hem. Pile fabrics (like velvet and velveteen) are cut with the nap running up because the color is richer in that direction. (Panne velvet is an exception. The nap has been pressed flat, so it is cut with the nap running down.) Corduroy is generally cut with the nap running down: it wears better in that direction.

To determine the direction of the nap, place your fingertips lightly on the surface of the material. Move them gently back and forth. Where there is resistance, there is nap. When the surface feels smooth, the nap is running down. When the surface is rough, the nap is running up. Mark the direction in which the nap moves with chalked arrows along the selvage (Fig. 96a).

Should you discover in cutting that the nap is running the wrong way, stick with it. It is better to be consistent and cut the nap in the wrong direction than to switch in mid-cutting and have two different colors or a patchwork of colors in the garment.

Long Naps and Furry Fabrics

The long-napped fabrics such as fleece, brushed wool, camel's hair, broadcloth, fake furs, and shaggy cloths are cut with the nap going down as if they were fur. Just remember the way in which you would stroke a pet. You start at the head and stroke down. If you were to start at the tail and stroke up, you would be "rubbing it the wrong way." Pattern pieces in long-nap fabrics all go in one direction—neck to hem.

Long-float Fabrics

Like pile fabrics, long-float fabrics catch the light, producing a sheen and color that vary with the direction of the light. Satin, sateen, polished cotton, and brocades must be treated like napped fabrics. All pattern pieces must be placed in the same direction lengthwise.

NOTE: Fabrics with pile, short or long nap, or sheen should not be cut on the crosswise grain.

PLACEMENT OF DESIGN UNITS

A real consideration in the use of your fabric is the judicious place-ment of its design units. Drape the fabric over yourself and study the effect in a mirror. Choose what is most effective or most flattering.

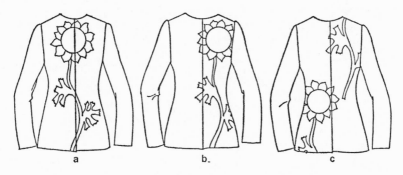

a   b.   c

Fig. 101

Centering the unit makes for formal balance (Fig. 101a). The unit placed to one side results in an asymmetric balance (Fig. 101b). An unusual or unexpected placement produces a dramatic effect (Fig. 101c).

When a fabric has a repeat of a design motif, whether woven or printed, study the direction and movement of the design units. If they are *moving in one direction, a one-way placement of pattern pieces* must also be observed.

PLACEMENTS OF STRIPES AND PLAIDS

Place the dominant vertical stripe, bar, or color at the center front and center back with the stripes or plaids evenly balanced on either

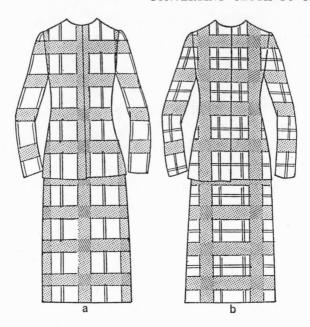

Fig. 102

side. A similar stripe, bar, or color is placed at the center of the sleeve (Fig. 102a).

OR

Place the dominant vertical stripe, bar, or color toward the side seams, equally spaced from the center (Fig. 102b).

Place the dominant crosswise stripe where it will be most flattering to the figure and in a corresponding position on the sleeve (Fig. 103a).

Often, for design interest, the dominant lines are used vertically in one part of the garment and horizontally or on the bias in another (Fig. 103b).

Even a check that appears to have an over-all look (Fig. 104a) may have a dominant stripe—the dark one. The darker bar of a simple stripe (Fig. 104b) is the dominant one. So these, too, need to be considered for placement.

Fig. 103

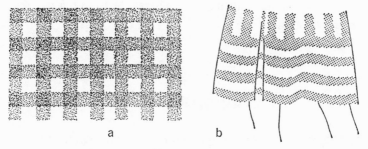

Fig. 104

MATCHING STRIPES, PLAIDS, CHECKS

Whether printed, woven, or knit, all stripes, plaids, blocks, and checks must be matched. The matching is not only horizontal at the construction seams but vertical as well.

In a suit, all dominant lines must be so placed that the finished look is one of continuous stripes, plaids, or checks with no break between the jacket and skirt or the jacket and pants.

Every part of a garment that joins or overlaps another part must match or complete the unit. This takes some doing!

The garment should close with the crosswise dominant lines matching. Stripes and plaids are closed over each other so that a complete plaid or stripe or group of stripes is directly on center.

The center back of the collar should match the center back of the coat or jacket.

The undercollar should match the upper collar if they are cut on the same grain.

Crosswise lines must match at the side seams, control seams, center front and center back, sleeve seams, lapels, and facings.

The dart legs should be centered on straight lines and match.

Pockets, belts, and buttonholes must match the area in which they are located.

The sleeves are set so that the heaviest crosswise lines match the heaviest crosswise lines of the jacket or coat.

In kimono sleeves, the dominant lines must match at the seams that join back to front.

It is wise in using stripes, checks, or plaids to let the sleeve pattern and the collar, pinned and uncut, each rest in the area in which it is tentatively located. Leave sufficient room around it so it can be moved for exact matching after the shoulder seams and the undercollar have been fitted.

ODDS OR EVEN?

Stripe and plaids are designed with an even (balanced) or uneven (unbalanced) placement of lines, bars, and colors. Before you can decide how to use them, you must determine which type they are.

Does the fabric have an up-and-down effect? Find the center or dominant horizontal line or bar or color. "Read" the lines above and below this. If they are the same (Fig. 105a), the plaid or stripe is balanced or even. If they are different (Fig. 105b), the plaid or stripe is unbalanced or uneven.

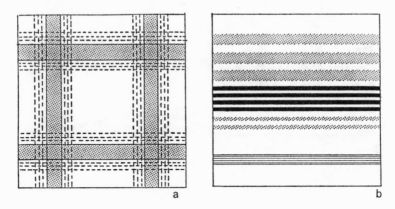

Fig. 105

Does the fabric have a right-and-left effect? Find the dominant vertical line or bar or color. Read the lines, bars, or colors to the right and left of this. If they are the same on both sides, the stripe is balanced or even (Fig. 106a). If they are different, the plaid or stripe is unbalanced or uneven (Fig. 106b).

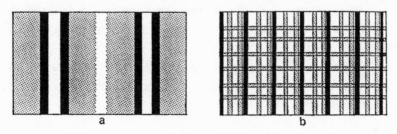

Fig. 106

It is very possible to get fabrics where the lines, bars, or colors are even in one direction and uneven in another, or even in both directions, or uneven in both directions. And designers, being the devilish ones they are, often complicate matters by using a lovely diagonal twill weave along with stripes or bars or colors.

When the movement is up and down, place all pattern pieces going in the same direction—neck to hem (Fig. 107).

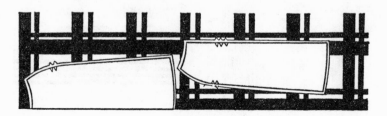

Fig. 107

When the movement is right to left, you have a choice. The stripes may move around the body, all heading in the same direction (Fig. 108a) or may be arranged in a mirror image (Fig. 108b), one side the reverse of the other.

To have the stripes move around the body in the same direction (Fig. 108a), choose the stripe you want for the center, fold the material lengthwise, and place the pattern in a directional layout (Fig. 108c).

To achieve a mirror image (Fig. 108b), fold the material crosswise, matching stripes. Place the center line on the exact center of a vertical stripe (Fig. 108d).

When the Movement Is Up and Down and Right and Left

A plaid that is unbalanced in both directions is definitely not for novices (Fig. 109a).

If the fabric has a right and wrong side, you will just have to settle for the imbalance. Use the layout for Figs. 108a and 108b.

a

b

c lengthwise fold

d crosswise fold

Fig. 108

If the fabric is reversible, the crosswise imbalance can be balanced by using the following layout:

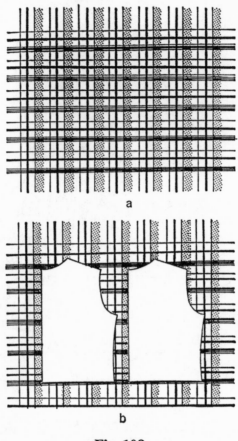

Fig. 109

On a single thickness of the fabric cut two identical pieces, using the same pattern, and going in the same direction on similar lengthwise and crosswise plaids (Fig. 109b). Use the reverse side of one as the right side.

This method is workable in diagonal materials, too.

LINE UP!

To make sure that upper and under layers are cut on the same stripes of the material, pin the two layers together every few inches or so, matching the lines. (It's easier to do this when the fabric is folded with the right side outside. Right side outside also makes it easier to match the plaid, checks, and so on.)

When you are working with plaids, stripes, or checks, you have a line in the fabric to go by instead of measuring the grain.

The key pattern piece is the front. Place it first on the fabric. Note the position of the notches in relation to the fabric design but remember that it is the *stitching lines* that *must be matched,* not the cutting lines. Next place the section that joins it, matching corresponding notches on similar lines or figures of the fabric. Continue in this way until every piece has been correctly placed to match those it must join.

Sometimes it is impossible to make every pair of seam lines match. For instance, you may be able to match the front sleeve cap to the front armhole, but this may not necessarily make the back sleeve cap and back armhole match. The bodice side seams may match, but the shoulder seams may not. Darts always interrupt the matching, so that the underarm sleeve seams can match only to the elbow either from the wrist up or from the shoulder down, but not both. What to do? Make the seams match that will be most prominent and hope for the best from the rest.

TRIAL LAYOUT

Have you ever had the experience of starting your cutting at one end, and proceeding merrily for most of the length of the fabric only to find, as you near the end, that there is not quite enough material to finish? A trial layout would have prevented this disaster.

Place the fabric on a flat surface. Line up the straight edges of the fabric with the straight edges of the cutting surface. Place the pattern in the position indicated on the layout chart.

Start at one end of the fabric. Support the weight of the rest of the cloth at the other end of the cutting table, on an ironing board, or on a chair. This prevents the pull on the cloth by its own weight. When the pattern has been temporarily pinned to the material, fold the finished end to make room on the flat surface for the new part.

Place the grain of the pattern parallel to the selvage of the material.

Place the pattern pieces close to each other. Spaces between may result in a shortage of as much as five or six inches—crucial inches. This could mean the difference between being able to get the pattern out of the length of cloth and not.

Arrange the pattern pieces so that, if any fabric is left, it will be in one usable piece either at the end or in the middle. You may find use for a larger piece—a hat, bag, scarf, or trimming. Otherwise you may accumulate pounds of unusable scraps.

Since this is only a trial, use as few pins as will give you the information you want. If changes need to be made, it won't take hours to unpin.

If the trial layout reveals that there is not enough material:

1. Make smaller seam allowances and/or a narrower hem.

2. Piece the material. (The "piece" is on the same grain.) It is as if you were adding another piece to make it wider or longer. Piece in some place where the joining seam will be least conspicuous.

3. Face or trim in another color or fabric.

4. Combine with another texture—suede, real or make-believe; leather; knitted sections.

5. Eliminate the cloth waistband of the skirt or pants. Use another material for the waistband or finish the waistline with an inside band.

6. Eliminate or change some detail. For instance, patch pockets could become bound pockets or welt pockets, both of which take less material.

7. If you are impossibly short of fabric, give up. Get another pattern with fewer pattern pieces and less detail. Or buy more material (if you can get it).

There's no doubt about it. The layout is hard, physically tiring work that at the same time requires the utmost alertness. Best save this part of the tailoring process for a time when you feel your freshest.

Chapter 11

Pinning, Cutting, Marking

Are you saying to yourself, "I've come almost halfway through this book and I'm only just starting?" Whether you think so or not, you really are well along even though you have little to show for it. Just think of all the thought, information, decision, and preparation necessary to get you this far. In ready-to-wear clothing all of this is done for you. Now you must work out every tiny detail of design and production yourself. Only after all these vital preliminaries are out of the way would one dare to put scissors to cloth.

PIN THE PATTERN TO THE FABRIC

When you are satisfied with the trial placement of the pattern on the fabric, go back and pin for the actual cutting.

1. Pin the grain line (straight of goods) parallel to the selvage in a number of places for the entire length of the pattern piece.

2. When the grain line is set, smooth the pattern toward the outer edges and pin the rest.

3. Keep the pattern and the fabric as flat as possible, trying not to raise them from the cutting surface any more than is necessary. The pins are placed whichever way will keep the cutting surface flat: either parallel to the seam line or at right angles to it.

4. Use one hand as an anchor and the other to pin. Keep smoothing the fabric as you go along.

5. The pins must go through the pattern and both thicknesses of cloth. Use pins large enough to do so. Place them 2 to 3 inches apart or as close as necessary to provide a true cutting edge. Curves require more pins than straight lines.

6. Use fine silk pins or fine needles used as pins on fabrics that bruise easily.

7. When additional seam or hem allowances are needed, mark them with tailor's chalk.

When you have finished the pinning, check the layout with the one on the layout chart. Check off each section to make sure you have them all. Double-check pattern sections that need to be reversed, such as sleeves. Double-check the matching of stripes, checks, plaids, or other motifs. This is the last chance to catch any errors before cutting. Cutting is so final!

8. Remove the pins from the grain line—there's no need for them any longer. The prolonged presence of pins may leave holes in the fabric.

A FEW WORDS OF ADVICE ABOUT THE CUTTING

Cut when you are fresh and alert and least likely to be distracted. You will be less apt to make mistakes.

Cut beside the cutting line of the pattern or the chalked line of your correction.

Use sharp scissors or shears. Bent shears are best for woolens. (Do not use pinking shears. It is too difficult to cut any but lightweight materials with them. Besides, pinking is meant to be an edge finish—one seldom used in tailoring.)

Keep the cloth as flat and smooth as possible. Move around the layout rather than shifting the fabric to meet you.

Use long, firm strokes for the straight edges, short strokes for the curved edges.

Cut with the grain. Many patterns indicate the direction of the stroke with a scissors symbol. When the fabric has a pile or nap, cut with the nap.

Notches may be cut into or out from the cutting edge, depending on the amount of seam allowance needed or the character of the fabric. Or notches may be marked in thread after the garment has been cut.

It is difficult to cut accurately through two layers of very heavy or very bulky fabric. Sometimes it is necessary, after the section has been cut, to correct the cutting of the underlayer. Use the pattern or the upper layer as a guide.

As the pieces are cut, lay them flat or hang them on a hanger. If folding is necessary, use as few folds as possible. Keep the pattern side out for easy identification and for protection of the fabric.

Where the pattern reads "clip" or "slash," it is the fabric, not the pattern, that is to be clipped or slashed. This should not be done until the seam line is first reinforced or stitched.

Cutting out the fabric is one of the backbreaking, tedious parts of sewing. Be comforted by the thought that, once the garment is cut out, you're well on your way.

MARK THE MATERIAL

All of the markings that deal with the assembling, stitching, and style details must be transferred from the pattern to the fabric. After all, it is the fabric that will be your garment, not the tissue pattern.

Mark everything you need to know!

The more time you take to mark now, the less work and guesswork when you come to join the sections of your garment.

Each pattern piece tells a complete story of its part in the construction. Even were you to lose that fateful sheet of pattern directions, you could still put your garment together with all the information you will find on the pattern itself.

These markings on your pattern DO NOT need to be transferred to the fabric

The identification markings: the name of the pattern company, the number of the pattern, the name of the pattern piece, its letter or number.

The markings that tell where to alter the pattern for a better fit.

The markings that show how the pattern is to be laid on the fabric and cut out: the fold of fabric, the grain line, the cutting line.

These markings DO need to be transferred to the fabric

All the markings that show how the garment is to be assembled: the notches, special markings like

that show points or spots to be joined—the position of buttons, snaps, joinings, and so on.

The markings that show how the garment is to be stitched on the wrong side.

The markings that show the placement of design details that appear on the right side: buttonholes, pockets, tucks, pleats, topstitching, and so forth.

Wrong-side Markings

The wrong-side markings are for the big construction seams and darts. The darts should always be marked precisely. The seams may or may not be marked.

Do mark the seam line when seams require precision stitching. Don't mark the seam line if fitting to your figure may create departures from the original seam line or if you can judge the seam allowance by eye. Many sewing machines have some measurements marked on the throat plate. If yours doesn't, you can make your own marking with masking tape or with a fine line of nail polish. It is a help to have the measurements right on the machine.

Wrong-side markings may be made with tailor's chalk, dressmaker's carbon paper, or basting thread.

Tailor's chalk makes safe, quick, and easy markings. It leaves no permanent marks on the material. This feature is at once an asset and a drawback. You can't mark now and sew later: there may not be any markings left. If you plan to use tailor's chalk, mark as you sew.

How to Use the Tailor's Chalk

1. Use a color that will show on the fabric.

2. Perforate the pattern in enough places to indicate a dart, seam, or spot marking. Use any suitable sharp instrument, such as an orange stick or an embroidery stiletto. Be careful not to mar the fabric when you punch the hole.

3a. Place a pin through each perforation, being sure to make it go through both thicknesses of fabric. Chalk the area caught by the pin on both upper and under sides (Fig. 110a).

OR

3b. Push the pin through the center of the perforation through both thicknesses of fabric. Mark with chalk the spot where the pin enters and emerges from the fabric (Fig. 110b).

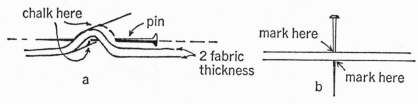

Fig. 110

Dressmaker's carbon paper and a tracing wheel make excellent markings but must be used with caution. (Note: dressmaker's carbon is *not* typewriter carbon.) The carbon lasts longer than chalk. Indeed, some of it lasts forever, which is one of its drawbacks. There are a few others: the tracing wheel may bruise touchy fabrics. The carbon doesn't show on varicolored or textured material. While it is fairly impossible to see the markings on some wools, they shine through brightly (and permanently) on white, light-colored, or sheer materials. Better test the marking on a scrap of your material before proceeding. Where you can use dressmaker's carbon, it is a wonderful stitching guide.

How to Mark with Dressmaker's Carbon Paper

1. Unpin a small section of one pattern piece. Unpinning the entire pattern to position the carbon is too risky: you may not get it back again precisely. Besides, the carbon doesn't come in sheet sizes large enough to do it that way.

2. Slip a sheet of dressmaker's carbon paper of a contrasting color between the pattern and the fabric. Place the coated side against the wrong side of the fabric.

3. Slip a second sheet of carbon paper under the lower thickness of cloth with the coated side against the wrong side of the fabric. In effect, you are enclosing the fabric with the carbon paper so both sides can be marked simultaneously.

4. Carefully replace the pattern and pin it in just enough places to hold it in position.

5. Slip a sheet of cardboard or a magazine under all. It provides a firm base that won't resist the tracing wheel. It will also protect the surface on which you are working.

6. Using the tracing wheel, carefully mark the seam line. Use a ruler for the straight lines; it's easier as well as more accurate to trace with one. Trace the curved lines freehand, carefully following the lines on the pattern.

7. Unpin the pattern, remove the carbon, slide it and the cardboard base along to a new section, and repeat as in steps 4, 5, and 6 (Fig. 111) until the entire piece is marked. Make sure the new marking is a continuation of the old.

8. In marking heavy fabrics, mark one side at a time.

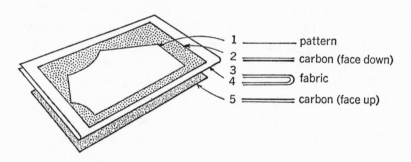

1 ——————— pattern
2 ═══════ carbon (face down)
3
4 ══════⟩ fabric
5 ═══════ carbon (face up)

Fig. 111

Right-side Markings

Some markings are necessary on the right side of the garment while work is in progress—the position of the pocket, a buttonhole, or a button, the center front, or a fold line for a facing or a pleat. You can't take chances with anything that may mar the beautiful surface of the cloth. Who wants to start with the cleaning fluid before a garment has even been worn?

The safest right-side marking is basting thread of a contrasting color. It can be easily removed when it has served its purpose and leaves no trace that it has been there.

When it is a line you want to indicate, use *guide basting*. Guide basting is a row of uneven basting with long stitches on the right side of the material and short stitches on the underside.

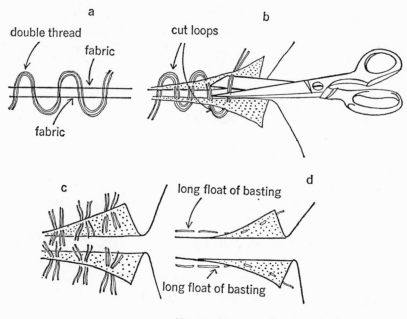

Fig. 112

1. Using a double thread of contrasting color, make a line of basting through the pattern and both layers of the fabric.

2. Leave 1-inch loops of thread between stitches (Fig. 112a).

3. Open the layers of the fabric carefully and cut the thread between, leaving small tufts (Fig. 112b).

4. Clip the stitches that appear on the surface of the pattern to release them (Fig. 112c).

5. Carefully remove the pattern.

6. Since the tufts of thread may pull out, immediately replace them with a line of guide basting on the right side (Fig. 112d).

7. Remove the tufts.

When it is a spot rather than a line you wish to mark, use *tailor's tacks*.

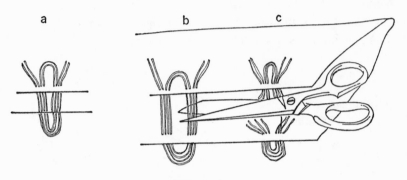

Fig. 113

1. Use a double thread of contrasting color.

2. Puncture a perforation in the pattern at the spot to be marked so the thread is not involved with the tissue.

3. Take a stitch through both thicknesses of the cloth, leaving a 1-inch end.

4. Take another stitch in the same place, making a 1-inch loop.

5. Repeat steps 3 and 4, making a double loop. Cut the thread, leaving a 1-inch end (Fig. 113a).

6. Carefully separate the two layers of cloth until a stitch appears on each outer side. This will hold the tufts in place.

7. Clip the thread between the layers (Fig. 113b). This produces tufts on the right side of the fabric called tailor's tacks (Fig. 113c).

8. Carefully remove the pattern.

The trick in successful tailor's tacks is not to cut the loops until the layers of fabric have been separated. If you cut them before, the tufts will pull out as you separate the two thicknesses.

If the fabric is too thick to make tailor's tacks through both layers, make them through the upper layer first. Push the needle through the center of the first tacks to mark the position of those on the underside. Make the tailor's tacks where indicated on the undersurface.

Different colors of basting thread can be used for the various markings. Don't use so many that you will need a legend (like a map) to identify the markings.

NOTCHES are those little triangular or diamond shapes on the cutting line of the pattern. They come singly, in pairs, or in groups. Sometimes they are numbered in the order in which they are put together. When you find a notch (or more than one) you will find its twin on another section of the garment. The two must be matched. With notches, you don't have to puzzle out which section goes with what. The notches tell. They speed up the assembling of a garment.

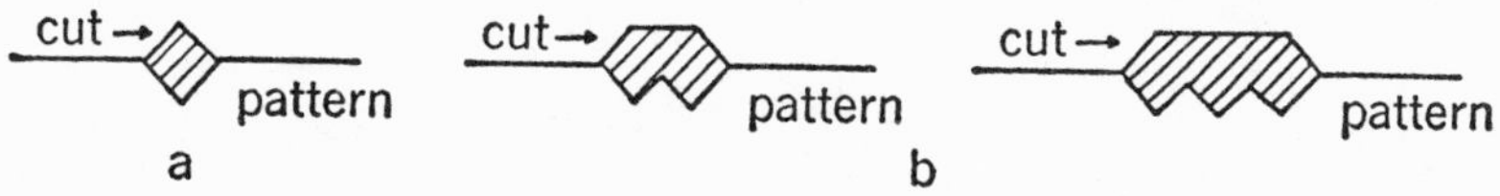

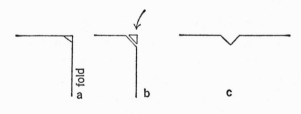

Fig. 114

Notches may be cut from the cutting line, either singly (Fig. 114a) or in twos or threes (Fig. 114b). The latter are not cut individually but as groups.

When it is safe to cut into the seam allowance (if, say, the material won't ravel or the seam allowance won't be needed for fitting), one may actually cut a notch into it (Fig. 115).

Fig. 115

To Cut a Notch

1. Fold the material where the notch is indicated on the pattern (Fig. 115a).

2. Snip diagonally across the corner (Fig. 115b).

3. When the fabric is opened out, the complete notch will appear (Fig. 115c).

The notch should be small. It is meant only for your eyes. Don't cut a big chunk out of the seam allowance.

Other Ways of Marking the Notches

1. A short snip into the seam allowance. This may be harder to see but will do if you are in a hurry.

2. Several loops of double thread of contrasting color. This is a very good method for very heavy or varicolored fabrics or fabrics that ravel.

PATTERN REMOVAL AND FABRIC PROTECTION

When the garment is completely marked, it is safe to remove the pattern.

To protect the length, shape, and grain of each cut edge, every garment section should be immediately stay-stitched.

Stay stitching is a line of machine stitching in the seam allowance close to the seam line.

Use any thread and 8 stitches to the inch. These are small enough to stay the edge and large enough for easy removal should that be necessary. Otherwise, the stay stitching may remain permanently in the seam allowance, where, we hope, no one will ever see it.

To preserve the grain, stay stitching must be directional.

Stitch with the grain. The rule is: stitch from a high point to a low one, from a wide point to a narrow one (Fig. 116a). The latter takes precedence over the former.

The threads of the material actually point the way. Examine the frayed edges for the direction. When the threads point down (Fig. 116b), stitch down. When the threads point up (Fig. 116c), stitch up.

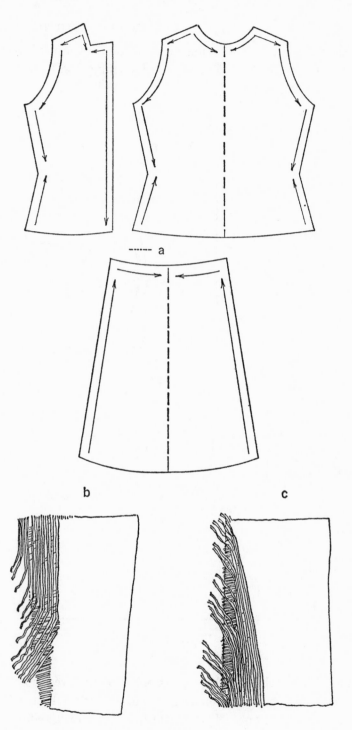

a

b   c

Fig. 116

Never make a continuous line of stay stitching around a corner. Break the thread at the end of a row of stitching and begin again in the new direction (Fig. 117).

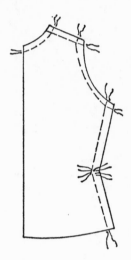

Fig. 117

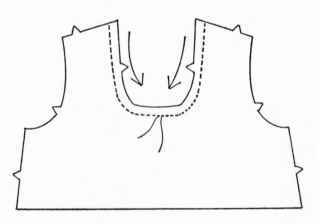

Fig. 118

On a curve, stitch from the highest point to the lowest point. Break the thread, start the second half of the curve at its highest point, and stitch to the lowest one, where it will meet the previous line of stay stitching. Break the thread (Fig. 118).

Just to make sure that your stitching has in no way affected the original size and shape of the section, compare your stay-stitched edge with the comparable edge of the pattern. Pull up the thread on any stretched edge. Clip the stitching in a few places to release a pulled-up edge. Stay stitching must preserve the line of an edge, not distort it.

What to Stay-stitch

Stay-stitch all curved and angled edges. If the fabric tends to ravel, it is wise to stay-stitch even straight edges.

What Not to Stay-stitch

These edges need not be stay-stitched:

Edges that will eventually be eased into others: for instance, a sleeve cap must be eased into the armhole. It does not get stay-stitched, but the armhole itself does, to preserve its curved line.

Edges that get stretched to fit others: for example, collar necklines are stretched slightly to fit the garment neck seam. They do not get stay-stitched, but the garment neckline does.

In each of the above instances, it is the *fixed edge* that *does* get the stay stitching, while the *edge to be eased or stretched* does not.

The hemline of a garment is not stay-stitched. It, too, must be eased into the adjoining area.

Hidden edges that don't join another section do not need stay stitching: for instance, the outer edges of facings.

True bias is not stay-stitched. Its charm is its hang and drape. It should not be restricted with stay stitching.

Stay stitching may seem a tedious task and you may be tempted to skip it. Don't: in the much handling during construction it is easy to stretch and pull the fabric out of shape. You certainly wouldn't want that.

Well begun is half done. When you've come this far, you've taken a giant step in the production of your garment.

Chapter 12

The Shape of Fashion

There are two ways to support the shape of fashion. One way is to let the body do all the work of propping up. Obviously, you can get out of that kind of garment only the shape you put into it. The second way is to build the shape right into the garment by means of a substructure. By doing this you can have any shape you want.

Contemporary (unstructured) tailoring, with its layers of fabric that envelop the body, falls into the first category. Classic (structured) tailoring, with its clean-cut sculptured lines, falls into the second.

With the look of a shirt and the comfort of a sweater, the unstructured, contemporary version of the suit or coat calls for little or no undercover support. What little there is appears only in areas that require reinforcement rather than shaping.

The charm of these "soft" tailored styles lies in the fluidity of line and the use of nonrestricted fabric. They come as a relief and a reaction to the massively structured "space-age" clothes of the sixties, of which the Courrèges models were a notable example.

Between the extremes of these two style periods are the present vast majority of coats, jackets, blazers, and suits. While stemming from the classic tailoring tradition, the new tailoring is modified by the use of softer fabric and less inner structure. This is as true now of men's tailoring as of women's.

Hard or soft, structured or unstructured, there's more to a jacket or coat than meets the eye. However little or however much, it's that unseen presence that gives a garment its definition or contour.

THE INTERFACING: SHIELD-LIKE SUBTLE OR FRANKLY FEMALE

Strictly speaking, an interfacing is a layer of supporting material placed between the facing and the outer fabric. In dressmaking, the interfacing is limited to the same size and shape as the facing. This is also the limit of the interfacing in many "soft," shirt-shaped jackets or coats.

In "hard" tailoring, the interfacing assumes more importance. It is extended to include part (for women) or all (for men) of the front shaping and often a back reinforcement as well. In addition, for women, the "shaping" can be as subtle as the shield-like shape of a man's jacket. Or it can be frankly female.

What you choose to do with the interfacing depends largely on the effect you want.

INTERFACINGS FOR "SOFT" TAILORING

Shirt Jackets

Interface collars and cuffs, front bands or edges, pocket flaps (Fig. 119, shaded areas).

Fig. 119

Wrap Styles

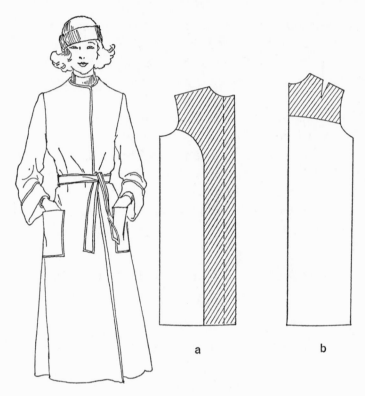

a   b

Fig. 120

FRONT INTERFACING

1. Make the front interfacing ½ inch wider than the front facing.

2. Extend the front interfacing to include the shoulder and arm-hole down to the point at which the armhole seam swings into an underarm curve. Generally a notch appears here. With a curved line, connect this point with the inner edge of the front interfacing (Fig. 120a).

3. Extend the interfacing to the hemline in a straight line.

BACK INTERFACING

Draw a slightly curved line starting 4 to 5 inches down from the neckline at the center back to the point on the armhole seam that swings into the underarm curve (Fig. 120b).

A Chanel-type Jacket

1. Extend the front interfacing to include the shoulder and arm-hole area.

2. Mark a point 3 to 4 inches down on the underarm seam. Make the front interfacing ½ inch wider than the front facing. With a

Fig. 121

curved line, connect the underarm point with the inner edge of the front interfacing. Extend the interfacing to the hemline in a straight line (Fig. 121a).

3. When the facing is cut all in one with the front of the garment, extend the interfacing ⅝ inch beyond the fold line of the front edge (Fig. 121b).

4. To firm the front edge of the interfacing turn under the front extension at the fold line and stiffen with close rows of machine stitching (Fig. 121c).

INTERFACINGS FOR "HARD" TAILORING

Time was when fine tailored clothes for women were always made by a man's tailor. When you went to him for a suit or coat, you knew exactly what you were going to get: no surprises in style or fabric. He made one thing only, a man's coat or suit—same fabric, same shaping —except that yours buttoned right over left. This type of tailoring showed its masculine origin all too clearly both in design and in contour.

The "man-tailored" suit for women today retains the classic styling but modifies the shaping to accommodate the curves of a woman's figure.

The Interfacing for a Traditional Man-tailored Woman's Jacket

In the traditional man-tailored woman's jacket the interfacing is extended to include the bust area in addition to the shoulder and armhole area.

Even if your interfacing pattern does not provide this extension, you can make your own pattern for it. While this may be a little extra work, it pays off by providing elegant shaping and support.

How to Make the Interfacing Pattern

1. On the adjusted style pattern, draw the over-all outline of the interfacing.

2. Either cut the original pattern apart (if you don't intend to use it again) or trace the interfacing pattern onto a fresh piece of paper (if you do intend to use the pattern again).

The Over-all Outline of the Front Interfacing

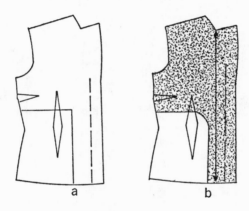

a   b

Fig. 122

1. Carry the interfacing across the shoulder and chest to the armhole and across the bust to the side seam (Fig. 122a).

2. Bring the interfacing 3½ to 4 inches down from the armhole on the side seam (excluding darts), or as far down as may be necessary to include any underarm shaping.

3. Make the remainder of the interfacing, from the cross line to the hem, ½ inch wider than the facing itself.

4. With a curved line, correct the corner where the horizontal and vertical edges of the interfacing meet (Fig. 122b).

5. Trace the grain line, the center-front line, and the notches.

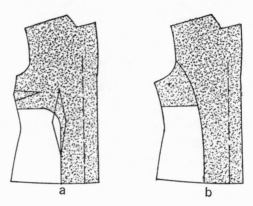

Fig. 123

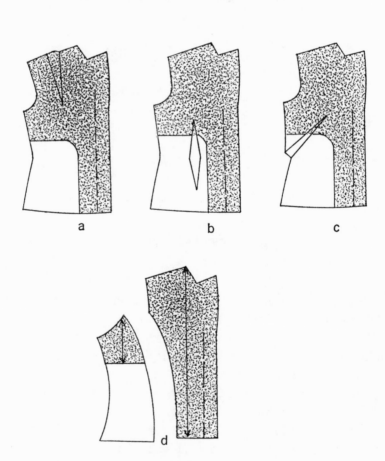

Fig. 124

Should the width of the interfacing bring the inner edge close to a dart or seam, carry the interfacing all the way over to the center of the nearest dart (Fig. 123a) or to the nearest seam (Fig. 123b). These are logical stopping places.

1. Include any darts that lie completely within the over-all outline (Fig. 124a).

2. Include 1½ to 2 inches of the tops of any vertical darts (Fig. 124b) or any angled darts (Fig. 124c).

3. Include any shaping seams that lie within this area. Cut as many sections of interfacing as there are sections of outer fabric (Fig. 124d).

When the Facing Is Cut All in One with the Garment

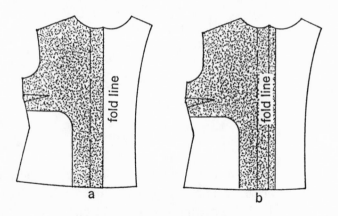

Fig. 125

When the facing is cut all in one with the jacket or coat, cut the interfacing only to the fold line for a crisp edge (Fig. 125a), or extend it ½ to ⅝ inch beyond the fold line for a soft edge (Fig. 125b).

The extension can be stiffened with close rows of stitching, as in Fig. 121c.

Keep in mind that it is the garment that gets interfaced, not the facing.

The Over-all Outline of the Back Interfacing

1. Bring the back interfacing 3½ to 4 inches down on the center back and a distance down on the side seam to match that of the front interfacing.

2. Join these two points with a flattened S curve from the center back to the underarm seam (Fig. 126).

Fig. 126

The long, bias sweep of the S curve provides give for the forward movement of the arms. A no-stretch straight line would restrict such action. Often the back interfacing is cut on the bias to provide even more ease of movement.

Some schools of tailoring omit the back interfacing, but it has its obvious advantages, not the least of which is that it blocks out the shoulder-pad ridge so that it doesn't show through.

1. Include any darts that lie within this over-all outline (Fig. 127a).

2. Include any seams that lie within this over-all outline (Fig.

127b). Cut as many on-grain sections of interfacing as there are sections of outer fabric.

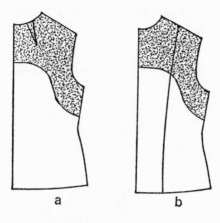

Fig. 127

When there is an underarm section rather than an underarm seam, follow the same general outline as for the front and back interfacings but divide the area into its several parts (Fig. 128).

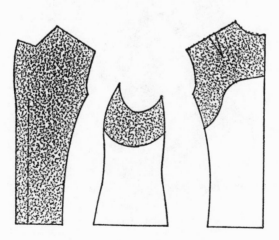

Fig. 128

THE FEMININE TOUCH

Can a man-tailored suit look feminine? You bet it can. Soften the severe look with a chiffon bow-tied blouse (Fig. 129).

Fig. 129

Or soften the jacket itself by subtracting some of the interfacing suggested in Fig. 122 (Fig. 130). (One way to deal with bust shaping is to circumvent it.)

Same Style, Different Effect: It's the interfacing that makes the difference.

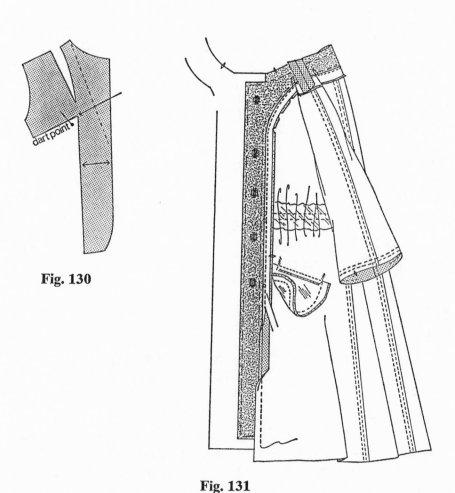

Fig. 130

Fig. 131

In this raglan-sleeve coat, only the decorative bands are interfaced (Fig. 131). The effect is soft at the shoulders.

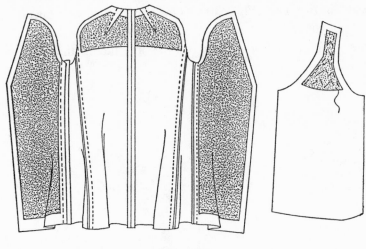

Fig. 132

In the raglan-sleeve coat of Fig. 132, the entire front, the entire shoulder, part of the back, and the shoulder area of the sleeve are interfaced for a firmer effect.

DELINEATE THE DESIGN DETAILS

And as if this were not enough, all important design details are interfaced for body and shape retention (Fig. 133a).

Collars and cuffs (Fig. 133a), pockets, welts, flaps (Fig. 133b), yokes (Fig. 133c), hip interest (Fig. 133d), belts and waistbands (Fig. 133e), and any other unusual details are interfaced.

All outside edges that have not already been interfaced are now interfaced with bias strips of interfacing material.

Hems, sleeve closings and hems, and back vents are interfaced (Fig. 134).

a

b

c

d

e

Fig. 133

Fig. 134

INTERFACING FOR AN UNLINED JACKET OR COAT

All these extensive interfacings are fine for garments that are to be lined. However, one would hardly want them in full view in an unlined coat or jacket. For such garments, interface only the faced areas. Make the interfacing slightly narrower than the facing. In that way not only will you make certain that the interfacing won't peep out from under the facing but you will have graded the two thicknesses, making for a smoother construction.

TOTAL SUPPORT: THE UNDERLINING, OR BACKING

Some fabrics, either alone or interfaced, may not be able to sustain the lines of the design. *They need total support.* Total support is supplied by an *underlining,* often called a backing.

The underlining is cut from the same pattern as the outer fabric and applied to its underside. When the two are joined, a new fabric is created that has the surface appeal of the original plus the character of the underlining. For instance, a loosely woven wool underlined with Siri is no longer a loosely woven wool and no longer Siri; it is Siri-backed wool. Now, instead of being limp, the wool is firm and can be used for styles calling for a firm fabric.

Generally, the same underlining is used throughout the garment so there is consistent color and texture in all parts. However, if the underlining used in the rest of the garment proves too heavy for comfort in the sleeves, then a lighter-weight underlining of the same color may be substituted.

Undoubtedly, it may seem more logical to use a firm material to begin with. But then fashion isn't logical. Besides, the use of an underlining opens up limitless possibilities in the choice of fabric for any design.

EITHER OR BOTH: UNDERLINING/INTERFACING

If you underline a garment do you also need an interfacing? That depends on the design and the fabric.

For a sweater-like or Chanel-type jacket an underlining is sufficient (Fig. 135a).

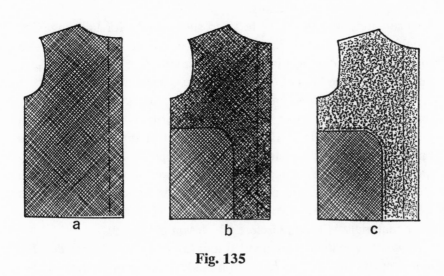

Fig. 135

A loosely woven or lacy fabric may be underlined first, then interfaced (Fig. 135b).

A closely woven but supple fabric may be firmed up by a combination of interfacing and underlining joined as one layer (Fig. 135c).

Interface the parts you normally would; underline the rest. Join the two by overlapped seams (see page 228).

Sometimes several different kinds of supporting material are used in one garment, each performing a specific function in a particular part of the garment.

THE SHAPING AND FOUNDATION FABRICS

When it comes to buttressing the shape of fashion, anything goes—from chicken wire to foam rubber!

Thumb through the costume design books and what do you find? All sorts of contraptions of bone, steel, wire, and wood. There have been steel girdles and whalebone corsets, farthingales and panniers, crinolines and hoopskirts. There have been stays and bustles, inflatable bras and padded posteriors.

Fortunately we don't have to go to such lengths for tailoring. One should, however, retain the same freedom to use any materials—if they work! The only test is whether *this* supporting material will produce and hold the lines of *this* design in *this* particular fabric.

Theoretically, almost any fabric can be used as an interfacing or underlining. (Every sewer has drawers full of odds and ends that can be pressed into service.) However, a number of supporting materials have been especially developed for such purposes. So great a variety are commercially available for the home sewer as to be bewildering. You probably know the names from the extensive advertising with which each company makes its extravagant claims. Experience with these materials will soon disclose which you prefer.

Supporting materials are divided into three classes: *the wovens, the non-wovens, and the fusibles* (iron-ons). They vary in character—limp to stiff. They vary in weight—light to heavy. They vary in width—18 inches to 72 inches. They vary in price. They vary in cleanability: some are washable, some are dry-cleanable. Some come in an array of colors, some come in neutrals.

Interfacings are generally compatible in weight with the fabrics they interface. That is, lightweight fabric—lightweight interfacing, medium-weight fabric—medium-weight interfacing, heavyweight fabric—heavyweight interfacing.

Underlinings, however, may be of any weight or any texture that will give the desired effect.

Interfacing and underlining materials are used interchangeably.

What is underlining in one garment may be interfacing in another; what is interfacing in one can be underlining in another. There are no rules. It's a case of using your judgment.

Woven fabrics can be eased, stretched, and blocked to fit the figure. *Non-woven* materials cannot.

For example, wool, a woven fabric, can be molded into a figure-conforming shape, while the non-woven felt cannot. The same holds true for interfacings and underlinings. Those that are woven can be blocked into the same shape as the outer fabric. Non-woven ones cannot. Since shaping is a very important part of the tailoring process, it is wise to choose woven interfacings and underlinings for this purpose.

Generally, the *fusibles* (iron-ons) are best used in small areas. Use them to stiffen standing collars, cuffs, and belts, and as reinforcement for areas to be slashed, like buttonholes and bound pockets. There are many of these iron-ons. They come in varying weights: sheer webs to canvas.

The ordinary life span of a book does not lend itself to keeping up (by name) with the many interfacings—woven, non-woven, or fusible—that appear on and disappear from the market with such frequency. For that reason we have stayed with generic rather than brand names.

The classic interfacing material for tailoring is hair canvas. Pull a crosswise (filler) yarn of the hair canvas. Note how a strand of horsehair or goat's hair is wound around it (Fig. 136a). It is this that gives the canvas its springiness, its resilience, its ability to cling to wool.

Always cut the lapel on the lengthwise grain to take advantage of the crosswise roll of the hair-wound filler yarns (Fig. 136b). This will produce that beautiful, soft turnback so characteristic of a tailored lapel (Fig. 136c).

Hair canvas comes in light, medium, and heavy weights and in a variety of fibers—cotton, wool, linen, synthetics, and blends.

The softest hair canvas is made of wool. Use this for any soft style and for any soft fabrics: cashmere, camel's hair, and the like.

The stiffest hair canvas is that made of synthetic fiber. Use it *only* in places where considerable stiffening is necessary.

Fig. 136

The most generally used hair canvases are those of medium-weight linen, cotton, or blends. The texture of these falls somewhere between the two extremes. They are firm yet pliable. They provide the shaping of most jackets and coats.

For *softer styles* and *lighter-weight fabrics* there is a group of *woven sheer canvases* (without the hair) that can be used in place of the hair canvas.

The Classic Tailored Collar

The collar most associated with classic tailoring is a neck-hugging, notched, set-on collar (Fig. 137a). The best interfacing for this collar

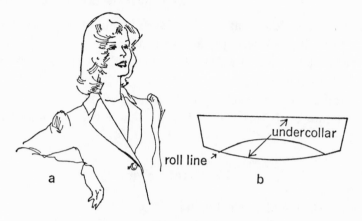

a

roll line ↗

undercollar ↗

b

Fig. 137

a   b

Fig. 138

is *tailor's linen.* When cut on the bias from the undercollar pattern (Fig. 137b), it molds well and fits beautifully.

For a similar collar on a dropped neckline (more usual in women's tailoring), use hair canvas.

For some types of construction, melton cloth is recommended. When melton cloth is not available in suitable colors, try a firm felt instead.

The Shawl Collar

The interfacing of a shawl collar is often cut as an extension of the front facing in the same way that the outer fabric is cut (Fig. 138a), though often these days the shawl collar is cut with a separate under-

Fig. 139

collar (Fig. 138b), in which case this gets interfaced, like any other undercollar. Use any of the recommended interfacing materials suitable for the fabric.

Flat collars: Peter Pan (or any version thereof) and cape collars. Use hair canvas for woolen fabrics, sheer canvas for lighter fabrics (Fig. 139).

Standing collars: Use any appropriate stiff material or stiffen the chosen material with many rows of machine stitching (Fig. 140).

Fig. 140

More Interfacings

Cuffs: use hair canvas or sheer canvas.

Flaps and welts: use hair canvas, sheer canvas, or the underlining material.

Patch pockets: use hair canvas, sheer canvas, or the underlining material.

Hems: use a bias strip of muslin, canvas (hair or sheer), or the underlining material.

Waistbands: use hair canvas, sheer canvas, French belting, or fusibles.

Since there is such a variety of interfacing and underlining materials to choose from, it isn't always easy to make a decision which to use. The safest thing to do when you shop for supporting material is to take with you a sample of your fabric and a picture of the design. Slip the interfacing or underlining under the fashion fabric. Study the effect. Decide whether the weight, finish, degree of flexibility, softness, firmness, or crispness of the supporting material will produce the design of the pattern in your chosen fashion fabric. There are no hard and fast rules. You must be the judge.

MORE OF THE INSIDE STORY

Anything that goes inside a garment adds to its shape and body. For this reason, it is also important to consider two other possible inner layers of cloth. They are interlining for warmth and lining for finish.

THE INTERLINING

Any coat or suit may be winter-proofed for warmth by the insertion of a lamb's-wool interlining between the interfaced garment and the lining. Lamb's wool comes in several colors and several weights. Choose the color and weight that best suit your personal needs and your fashion fabric. Since everything else in the coat has been sponged, play it safe and sponge the interlining, too.

You may interline as much or as little of your coat or jacket as you would like. If you are the type that never thaws out till the end of spring, better interline the whole coat—sleeves and all.

If a double layer of interlining will help you face the winter winds, here's your chance. The usual bought coat never does seem to have enough interlining for warmth.

Even if the pattern doesn't call for it, it is possible to interline a coat or jacket. (Patterns rarely include a pattern for an interlining. Generally one must work out one's own pattern and layout.)

Use the adjusted lining pattern with the modifications described below for an unfitted coat or jacket (Fig. 141) and the adjusted original pattern for a fitted garment. In the latter case you will, in effect, be backing the garment with a layer of interlining material. Keep this in mind when you are considering the use of an underlining in a winter coat. Often the interlining can replace it. And, of course, make certain that your pattern has sufficient ease to accommodate this extra layer.

One-piece sleeves may be completely interlined with lamb's wool before being stitched (Fig. 141a). In a two-piece sleeve, generally only the upper sleeve is interlined (Fig. 141b). In a kimono sleeve, the gussets (when present) are *not* interlined.

1. Start with the lining pattern (Fig. 141c).

2. Eliminate the center-back pleat (Fig. 141d).

3. Extend the lines of the front-shoulder dart-tuck until they converge to form a dart. Retain the back-shoulder dart.

4. Trim away the interlining at all outside edges so it will just meet the front facings, the back facing, and the hem.

5. Allow only ¼-inch seam allowances at the shoulder, the armhole, and the sleeve cap for overlapping seams.

Another presently fashionable way to add warmth is via *a quilted, knit, or pile-fabric lining.* Such bulky linings double as lining-interlinings. They contain features of both. The pattern is like the one for the interlining. The construction and insertion are like that of the lining except for the outside edges. Obviously, it is important to reduce the bulk of such linings wherever possible.

1. Choose a style that has enough fullness to accommodate the bulkiness.

2. Eliminate the center-back pleat of the lining pattern. Convert the front-shoulder dart-tuck into a dart.

3. Trim away the interlining on all outside edges so it will just

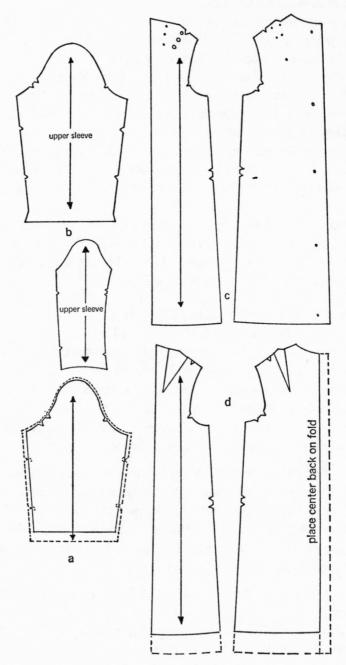

Fig. 141

meet the facings and the hem. Finish with seam binding. Attach the binding to the garment.

4. Make the sleeves of an easy-to-get-into silky material.

5. Avoid turn-unders and double thicknesses wherever possible.

THE COVER-UP OF ALL THESE INNER WORKINGS IS THE LINING

Most linings are made of silky materials so they will slide on and off easily. Happily, that silky feel also adds a feeling of luxury.

The lining must not interfere with the already considerable shaping of the garment. It is designed, stitched, and inserted in such a way as to permit freedom of movement. Hence its considerable ease: the pleat at the front shoulder for shaping the bosom instead of the usual dart, a pleat at the center back, and a little extra length in the form of a tuck at all hems.

The Lining Pattern—Ready-made or Created by You

When there is one, use the pattern for the lining that comes with the garment pattern. This does a good job of eliminating unnecessary details and stitching. Make the same alterations on the lining as were made on the garment.

If you wish to make a lining when none is included in the pattern, this is how to do it. Use the adjusted pattern of the coat or jacket. Add a 1-inch pleat at the center back. Trace the facings on the pattern front and back. Cut away the facings, but add seam allowance to the cut edges.

For an attached hem, cut off the pattern at the hemline of jacket, coat, or sleeve. For a free-hanging coat hem, add 1½ to 2 inches for a hem. The original shaping may be retained or the dart control may be converted to a shoulder dart-tuck laid in a soft fold.

MORE INSIDE STUFF

And that's not all one may find on the inside of a tailored garment!

The method of interfacing and reinforcing suggested in this chapter gives a reasonable degree of support in the shoulder area. Sometimes, however, some additional reinforcement or light padding is desirable to ensure a firm, trim look.

If you are one who doesn't like shoulder padding, try this for achieving a typical man's suit look. Add a layer of *hair canvas reinforcement* at front and/or back armholes to fill out the hollows at the armhole edge of the chest or back.

1. On the pattern, trace the armhole reinforcement as follows: mark a point 4 inches up on the shoulder seam, measuring from the

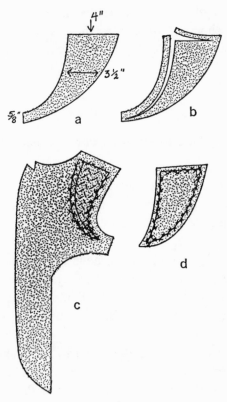

Fig. 142

armhole toward the neck. Mark a point 3½ inches over on the cross-wise grain at the point where the armhole seam swings into the underarm curve. Mark a point ⅝ inch down on the side seam.

2. Trace the shoulder, armhole, and side seams. Draw a curved line to connect the shoulder and side seam (Fig. 142a).

3. Trim away all seam allowances on the reinforcement (Fig. 142b). Mark the same grain as the pattern.

4. Using this newly created pattern, cut the reinforcement out of the interfacing material.

5. Superimpose the shoulder reinforcement on the front (or back) interfacing. Set into position *on the seam lines.*

6. Join the two with long basting stitches along the edges and diagonal basting to hold the rest (Fig. 142c).

As many additional layers of reinforcement may be used as will provide the desired effect. Grade each layer (Fig. 142d). Use hair canvas or layers of fleece between the hair canvas layers.

Make enough of these layers and you will be creating one kind of shoulder pad. And that's a fine way to do it. Often ready-made pads are not quite right for the lines of the garment or for your figure. You're better off when you make them yourself.

SHOULDER PADS

Despite the fact that the shoulder area has been firmed with interfacing, many tailored garments look trimmer with the additional support of some light shoulder padding.

The most effective shoulder pad for a set-in sleeve is squared off at

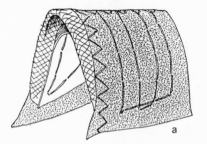
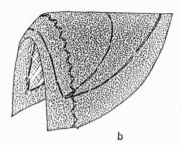

a

b

Fig. 143

the front shoulder and tapered at the back (Fig. 143a). A shoulder pad for a kimono or raglan sleeve should be shaped to cup the shoulder (Fig. 143b).

Such pads are commercially available but a little hard to find. You can make your own with a little stiffening, a little wadding, and, if the garment is unlined, a covering fabric.

These materials may be used for stiffening: hair canvas or any other canvas, Pellon, crinoline, or any other sufficiently stiff foundation fabric.

The materials used for padding are flannel, felting, cotton wadding, quilting cotton, foam rubber, or any other similar materials you may have in your collection.

A covering fabric may be a lightweight silk or self fabric.

Pad pattern: Use the adjusted garment pattern. If the pattern is in several sections, pin together all those that make the front shoulder and armhole area and those that make the back shoulder and armhole area.

A Shoulder Pad for a Set-in Sleeve

1. Draw the shape of the shoulder pad on the front and back patterns. Come halfway down the armhole at both front and back. Square off the front; taper the back. (That square front helps to fill out the hollow just below the shoulder.) Make the shoulder length of the pad equal to the shoulder measurement from the neckline to the armhole seam (Fig. 144a).

2. Trace the front and back shoulder pad patterns onto a piece of paper.

3. Cut them out of hair canvas on the straight grain.

4. Join the front and back canvases by overlapping at the shoulder seams. Stitch. Trim away the seam allowances close to the stitching (Fig. 144b).

5. Cut a strip of bias muslin 9 inches long by 2½ inches wide. Fold it in half lengthwise. Insert a layer (or layers) of wadding (cotton batting, quilting cotton, or flannel). Make diagonal rows of machine stitching to hold the padding in place (Fig. 144c).

6. Stitch the padded muslin strip to the underside of the hair can-

vas, extending it about ¾ to ½ inch at the shoulder-armhole edge
and tapering it to nothing at each end.

7. Pad with layers of wadding cut to shape. (This is your great
chance to get a shoulder pad just to your liking—not too thick, not
too thin.) The thickest part of the pad should be at the armhole edge
of the shoulder. Taper the thickness toward the neck and toward the
ends.

8. Quilt the pad with rows of hand or machine stitching to hold all
the stuffing in place (Fig. 144d).

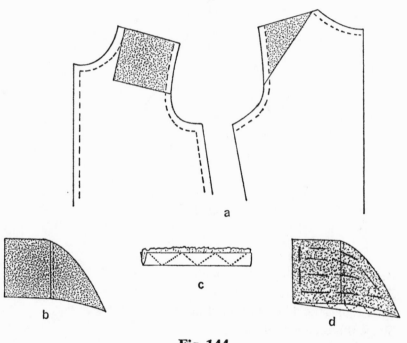

Fig. 144

An even lighter pad may be made by substituting a layer of felting
or flannelette for the cotton wadding. A very satisfactory pad may be
made of the hair canvas and several graded layers of Pellon. If a commercial pad is used, you may remove enough of the stuffing to suit
your needs.

A Shoulder Pad for a Dropped-shoulder, Kimono, or Raglan Sleeve

Your chances for getting away without shoulder pads are best in kimono or raglan sleeves and dropped-shoulder styles. The soft, sloping lines are part of the charm of these designs. If padding is used to define the shoulder, it looks best when it is light and when it cups the shoulder.

Here is an easy-to-make pattern for this type of pad (Fig. 145).

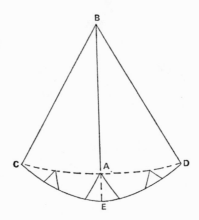

Fig. 145

A–B equals the shoulder length.
A–C equals half the front armhole.
A–D equals half the back armhole.
A–E equals the desired depth of the pad over the shoulder.
Shape this area with darts.

1. Using this pattern, cut the pad of stiff shaping material.

2. Slash one dart leg of each dart and overlap on the other dart leg. Pin. Fit the pads carefully to your shoulder. Curved darts provide a better cupping.

3. Stitch the darts. Trim away the excess.

4. Pad with any of the wadding materials suggested for the set-in sleeve pad to the desired thickness.

5. Pad-stitch to hold all the thicknesses in place.

Cap Contour

Sometimes sleeves of soft fabrics have a tendency to collapse at the cap. Sometimes the design calls for a more than usual firmly rounded cap. In both of these cases, the cap needs support.

One way to support the cap is with an *underlining* of lamb's-wool padding. Use the sleeve pattern to cut the cap (Fig. 146a). Directions for inserting the cap support will be found on page 400.

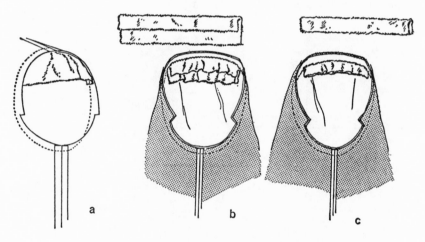

Fig. 146

Another way of providing soft support is with a *sleeve head*. Sleeve heads are commercially available by the yard, but they can easily be made with any appropriate fabric.

Cut a bias strip of lamb's-wool padding. (Self fabric, flannel, Siri, muslin, or any other similar soft fabric will also do.) Make the strip at least 8 inches long by 3 inches wide.

For light padding, make a 1-inch lengthwise fold (Fig. 146b).

For more thickness, fold the strip into thirds lengthwise (Fig. 146c).

See page 400 for insertion.

YOU CAN KEEP A GOOD HEM DOWN

Gravity alone won't do it, but a little assistance from interfacings, underlinings, and weights will keep a good hem down.

Interfacings and underlinings do the trick in the structured garment. (Weights for these garments are optional.) It's the unstructured garment that needs particular attention at the hem to compensate for the lack of an inner structure. A case in point: the famous Chanel chain applied to the hem of her otherwise unstructured jackets to keep the soufflé woolens from floating off.

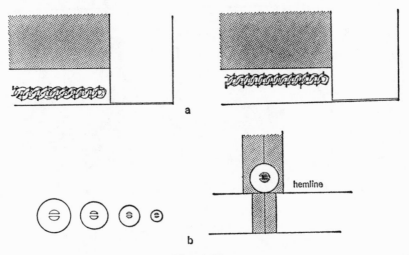

Fig. 147

A hem may be *weighted uniformly* with a chain. Chains are available in assorted lengths, weights, and metals (Fig. 147a).

A hem may be *weighted in spots.* Use dressmaker's weights: lead disks that come in a range of sizes up to 1½ inches in diameter (Fig. 147b).

Who knows the shape of things to come? The vagaries of fashion being what they are, there is no way of foretelling the shaping need of future styles. It's enough to keep up with the present ones. Unfortunately for the sewer, there is no one ready-made formula that will do for everything.

It is to be hoped that this chapter has provided an approach to and a method for solving types of shaping problems. Use this basic information with ingenuity and freedom. Just remember that if it works to produce the lines you want, it's right. When it comes to shaping— anything goes!

Part III
TAILORING TECHNIQUES

Chapter 13

And Sew a Fine Seam

Whether the design is avant-garde or classic, the garment lined or unlined, constructed or unconstructed, hands and machine are what put it together. Though the present tendency is to use machines for more and more operations, even the machines cannot work without loving hands to guide them. In truth, there is really not much that a sewing machine can do that hands cannot. Hand sewing just takes longer. Even skilled sewers find it easier to control many operations by hand rather than by machine.

This does not mean that one should entirely revert to hand sewing in a machine age. It would be somewhat anachronistic to put a suit together by hand while the dishwasher is chugging away, the clothes dryer is whirring, the TV is blaring, and supersonic planes are zooming overhead.

Tailoring, however, entails a considerable amount of handwork (even in factories). It is the handwork that gives custom-made clothes their superior look and higher price tags.

By adding these hand techniques you can turn out expensive-looking clothes. After all, the major cost of any garment is the labor.

Both machine and hand sewing are necessary for fine craftsmanship. Use machines where they are effective and where they will shorten the work. Use your hands for those thousands of tiny, invisible stitches that ensure the subtle shaping, the superb fit, and the long life of a good tailored garment.

MACHINE CONSTRUCTION

Aside from a sewing machine in good working order, successful machine stitching depends on the combination of needle and thread best suited to the fabric. There is a sufficient range of needles and thread to accommodate every fabric.

It is always a good idea to make a test seam on a scrap of the garment fabric to check the correctness of the machine stitching. It should "ride" smoothly. The tension should be neither too tight nor too loose. Balanced stitches should lock properly on both upper and lower thicknesses. There should be no puckering or creeping of fabric. The pressure should be neither so light as to raise the fabric with the feed nor so heavy as to leave an imprint of the feed on the material. Check the length of the stitch. If any adjustment should be necessary to the upper or lower tensions or to the pressure of the presser bar, consult your sewing-machine manual for directions. *Key your stitching to your fabric.*

TO BASTE OR NOT TO BASTE

Many a would-be sewer has been discouraged by the prospect of endless and laborious basting before stitching. In many instances, basting is long, tedious, and not necessarily effective. However, there are times when it should be used—on silks and other slithery fabrics, and when basting will provide a clear idea of the fit.

Fig. 148

Basting is a basic stitch with many variations. It consists of a succession of stitches and spaces either large or small, even or uneven. The size of the stitch varies with the use and the amount of strain exerted on the seam. Where the strain is great—as in fitting—use small basting stitches; where there is no strain, use longer stitches.

In *even basting* (Fig. 148a), both stitches and spaces are of equal length on both sides of the fabric.

In *uneven basting* (Fig. 148b), stitches and spaces are unequal in length, being longer on the surface and shorter on the underside.

Use a single thread of convenient but not too long length. Start with a knotted end and finish with several over-and-over stitches.* Use silk thread for basting velvets, fine silks, and some woolens: it is less likely to leave marks. Baste beside the seam line to facilitate removal. To remove, clip the bastings at intervals and remove the threads. Pulling out a long basting thread may mark or cut the fabric. Tweezers are a fine instrument for this purpose. Remove bastings *before* pressing, since pressing will leave the imprint of the basting.

*OVER-AND-OVER STITCH

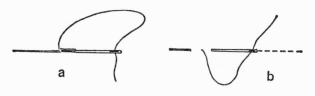

a   b

Fig. 149

An over-and-over stitch (Fig. 149a) consists of two or more backstitches** sewn on top of one another. It is used as reinforcement.

**BACKSTITCH

For backstitches (Fig. 149b), start at the right-hand end. Bring the needle up on the right side one stitch ahead. Working back to the right, insert the needle at the point where the preceding stitch ended, slide it along the underside, and once more bring it out one stitch ahead. You are really encircling the cloth with the stitches. This produces a line of hand stitching that closely resembles machine stitching.

Machine stitching is done beside the basting, never directly over it. (The latter would make it difficult, if not impossible, to remove the basting when the stitching is complete.)

PINNING PREFERRED

In contrast, pinning is fast and easy and holds the fabric securely in place as it is fed into the machine. Pinning is the best way to match stripes, plaids, checks, motifs, and cross seams perfectly.

Discard old, bent, rusted, or coarse pins. Use sharp, new pins appropriate for the fabric.

Compare the pattern seam lengths of the sections to be joined. If they are equal, you must pin and stitch so they remain so. If one length is really longer than the other, the extra amount must be eased in.

Pin at the beginning and end of a seam line, at all notches, and at a sufficient number of places between. Pins may be placed at right angles to the seam line (Fig. 150a), or lengthwise—with points facing the top of the seam (Fig. 150b). Fabrics that bruise easily are pinned in the seam allowance rather than on the stitching line (Fig. 150c), so the pin marks won't show.

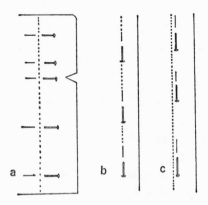

Fig. 150

One has to admit that stitching over pins has its hazards. There is always the chance that the needle may hit a pin, bending it and, what's worse, breaking the needle.

If you use pins instead of basting, remove them just before the presser foot reaches them. While this does slow up the stitching, it is safer. The exception to this advice is the stitching of plaids, stripes, checks, and cross seams. Stitch slowly over the pins, hold your breath, and pray for the best.

Professional machine operators can simply put two thicknesses of material together and stitch away without the preliminary folderol of pinning or basting. When you get that proficient, you can, too. Meanwhile, give yourself some help. Pin wherever it will work. Baste wherever it appears necessary.

If you intend to baste before stitching, this is the point at which to do it. If you are machine-stitching over the pins, start now.

AND SEW A FINE SEAM

1. In general, it is a good idea to lock the stitches at the beginning and end of each seam with back-and-forth stitching.

2. Stitch the seam slowly. Speed stitching is of no particular value to home sewers. There are not so many yards of machine stitching in any garment that the time saved is worth the risk of faulty stitching.

3. Keep your eyes on the stitching. Guide the cloth with one hand and anchor it with the other.

4. If you need to go back over a line of stitching to correct it, be sure to remove the first stitching. Every added row of machine stitching makes the area that much stiffer.

5. Seam stitching, like stay stitching, is directional to preserve the grain, the length, and the shape of the fabric.

FOR EXAMPLE:

In stitching a flared skirt, start at the hem and stitch to the waist. Were you to reverse the direction (waist to hem), the action of the feed and the presser foot on the angle of the seam would tend to stretch and distort it.

6. Be sure to stitch the full seam allowance—either that planned for in the pattern or that determined by your fitting. An eighth of an inch may not seem much to you at the time, but a little arithmetic will quickly disclose that ⅛ inch on each of two thicknesses equals ¼ inch. Two ¼ inches equal ½ inch. Four ¼ inches equal 1 inch. Without much ado you could be adding anywhere from 1 to 2 inches on your garment, which grades it up to the next size.

7. If the seam puckers despite the correct setting, try the taut-stitching technique on page 246.

PROPER PRESSURE IS ESSENTIAL

When the pressure is not properly adjusted for the fabric, there is a tendency for the feed to carry along the underlayer of cloth faster than the presser foot does the upper layer. As a result, you may wind up with an extra length of top-layer fabric at the end of the seam. (Long seams on thick woolens and pile materials are particularly vulnerable in this respect.)

Some of the newer sewing machines have built-in devices for feeding the fabric evenly into the machine whatever the thickness or thinness of the material. If your machine doesn't have this feature, investigate the possibility of buying an even-feed attachment. This is a small, inexpensive, and easy-to-use mechanism.

Lacking an even feed, regulate the pressure by adjusting the presser bar according to the thickness of the fabric.

HOW TO JOIN MATCHING CROSS SEAMS

1. Stitch each seam and press it open.

2. Free the cross-seam areas of bulk by trimming away some of the seam allowances (Fig. 151a).

3. Place both thicknesses of fabric together so that the seams match.

4. Put the point of a pin through the matching seams of both thicknesses (Fig. 151b). Slide it along the seam line of the undersurface and bring it up on the seam line of the upper surface. The pin spans the area of the cross seams.

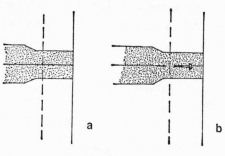

Fig. 151

5. Stitch across the pin very slowly and very carefully to run less risk of striking it.

If you insist on using thread to hold the cross seam in place, use a backstitch rather than a basting stitch. It fastens more securely.

HOW TO JOIN MATCHING PLAIDS, STRIPES, AND CHECKS

Matching plaids, stripes, and checks can be stitched by the same method used to join cross seams.

1. Place the corresponding bars of both thicknesses of the fabric together.

2. Pin and stitch as above, matching bars instead of cross seams.

VARIATIONS ON A SEAM

Here is a group of seams most often used in tailoring. The type of seam used for any particular garment or any special part of it depends on the fabric, the style, and whether or not the seam will be exposed.

Plain seam (Fig. 152a) is the one most frequently used in tailoring, since the seams are generally covered by a lining. With right sides together, stitch the seam on the stitching line, trim the seam allowances, and press it open.

Topstitching a plain seam (see Fig. 155) adds not only strength but decorativeness. It is a very important trimming detail for skirts, jackets, and coats.

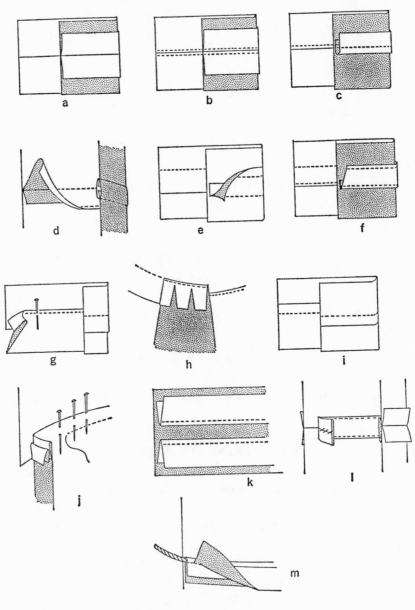

Fig. 152

VARIATION NO. 1 looks like a slot seam (Fig. 152b). Make the plain seam and press it open. On the right side, make two rows of top-stitching equally distant from the seam line.

VARIATION NO. 2 looks like a welt seam (Fig. 152c). Make the plain seam and trim only one seam allowance. Press both seam allow-ances to one side, the longer enclosing the shorter. On the right side, make one row of decorative stitching an even distance away from the seam line, catching both seam allowances.

Fell seam (Fig. 152d) is used on unlined or reversible garments. Stitch the seam. Press the seam allowances to one side. Trim the under-seam allowance. Turn under some of the upper-seam allowance and topstitch by machine or by hand. This may be made on either the right or the wrong side.

Welt seam (Fig. 152e) is used on heavy and very heavy fabrics. It is a strong seam and resembles variation No. 2 in appearance. Stitch with right sides together. Trim one seam allowance. Press both seam allowances to one side, the longer enclosing the shorter. On the right side, make a row of decorative stitching the desired distance from the seam, catching the longer seam allowance. Do not catch the shorter width of the graded seam.

Double-stitched welt seam (Fig. 152f) is made the same way as the welt seam. Add a second row of decorative stitching.

Lapped seam, or overlap seam (Fig. 152g). Turn under the seam allowance of one raw edge; press to position. Overlap the turned edge on the other, matching the raw edges. (It is easier to match the raw edges from the wrong side.) Pin and stitch on the right side an even distance from the fold.

Lapped seam on a curve (Fig. 152h) is frequently used on yokes. Stay-stitch, and clip the seam allowance on the edge to be turned. Turn under the seam allowance and press to position. Overlap on the under section, matching raw edges. Pin or baste to position. Stitch on the right side an even distance from the fold and close to it.

Tucked seam (Fig. 152i). When a straight lapped seam is top-stitched a wider distance in from the edge, it looks like a tuck.

Faced, lapped seam, or curved tuck seam (Fig. 152j). The curved tuck seam is similar to the straight tucked seam in that the line of decorative topstitching is a distance in from the edge. This presents a problem. To lie flat, the curved seam allowance must be clipped at intervals before being turned under. To reinforce this slashed edge and to hide the slashes, the curved edge needs a facing with a similarly slashed seam allowance. Grade the seam allowances, turn to the right side, roll the joining seam to the underside and press to position. Overlap the faced edge on the under section. Pin and topstitch.

Slot seam (Fig. 152k) can be used as a decorative feature for an otherwise simple design. It is a beautiful method for joining the sections of suede skins when they are used for dresses, jackets, and coats.

Turn under the edges of the fabric and press to position. Overlap the folded edges on the right side of a lengthwise strip of fabric. The folded edges may meet at the center or leave a space between to reveal the strip. Topstitch in from the folded edge.

Strap seam (Fig. 152l) is a decorative device for hiding a seam. Make a plain seam on the garment, on either the wrong side or the right side. Trim the seam allowance and press it open. Make the strap as follows: cut a strip of fabric twice the width of the finished strap. Turn under the edges until they just meet. Join the edges with permanent diagonal bastings. Place the strap over the garment, matching its seam to the garment seam. Topstitch each edge close to or in from the fold.

Corded seam (Fig. 152m) is an interesting finish, whether made of self fabric or of contrasting color or texture. Cut a strip of fabric on the true bias (see page 217) wide enough to cover the cord, plus two seam allowances. Fold the strip right side out. Slip the cord into the fold. Backstitch close to the cord with matching thread, or machine-stitch using a cording foot. Baste the corded strip in place on the seam line, on the right side of one thickness of the fabric, raw edges matching. Place the second thickness over it, right sides together, matching all seam lines and all raw edges. Machine-stitch through all the thicknesses, using the cording foot. Grade the seam allowances.

Piped seam is made in the same way as a corded seam, except that the cord is omitted.

HOW TO MAKE A BIAS STRIP

1. Bring the lengthwise grain to meet the crosswise grain (Fig. 153a).

2. Cut along the fold, which is the bias. (There is no such thing as "near 'ems" when it comes to bias. It either is or isn't.)

3. Rule off strips of the desired width parallel to the bias edge, and cut (Fig. 153b).

4. On the straight grain, join as many strips as will give the needed length (Fig. 153c).

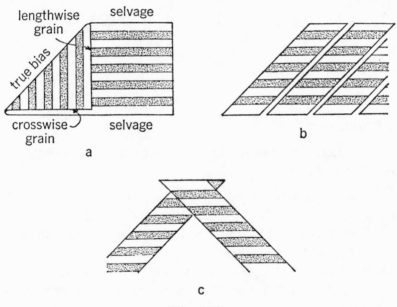

Fig. 153

HOW TO STITCH AN ENCLOSED OR ENCASED SEAM

This technique is used in welts, flaps, collars, lapels, facings, and so on.

Whenever a section of a garment consists of two layers, the seam that joins them should never be visible from the surface. The seam is rolled to the underside. This calls for a little extra material on the upper layer to negotiate the turn (see page 132) and some extra stitching to guarantee that the seam never slips from its position. There are two methods by which this may be accomplished.

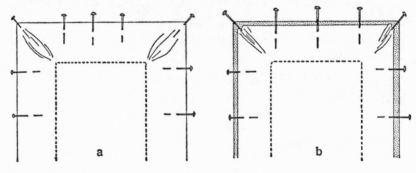

Fig. 154

METHOD I

(Fig. 154a) This is used when the upper layer is cut slightly larger than the underlayer.

1. With right sides together, pin the corners diagonally, edges matching.

2. Push a little bubble of fullness into each corner on both sides of the corner pin. Pin to position.

3. With the shorter layer on top, stretch it to match the longer one. With edges aligned, pin at the center and at intervals between the center and the end.

4. With the shorter layer on top, stitch an even distance in from the edge.

METHOD II

(Fig. 154b) This is used when both layers are cut the same size.

1. With right sides together, set the raw edge of the upper layer down from the raw edge of the underlayer. How much down depends on the thickness of the fabric—less for thinner materials, more for heavier ones.

2. Trim away the excess seam allowance of the underlayer so all raw edges are aligned.

3. Stitch the two layers an even distance in from the edges. Straight seams may be handled the same way except that there are no corners.

To guarantee that the seam that joins the outer fabric and its facing never slips into view (despite all one's efforts), the two thicknesses are further held in place with either topstitching or understitching, depending on which is appropriate to the design and the fabric.

Topstitching is a line of machine or hand stitching placed an even distance in from a seam or an edge.

Understitching is a line of stitching that fastens the seam allowances to the facing (in dressmaking) and to the interfacing (in tailoring).

Topstitching

Topstitching is one of the prime examples in design when a structural necessity becomes a decorative feature. It can make any seam line or edge more interesting and more important. It emphasizes the architecture of the design (Fig. 155).

Since topstitching becomes a feature of the design, one may choose whatever kind of stitching, whatever stitch size, however many rows of stitching and whatever thread will be most effective. It may be necessary to do a little experimenting to decide just what kind of topstitching is most effective for your purposes.

Buttonhole twist is the thread generally used for *machine topstitching*. If it is difficult to get the color you need, try a double strand of mercerized cotton thread instead. It comes in a greater range of colors. Often its lack of shininess makes it preferable to the buttonhole twist. On a single-needle sewing machine, use the double thread from two bobbins set one over the other on the spool holder. On a two-needle sewing machine, use the double thread from two spools set on the two spindles. Thread as usual, through one needle, as if the double were a single thread.

In any style where the fabric reverses itself—for instance, the front

closing and lapel or a convertible collar—use the buttonhole twist or
the double-strand cotton for both the bobbin and the upper thread.
Where there is no reversal, use the buttonhole twist or the double-
strand cotton for the upper threading and a single strand of silk or
cotton thread for the bobbin.

Use a machine needle with a large enough eye or one of the self-
threading kind that can take the thicker thread. Adjust the tension.

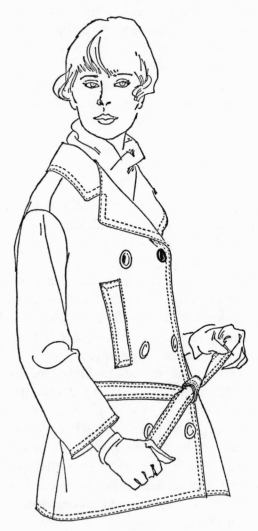

Fig. 155

Topstitching may be done when the garment is completed, as it would be around the edges of a coat or jacket or skirt. Often, however, it must be done during construction, either because it is easier or because it is more logical. Your pattern directions will indicate this.

There are a number of devices for guaranteeing that the stitching is an even distance from the edge.

1. Mark with guide basting.
2. Mark with a gummed tape designed for this purpose.
3. Use the gauge on the throat plate of the machine.
4. Use a quilting foot.
5. In machines with a zigzag stitch, set the bight over as far as it will go in either direction that is suitable. Keep the presser foot aligned with the edge of the garment.

When the stitching is finished, draw the ends of the thread through to the wrong side. You may tie them in a square knot. Safer yet, thread a needle with the ends and weave them into the topstitching for a very short distance.

If the *topstitching is hand stitching,* one of several stitches may be used: *glove stitch* (small basting ¼ inch to ½ inch long, even on both sides); *saddle stitch* (uneven basting with longer stitches on the outside and shorter stitches on the underside); *seed stitch* (tiny backstitch or half backstitch made with two or three strands of embroidery floss, pulled up unevenly, making a tiny irregular stitch on the surface).

Understitching

There are many styles that would be spoiled by topstitching and yet need some kind of permanent positioning. For such designs the answer is *understitching.* While topstitching is there for all the world to see, understitching quietly goes about its business unseen.

In dressmaking, the understitching consists of fastening the seam allowances caught between the facing and the outer fabric to the fac-

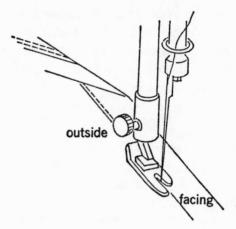

Fig. 156

ing by machine stitching (Fig. 156). In tailoring, the seam allowances are fastened to the tape or interfacing by hand stitching (see Fig. 158c).

1. After the layers have been stitched and pressed open, the seam allowances are graded* by making the one on the underlayer narrower than the upper layer.

*GRADING

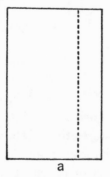
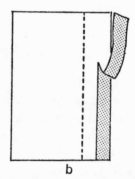

a   b

Fig. 157

In tailoring (indeed, in all fine sewing) we never permit one edge to end directly over another as it does in Fig. 157a. This produces a bumpy ridge. Instead, we stagger or layer or *grade* widths of seam allowances so that the bulk is diminished gradually—hence the word *grading*. This beveling eliminates unsightly bumps (Fig. 157b).

The width of each trimmed seam allowance is determined by the thickness of the fabric. Lightweight fabrics can be trimmed to a narrower width than can heavy fabrics.

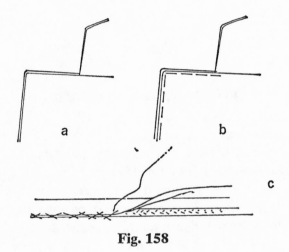

Fig. 158

2. Turn the facing to the right side. Steam-press the edges with the seam rolled into its proper position (Fig. 158a).

3. Edge-baste firmly to hold the pressed seam in position (Fig. 158b). *Edge basting* is a line of small, firm basting stitches on the right side close to the finished edge of the garment.

4. Lift the upper layer gently and fasten the wider seam allowance to the tape or the interfacing with either permanent basting or catch stitching* (Fig. 158c). This will automatically enclose or encase the narrower seam allowance.

*CATCH STITCH

A catch stitch (sometimes called a feather stitch) resembles a cross-stitch, and is used a great deal in tailoring (Fig. 159).

Take a tiny backstitch a little to the right on an imaginary line, picking up only one or two threads. Complete the stitch by taking a similar tiny backstitch on an imaginary lower line. Repeat. The movement is to the right; the needle points to the left shoulder each time.

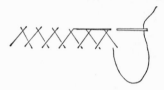

Fig. 159

FINISH WITH A FLOURISH

Pride in craftsmanship dictates that the inside of a garment be just as beautiful as the outside. Often beauty and function go hand in hand. An attractive finish for a raw edge may enhance its appearance; it also prevents it from raveling. There are as many types of finishes as there are functions, fabrics, and fancies of creative sewers.

When a lining is used, no special finish is necessary unless the fabric tends to ravel. The best way to prevent this is with overcasting, either machine or hand.

Hand overcasting (Fig. 160a): This is a series of slanting stitches

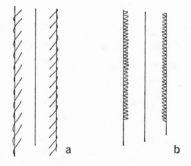

Fig. 160

worked over either single or double raw edges. The stitches are evenly spaced and even in depth.

Machine overcasting (Fig. 160b): Set the sewing machine for a zigzag stitch wide enough and close enough to protect the edge. How wide and how close depend on the fabric. Test.

When a lining is not used, the finish must not only be functional, it must also be attractive.

Very much in favor these days is the bulkless construction of a trimmed-back seam allowance. Since this places the seam itself in peril, a strong finish is absolutely necessary.

Once more, overcasting to the rescue. This time it is done by machine over the double raw edges, finishing them as one. Or, if you prefer, overcast each edge separately.

Here are a few other commonly used seam finishes for tailored unlined garments.

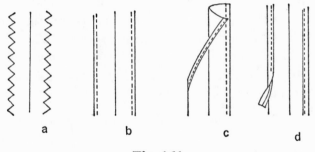

a   b   c   d

Fig. 161

1. Pinking—pretty, but marginally effective (Fig. 161a).

2. A row of machine stitching on each seam allowance—functional: it stops the raveling at the seam line, but is not particularly beautiful (Fig. 161b).

3. A line of machine stitching on a turned-under edge—good for lightweight fabrics (Fig. 161c).

4. Edges bound with bias strips—very attractive and very functional, but takes time to do (Fig. 161d). This finish is excellent for unlined garments.

HOW TO STITCH SINGLE-POINTED DARTS

1. With right sides inside, fold the dart and match the dart legs (seam lines). Pin to position.

2. Place the fabric in the machine with the wide end of the dart at the top and the point of the dart toward you. Set the fabric in the machine so that the stitching line (rather than the fold line) is directed toward your body at a right angle (Fig. 162a). (Any other position than this and you would be stitching sidesaddle.)

3. Lock the stitches at the wide end by back-and-forth stitching. Stitch to the dart point. You will have more control of the stitching if you *slow up as you approach the dart point*. Keep the last two or three stitches practically parallel to the fold (Fig. 162b) before tapering off to nothing at the point. If you swoop in suddenly as you realize you are getting close to the end of your stitching, you will only produce a bubble or a pleat instead of a perfect blending at dart's end.

4. Cut the thread. Tie the ends in a square knot: right over left, left over right (the knot used in macramé) (Fig. 162c). Don't attempt any back-and-forth stitching here. It is practically impossible to get back on the stitching line accurately. Besides, the additional stitching would make the point too stiff.

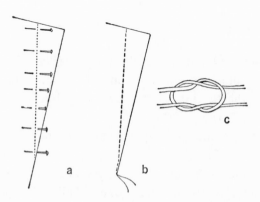

Fig. 162

Double-pointed Darts

The double-pointed dart is used for waistline fitting. The temptation in stitching a double-pointed dart is to start at one point and
stitch to the other. This can be done if one is very careful to bring the
machine needle exactly into and out of the points of the dart.

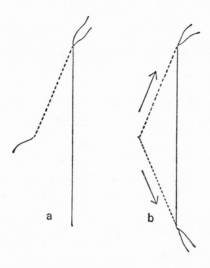

a   b

Fig. 163

An easier and safer method is to follow the rule for the single-
pointed dart.

1. Start at the widest part of the dart and stitch to the point in one
direction (Fig. 163a).

2. Bring the threads at the wide end through to one side.

3. Tie square knots at both ends of the stitching.

4. Once again, let the needle down into the wide part of the dart
and stitch to the second point (Fig. 163b).

5. Repeat the procedure for tying the threads.

HOW TO STITCH DARTS AND SEAMS IN
THE INTERFACING

"Smooth" is the word for the inner construction in tailoring. No lumps, no bumps, to even hint at what goes on under cover of cloth. This calls for a special stitching of all seams and darts in the interfacing, underlining, and interlining.

Join Seams by Overlapping Seam Lines

1. Mark each seam line carefully.

2. Overlap the seam line of one section on the seam line of the other. Pin to position.

3. Stitch. Make two rows of straight stitching—the first directly on the seam line, the second right beside it (Fig. 164a). Or, if your machine can do zigzag stitching, stitch directly over the seam line (Fig. 164b).

4. Trim away the seam allowances on both sides close to the stitching (Fig. 164c).

5. There may be times when the joining is better done by hand stitching. Use the catch stitch or the cross-stitch (Fig. 164d).*

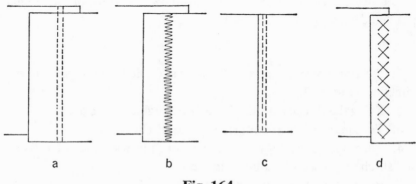

a   b   c   d

Fig. 164

*CROSS-STITCH

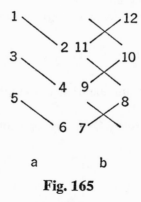

Fig. 165

Using a single matching thread, fasten the thread on the underside. Bring the needle out at 1, insert it at 2, bring it out at 3, insert it at 4, bring it out at 5, insert it at 6. This makes three diagonal stitches going in the same direction (Fig. 165a). To complete the stitches, make three diagonal stitches going in the opposite direction. Bring the needle out at 7, insert it at 8, bring it out at 9, insert it at 10, bring it out at 11, insert it at 12 (Fig. 165b). Fasten the thread on the underside.

Join Seams over Tape

This abutted seam is an excellent method for stitching a shaping seam or one that needs special reinforcement.

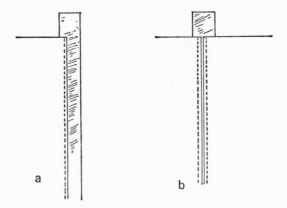

Fig. 166

1. Mark each seam line carefully.

2. Trim away the seam allowance.

3. Cut the required length of preshrunk tape or a narrow strip of interfacing.

4. Bring one seam line to the center of the strip. Stitch (Fig. 166a).

5. Bring the second seam line to meet the first. Stitch (Fig. 166b).

Join Darts by Overlapping Seam Lines

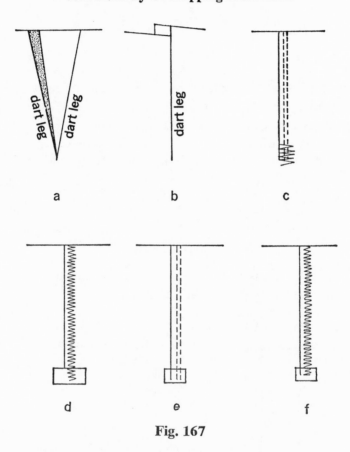

Fig. 167

1. Mark the dart seam lines (legs) carefully.

2. Slash one dart leg to the dart point (Fig. 167a).

3. Overlap the slashed edge on the other dart leg (Fig. 167b).

4. Reinforce the point of the dart with either zigzag stitching (Fig. 167c) or a patch of tape or interfacing (Fig. 167d).

5. Start the stitching at the dart point—the point that requires precision stitching—and stitch to its end. Stitch close to the cut edge. Use either two rows of straight stitching (Fig. 167e) or one row of zigzag stitching (Fig. 167f).

6. Trim away the excess fabric close to the stitching.

Join Dart Legs over Tape

Darts, as well as seams, may be joined over tape in an abutted seam.

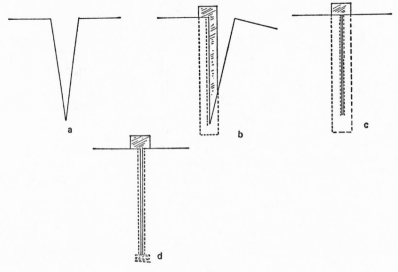

Fig. 168

1. Mark the dart, and cut it out entirely (Fig. 168a).

2. Cut a length of preshrunk tape as long as the dart plus ¼ inch at each end. (You could use a narrow strip of interfacing material instead of the tape.)

3. Bring one dart leg to the center of the strip. Pin and stitch (Fig. 168b).

4. Bring the second dart leg to meet the first. Pin and stitch (Fig. 168c).

5. Reinforce each dart point with lock stitching or zigzag stitching (Fig. 168d).

This is also a good method for joining a shaping seam.

HOW TO STITCH THE DARTS AND SEAMS IN UNDERLINED GARMENTS

METHOD I— *for Sheer and Very Lightweight Fabrics*

1. Cut the fabric and the underlining from the same pattern.
2. Transfer the pattern markings to the underlining only.
3. Stay-stitch or baste the outer fabric and the underlining.

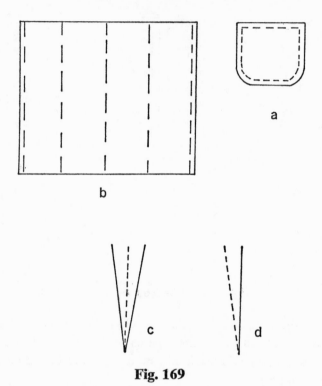

Fig. 169

To join two flat unshaped sections:

1. Match the centers of both sections, pin, and baste.
2. For small sections: continue basting around all edges (Fig. 169a).
3. For large sections: work from the center toward the outer edges, making rows of basting every few inches (Fig. 169b).

4. To stitch a dart: machine-stitch directly down the center, ending at the point, through both thicknesses of material (Fig. 169c).

5. Fold the dart on the line of stitching, smoothing the material away from it.

6. Pin and stitch through all the layers of the material (Fig. 169d). Stitch from the wide end to the dart point, being particularly careful to smooth the fabric at the point and to taper the stitching off the fabric for a perfect blend.

7. If the finished dart is not too bulky, leave it uncut. If bulky, slash the dart and press it open as previously directed.

It is very difficult to get a perfectly stitched dart by this method in any but sheer or very lightweight material. Method II produces a much more accurate dart in heavier materials.

8. Include the underlining in all construction seams.

METHOD II—*for Lightweight Outer Fabric and Underlining*

1. Cut the fabric and the underlining from the same pattern.

2. Transfer the pattern markings to the fabric *and* the underlining.

3. Pin and stitch the dart in the outer fabric. Pin and stitch the dart in the backing.

4. If the finished dart is not too bulky, leave it uncut; if bulky, slash the dart and press it open. When the darts are cut, place them one over the other. If uncut, press the garment dart in one direction, the underlining dart in the opposite direction, to avoid bulk.

5. Join the outer layer and the underlining with basting.

Since this section of the garment has been shaped by the darts, it cannot be worked flat as a straight or unshaped section might be. To preserve the shaping, the two are joined over a curve of the tailor's ham in the following way.

1. Place the backing over the tailor's ham wrong side up.

2. Place the outer fabric over the backing right side up. This places the material and backing in the same relative position and shaping in which the garment will be worn—fashion fabric topping foundation fabric, with the tailor's ham representing the body.

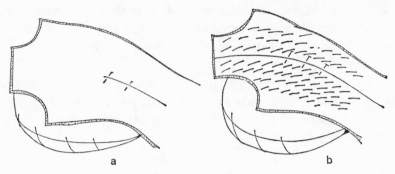

a   b

Fig. 170

3. Match the darts and pin (Fig. 170a).

4. Using the dart point as a hub, smooth the fabric toward the outer edges in strokes like the spokes of a wheel; pin (Fig. 170b).

5. Baste or tailor-baste* the two thicknesses in rows about 2 to 3 inches apart. Start with the dart and work to the outer edges. The long stitches are on the right side of the fabric, the short stitches on the underside.

6. Include the underlining in all construction seams.

*TAILOR BASTING

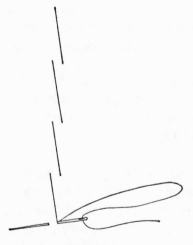

Fig. 171

Tailor basting is worked through two (or more) layers of fabric to hold them in place while the garment is in construction. It consists of a long diagonal stitch on the upper side and a short horizontal stitch on the underside (Fig. 171). Don't pull up the thread tightly. This is a "relaxed" stitch to avoid a quilted effect.

METHOD III—*for Medium to Heavy Outer Fabric and Crisp or Springy Interfacing (like Hair Canvas) or Underlining*

(Strange as this may seem to you now, it is possible that one day fashion will again call for shapes heavily supported in this manner.)

1. Cut the fabric and the underlining from the same pattern.

2. Transfer the pattern markings to each.

3. Pin and stitch the dart in the outer fabric. Slash the dart and press it open.

4. Stitch the dart in the underlining or interfacing by the slash-and-overlap method. Trim away excess material close to the stitching line.

5. Join the outer layer and the underlining by the method described in Method II.

6. Trim away the seam allowances of the underlining or interfacing. Catch-stitch the cut edges to the outer fabric (Fig. 172).

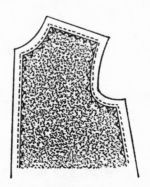

Fig. 172

7. Stitch the construction seams through the two layers of outer fabric only.

Use whichever of the three methods is least bulky and where the stitching is most accurate as it comes off the dart point.

To Underline a Garment with Fullness

METHOD I—*Good for Sheer or Lightweight Fabrics and Slim Figures*

Cut the underlining in exactly the same way as the outer fabric. Join the two with stay stitching on all edges. Or join as in Method I, Fig. 169. Gather them together. This produces a very full effect.

METHOD II—*Good for Heavier Fabrics and Heavier Figures*

Cut the underlining in exactly the same way as the outer fabric. Dart the underlining; shirr the outer fabric. Join the two with basting along all outside edges. In this way, the underlining acts as a stay for the fullness, keeping it in place while reducing the bulkiness.

METHOD III—*for Bouffant or Belled Shapes*

The same as Method I except that the underlined fabric is laid in pleats—pressed or unpressed.

METHOD IV—*for Crisp Pleats*

Omit the underlining.

THE NO-LINING JACKET OR COAT

Seams and Darts

In making an unlined garment, you may choose any of the seams (page 214) that appear suitable to the design and fabric.

However, the seams most often used for such tailored jackets or coats are the flat-fell seam, the welt seam, and the double-stitched welt seam.

Darts in unlined garments generally remain uncut. They may be stitched to resemble a single- or double-stitched welt seam.

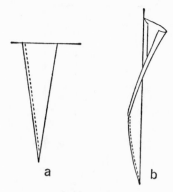

Fig. 173

Press the dart to one side and stitch the folded edge (Fig. 173a).
A wide dart may be treated like a welt seam (Fig. 173b).

1. Trim one side of the dart to a narrow width.

2. Fold under a narrow seam allowance on the second side.

3. Press the longer seam allowance to one side so it encloses the narrower seam allowance.

4. Stitch from the wide end to the dart point close to the folded edge.

The foregoing methods of stitching the seams and darts are also applicable in the making of a reversible garment from a reversible fabric.

HOW TO STITCH A CORNER

Place the two thicknesses of fabric together.

In very sheer fabrics (Fig. 174a):

1. Stitch the seam, ending with the needle in the fabric at the corner.

2. Raise the presser foot and pivot a 90-degree angle.

3. Lower the presser foot and continue stitching in the new direction.

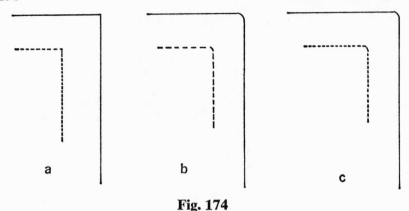

Fig. 174

In medium-weight fabrics (Fig. 174b):

1. Stitch the seam almost to the corner.
2. Take one stitch across the corner.
3. Continue stitching the second side.

In heavy fabrics (Fig. 174c):

1. Stitch the seam almost to the corner.
2. Take three stitches to round the corner.
3. Continue to stitch the other side.

Needless to say, in sewing, as in driving a car, slow up when rounding a corner.

In all cases, press the seams open over a point presser, (the point is inserted into each corner), grade the seam allowances, free the corner of bulk,* and turn to the right side. *Gently* work out the corners with an orange stick or a blunt needle.

*TO FREE A CORNER OF EXCESS BULK

Make three slashes—one diagonally across the corner, a second diagonally farther into the seam allowance on one side, a third diagonally farther into the seam allowance on the other side. Cut close to the stitching line (Fig. 175).

If you're worried about the stitching coming apart, perhaps you'd better reinforce the corner with very small machine stitches.

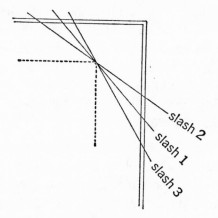

Fig. 175

HOW TO STITCH A STYLE LINE THAT COMES TO A POINT OR A CORNER

(Fig. 176)

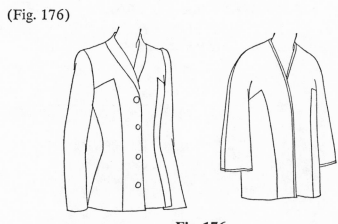

Fig. 176

1. Mark the matching points very carefully.

2. Reinforce each with stay stitching or an organza facing.

3. With right sides together, match the markings. Pin.

4. Bring the needle down directly on the matched points. Stitch away from the marking to the end of the seam.

5. Pull the threads at the corner through to one side and tie them in a square knot.

6. Clip the seam allowance at the corner to the stitching line in order to facilitate the matching and stitching of the second side.

7. Once more, bring the needle down into the marking at the point where the previous stitching started. Stitch away from the marking in the opposite direction to the end of the seam.

8. Again, pull the ends of the thread at the marking through to one side and tie. Make sure that the two lines of stitching just meet at the corner.

Stitch one side at a time. Stitching the entire corner in one continuous line is not only too difficult, but hazardous. The action of the presser foot and the feed may displace the fabric at the point that calls for precision.

A safe rule to follow in stitching: always *start the stitching at the point where precision is most needed;* stitch away from it.

HOW TO MITER A CORNER

In lightweight or medium-weight material:

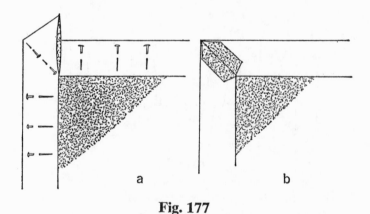

a   b

Fig. 177

1. Turn the hem (or the seam allowance) to the outside, right sides together (Fig. 177a).

2. Pinch the corner into a dart (Fig. 177a) and pin. It must be tight against the underlayer.

3. Stitch the seam line of the dart. Trim and press open over the point presser (Fig. 177b).

4. Turn the mitered corner to the inside, gently working out the corner with an orange stick or a blunt needle.

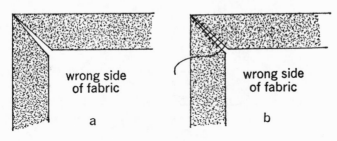

Fig. 178

In heavy fabric:

1. Turn the hem (or seam allowance) to the inside, with wrong sides together.

2. Pinch the corner into a dart, keeping it tight against the underlayer.

3. Trim the excess fabric that forms the dart diagonally across the corner (Fig. 178a).

4. Stitch the raw edges securely in place with overhand stitches* (Fig. 178b).

*THE OVERHAND STITCH

The overhand stitch is used whenever a strong, flat seam is desired: for instance, when working with lace or fur.

The needle (a short one is advisable) is inserted at an angle, but the stitches are vertical, at right angles to the miter, passing over and under the edges. The stitches are close, small, and even. Do not draw them up tightly. If you do, the seam will not lie flat.

HOW TO REINFORCE A CORNER THAT NEEDS
TO BE CLIPPED

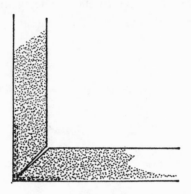

Fig. 179

1. Reinforce the corner to be clipped with a double row of tiny machine stitches.

2. Clip diagonally to the corner close to the stitching line (Fig. 179).

HOW TO REINFORCE A SLASH LINE

This method is used for gussets, sleeve openings, and so on.

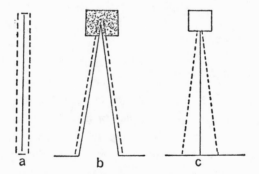

Fig. 180

METHOD I

Stitch either side of the slash, tapering toward the end of the slash. Take one stitch across the end to provide the space for turning (Fig. 180a).

METHOD II

Slash lines may be reinforced with a patch of seam binding, organza, or iron-on material. The first two are stitched to the right side and pulled through to the wrong side like facings—which indeed they are (Fig. 180b).

The iron-on material is applied directly to the wrong side (Fig. 180c).

HOW TO STITCH A CURVED SEAM WHEN THE SIDES ARE OPPOSING CURVES

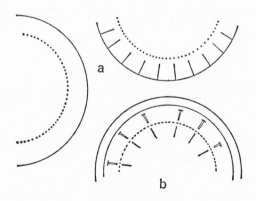

Fig. 181

1. Stay-stitch each side (Fig. 181a).

2. Clip the concave curve (inside curve) to within a short distance of each end.

3. Stretch the concave curve to match the convex curve (outside curve).

4. Pin to position and stitch (Fig. 181b).

SHORT CUTS

To release straining when an outside edge is shorter than the seam line: Clip all seam allowances that curve in (Fig. 182a). A clip is a short snip in the seam allowance made with the point of the scissors at right angles to the stitching line.

To eliminate rippling when an outside edge is longer than the seam line: Notch all seam allowances that curve out (Fig. 182b). A notch is a small wedge that is cut out of the seam allowance.

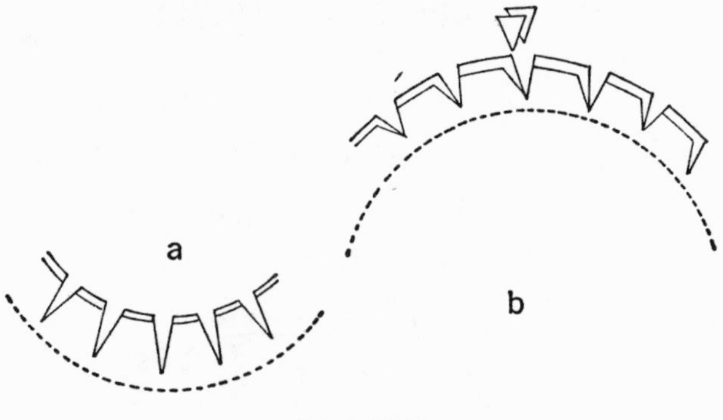

Fig. 182

Some seams, like a control seam over the bust, require clipping on one seam allowance to release the strain and notching on the other to eliminate the rippling.

Notch between the clips so there will not be too much stress on the stitching. If notches and clips are directly opposite each other, the seam will be literally "hanging by a thread."

A "HANDY" TECHNIQUE

The position of the hands and fingers can determine the ease or the tautness of the stitching. In ease stitching the fingers exert a horizontal pull on the fabric. In taut stitching, the pull is vertical.

Ease Stitching (off-grain stitching): Useful for easing a slight amount of fullness. Also a good way to prevent the top layer of fabric from slipping forward.

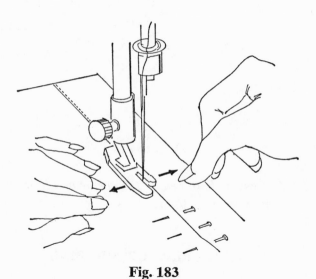

Fig. 183

1. Place the forefingers on *either side of the presser foot* (Fig. 183).

2. Pull the fabric horizontally as it feeds into the machine.

3. Stitch a little bit at a time, slowly, easing in the fullness to the desired amount.

Taut-stitching Technique: Useful for stitching knits and bias and stretch fabrics. It also prevents seam puckering.

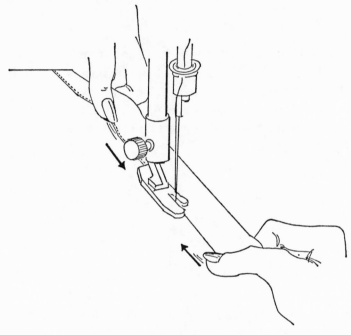

Fig. 184

Pull the fabric evenly *both behind the needle and in front of it* as it feeds into the machine (Fig. 184).

GATHERING OR SHIRRING

Gathering is fullness drawn up by a thread into a desired length. It may be done by hand or by machine.

For *machine gathering,* use a basting stitch. It is easier to pull up the bobbin thread when it is a buttonhole twist or coarse thread.

Hand gathering is made with running stitches—tiny even bastings (Fig. 185a). Work from the right to the left, using a double thread. The needle is woven through the material by an up-and-down hand motion while the fabric is held still. When the needle is full of the tiny stitches, the thread is drawn through.

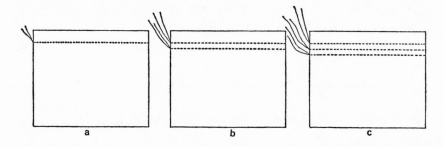

Fig. 185

Two rows of running stitches make for a more even distribution of the gathers (Fig. 185b). The first row is made in the seam allowance close to the seam line. The second row is made ¼ inch above the first toward the raw edge.

Shirring is three (or more) rows of gathering (Fig. 185c). Since it is generally used in a decorative manner, the stitches are made at and below the seam line where they can be seen.

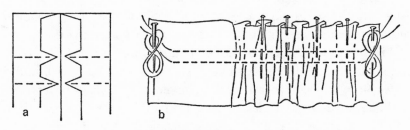

Fig. 186

1. Eliminate the bulk at all cross seams by notching the seam allowances almost to the stitching lines where the rows of gathering will be made (Fig. 186a).

2. Section off the length to be gathered into halves, quarters, eighths, and so on—as many sections as convenient for the length to be gathered.

3. Section off the length to which the fullness is to be joined in a similar manner.

4. Place a pin at right angles to the edge at each end of the area to be gathered.

5. Anchor one end of the gathering by winding the ends of the thread around the pin in a figure eight.

6. Draw up the fullness until it equals the exact fixed length (Fig. 186b).

7. Wind the ends of the thread around the second pin as at the other end.

8. Match the markings for each section. Pin at right angles to the stitching line.

9. Secure the fullness with basting or backstitching.

In dressmaking you might get away with simply pinning or basting a gathered area before machine-stitching. In tailoring, because of the heavier fabrics, it is wiser to backstitch. Backstitching locks the folds of the gathers in place. Fullness controlled in this way is not dislodged by the subsequent machine stitching.

This has been a chapter on techniques. Assuredly they are essential for fine production and one cannot minimize their worth. However, tools and techniques alone do not make artists. It's what an artist does with them that matters. Practicing from morning to night undoubtedly helps but does not necessarily make of every aspiring young pianist a concert star. Stitching miles of perfect seams and doing acres of fine needlework does not alone guarantee that a suit will turn out to look like a couturier's creation. A garment could be as well built in its way as a bridge or skyscraper and yet not have style or beauty.

While anything that can be described by the term "work of art" requires a knowledge of technique, technique alone never makes it such. So sew that you raise the *act* of sewing to the *art* of sewing.

Chapter 14

Special Fabrics — Special Handling

The previous chapter dealt with general techniques applicable to general stitching situations for most fabrics. This chapter covers the special handling required by several popular special fabrics.

KNIT OR NOT: STITCHING FABRICS WITH STRETCH

Knits are not the only fabrics that have stretch. Bias-cut woven fabrics have stretch, too.

When stitching fabrics with stretch, all seams must have enough "give" to match the stretch of the fabric and yet not break the thread. There are three ways this can be done: by straight stitching (if you must), by zigzag stitching (if you can), or by stretch stitching (if your sewing machine is equipped with this feature).

Because *straight stitching* itself has no give, some stretch comes by providing sufficient length of thread to accommodate the pull. Shorter stitches and less tension will do so.

The side-to-side movement of the *zigzag stitch* does provide give. Use the narrowest of the zigzag stitches, a reduced tension, and a stitch length appropriate for the fabric. Use this stitch for all the big construction seams—never for topstitching, which requires the straightest of seams.

The *stretch stitch* is built into many of the newer sewing machines and is a great boon to those who love to work with fabrics that stretch. Simply set your machine for stretch stitching.

SOME GENERAL SUGGESTIONS FOR WORKING WITH FABRICS THAT STRETCH

Use ball-point needles for both hand and machine stitching. Their rounded points slip between the threads of the fabric rather than piercing them as sharp-pointed needles do.

Use mercerized cotton thread, which is supple; silk thread, which has some elasticity; or synthetic thread, advertised to have even more.

PILES OF FUN

Even the *short-pile fabrics* have some depth. (That's the beauty of them. Double the depth as two layers are fed into the machine for stitching and you have problems. The machine is set for flat fabrics. The piles lock, and the upper layer has a tendency to creep forward. What to do? Try the following.

1. Instead of basting all sections together before stitching, back-stitch. It holds the layers together firmly.

2. Loosen the tension slightly and reduce the pressure on the presser foot. Raising the presser bar will provide room for the depth of the piles.

3. Keep the layers separated until they are fed into the presser foot to keep the piles from locking.

4. An even-feed either built into your sewing machine or added as an attachment is helpful in letting the fabric "ride" through the machine.

And do remember to sew in the direction of the nap or pile.

When it comes to sewing the *deep-pile fabrics,* multiply the problems of the short-pile fabrics by the depth of the surface surplus. And then some! What to do with the "hairs" that are caught in the seams and darts?

1. Use all the techniques for sewing the short-pile fabrics.

2. In stitching shaggy-haired fabrics, use a fine, long needle or hat-pin to work the hairs out of the seams and darts. When released, these hairs conceal the seam.

Another way to deal with the shaggy-haired fabrics is to eliminate the hairs from the seam area before stitching. Shear the pile from the seam allowance close to the fabric at the seam line. Use sharp scissors held parallel to the cloth.

When the pile or surface surplus is very heavy, treat the fabric as if it were fur—real or phony.

THE FABULOUS FAKES: THE PHONY FURS AND THE PSEUDO SUEDES

The most exciting of the new fabrics are fakes—real fakes, look-alikes for the skins they ape but with virtues of their own. The phony furs and the pseudo suedes have it going for them both ways. Sometimes they are handled like fabrics—which they are. And sometimes they are handled like the furs and suedes they pretend to be.

THE PHONY FURS

If your fur fabric is of short pile, treat it like any other short-pile fabric. If the "fur" fabric is the long-haired type, treat it like a deep-pile fabric. If it truly looks like real fur, handle it as one would the real thing.

Cut from the Wrong Side: Smooth, flat furs can be cut with sharp shears. Deep-pile furs are cut with a razor blade or an X-Acto knife. In this way, you will cut only the backing and avoid cutting the hair or pile. The uncut hair is used to cover the seam, thereby making the joining invisible.

It's a good idea to make a test seam or dart so you can get the feel of the fabric and determine the best method for stitching it.

When Machine-stitched: With the fur sides inside, align the edges to be joined and hold them in place with large paper clips. Should the fabric creep or pucker, baste or backstitch to hold it in place.

Use your zipper foot or cording foot to accommodate the difference in the thickness between the shaved and the unshaved fabric (above).

All stitching is done in the direction of the nap or pile. Keep the tension and pressure light or use an even-feed mechanism. Use a coarse needle and heavy-duty thread.

Finish all seam edges with machine zigzag stitching or hand overcasting.

When Hand-stitched: Trim away all but ⅛ inch of the seam allowances. Join the sections by overhand stitches (page 241).

It is easier to hand-stitch furs and fur-type fabrics with a Glover's needle No. 7. This is a suture needle. Its spearlike point pierces the "skin" without tearing it.

All hand stitches catch only the backing of the fabric. They must never come through to the right side.

If you want to give your phony fur the full fur treatment, tape the seams to reinforce them. Baste twill tape over the seam line so it extends ⅛ inch beyond the stitching line into the seam allowance and include it in the seam.

THE PSEUDO SUEDES

The pseudo suedes run the gamut from the comparatively inexpensive suede-surfaced fabrics to the luxury-item, status-symbol Ultrasuede. The former are treated like any other fabrics with napped surfaces. The latter is handled sometimes like fabric, more often like the leather it resembles.

What does it take to sew Ultrasuede (besides money)? Accuracy and time and a sewing machine that won't fight the fabric. If you've ever longed for a garment you could paste together rather than stitch, this is your big chance: so much of the "basting" and interfacing and finishing is done with a fusible web.

While silk thread, 100 per cent polyester thread, or polyester-core thread are usually recommended, mercerized cotton thread works just as well.

Use fine machine and hand needles. For the construction seams, use 10 to 12 stitches per inch. Small stitches will perforate the material as if it were paper and it can be torn just as easily along the perforations. Use an eased tension and the taut-stitching technique.

There are two ways in which darts and seams may be stitched: the standard (regulation) method and the flat (overlap) method. The first is the familiar method for sewing woven or knit cloth. The second is the method by which leathers are sewn together.

The Standard Method

Believe it or not, beautifully classic tailored garments of Ultrasuede can be made by the standard method, using all the regulation tailoring techniques, with this happy difference: the iron-on interfacings and the fusible webs replace all the laborious hand stitching! Just think—no basting, no catch stitching, no hemming, no pad stitching! The garment made by the standard method is not the least bit bulkier than any other cloth of comparable weight and texture, and it's nothing short of handsome.

The seam allowances are stitched in the regulation (right sides together) manner and pressed open. To hold them in place, the seam allowances may be fused, topstitched, or both. Avoid back-and-forth lock stitching, which tends to weaken or may even tear the fabric.

STITCHING THE DARTS

1. Fuse a ½-inch square or round patch of sheer iron-on material at the dart point. This both reinforces and prevents "bubbling" at the dart point.

2. Stitch from the wide end of the dart to its point.

3. Tie the thread ends in a square knot.

4. Slash the dart from the wide end as far as the points of sharp trimming scissors will go (about 1 inch from the point). Clip across the dart to the stitching.

5. Press the dart open over narrow strips of web fusing material.

STITCHING THE FACINGS

Stitch all facings in the regulation construction for encased seams. If no topstitching is to be used, the seam allowances may be the usual ⅝ inch. When topstitching is to be used, trim and grade the seam allowances, keeping them within the topstitched area. For instance: in topstitching ⅜ inch from the edge, trim the longer of the seam allowances short of the ⅜ inch.

It is especially important to observe all the tailoring techniques in regard to trimming, clipping, grading, freeing the corners of bulk, and pressing and rolling the joining seam to the undersurface.

Flat (Overlap) Method

In the flat method, all seams are overlapped and topstitched. The seam allowances of all faced and outer edges are trimmed away, aligned, and topstitched.

Hems may be raw (cut) edges, with or without a facing. No finish is necessary.

Knowing this, it is possible to save some fabric by eliminating or diminishing the seam allowance of all such edges.

STITCHING THE SEAMS

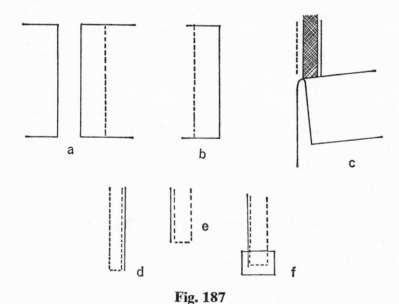

a   b   c   d   e   f

Fig. 187

1. Trim away the seam allowance from the overlap edge (Fig. 187a).

2. Trim back the seam allowance of the underlap edge to ⅜ inch or any other predetermined width, depending on where the top-stitching is to be.

In an overlap method, one would naturally think in terms of working from the right side, where the overlap actually occurs. To do so would mean to mark the position of the overlap on the right side of the underlap material. Since it takes considerable marking for an accurate overlap line, it is safer (and much easier) to work in reverse on the underside. Here's how.

On the Overlap

1. Working on the underside, mark a line ⅜ inch (or whatever width you've decided on) up from the cut edge. Use a soft lead or chalk pencil (Fig. 187b).

2. Bring the cut edge of the underlap to this line.

3. Slip a ¼-inch strip of fusible web between the two. Steam-press lightly to position—just enough to hold the two in place for top-stitching (Fig. 187c).

On the Right Side

1. Make a line of topstitching close to the cut edge of the overlap.

2. Make a second line of topstitching ¼ inch or more from the first (Fig. 187d).

Lap fronts over backs. If there is an underarm section, lap the front and back sections over the underarm sections. Generally, yoke seams are overlapped on joining sections. While the direction of the overlap is not crucial, being consistent is.

STITCHING THE DARTS

Darts may be made by the overlap method, but it is harder to produce as fine or as accurate a dart point.

If you insist, here is how it is done.

1. Slash one dart leg.

2. With right side up, overlap the slashed edge to meet the other dart leg.

3. Topstitch close to the edge from the wide end to the dart point.

4. Pivot at the dart point and stitch to a second point ¼ inch away. Pivot once more. Make a second row of stitching ¼ inch from the first (Fig. 187e).

5. On the underside, trim away all excess material. Place a ½-inch patch of sheer iron-on material for a reinforcement at the point of the dart, and press (Fig. 187f).

Combinations

You may use a combination of the standard and flat methods: for instance, standard method for the darts and sleeves, flat method for the rest.

Ultrasuede is a surprisingly easy fabric to work with. And the results? Well, that's what keeps the fabric stores running out of yardage despite its high price.

THE TWO-FACED FABRICS

You could ignore the potential of a two-faced fabric and treat it like any other—stitch it, line it, forget what it *could* be. That would be a pity.

To take full advantage of its double drama, try the hidden-construction method described below. Its sleight of hand will intrigue you and baffle your friends.

1. Separate the two layers of fabric at all edges to be stitched. Do this by slicing through the perpendicular threads that join the layers for about 1½ inches (Fig. 188a).

2. Machine-stitch the seams of one thickness (Fig. 188b).

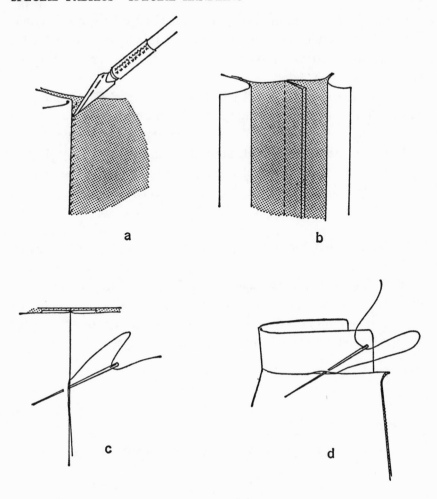

a

b

c

d

Fig. 188

3. Press open the seam allowances as best you can with the tip of the iron. (Being small, a traveling iron is great for this purpose.)

4. Trim and turn under the seam allowances of the second side so the folds meet directly over the seam line of the first side (Fig. 188c). Slip-stitch.

5. Set the hem. Add seam allowance. Trim the excess fabric.

6. For the hem and all outside untrimmed edges: separate the two layers of fabrics and slice the perpendicular joining threads as for the other seams. Turn under both seam allowances toward each other. Slip-stitch along the edge.

7. *The collar:* slice back 1½ inches of all edges. Turn under and slip-stitch all untrimmed outside edges. Turn under both seam allowances on the collar neck edge, but leave the edge open.

8. Slip the garment neck edge into the collar opening (Fig. 188d). Slip-stitch the folds of the collar edges to the neck seam line of the garment. (Cuffs can be attached in the same way.)

If you topstitch for trimming, you can create a great welt-seam look.

If all this seems like too much work for you, decide which of the two sides you are most apt to wear for the outside. Use a welt-seam construction throughout. Either bind the outside edges or turn the seam allowances to the underside and stitch the edges.

HALF THE MATERIAL CAN DOUBLE THE FUN

Instead of limiting yourself to the edges, separate the entire two layers of the fabric by slicing through the perpendicular threads that join them. Now each layer is a complete and usable fabric by itself. Though half the original, it has double the possibilities. Use half for a skirt and half for a top (Fig. 189), or in any other way you can devise.

Admittedly it's a chore to put asunder what the factory hath joined together, but where would you ever find such matching fabrics otherwise?

Fig. 189

Chapter 15

Pressing Problems

There comes a time in the tailoring process when one wonders whether those limp little pieces of cloth so carefully stitched together are ever going to look like anything. This is usually just before a good pressing.

Pressing makes the difference between a limp length of cloth and a shapely section of garment.

As important as pressing is to the rest of your sewing, in tailoring it is raised to a fine art. Indeed, one cannot think of tailoring without also thinking of those crisp edges, those flat seams, and that subtly blocked-to-shape sculptured form.

The equipment is so varied, the process so fascinating, the results so spectacular, that even people who ordinarily hate ironing actually enjoy the pressing in tailoring.

Sewing without pressing is an incomplete act. The iron is just as important to the tailoring process as the sewing machine. You cannot wait until your sewing is finished for one mighty pressing binge. It simply won't work. Once the layers are applied to each other, one can never get back inside again. A right-side touch-up (or even a more thorough pressing at the tailor's) can never accomplish what pressing and shaping as you sew can do for the garment.

SEW AND PRESS

Press every dart and seam open before stitching it to a cross seam. Press **each** section of a garment before stitching it to another.

Press open every enclosed seam before turning the facing back to the underside (collars, cuffs, welts, flaps, lapels, closings, and so on).

Block over appropriate press pads all darts and shaping seams, as well as all straight pieces destined to fit curved areas. This applies to collars, lapels, sleeve caps, and so forth.

Press and shape each unit of work separately in outer fabric, interfacing, underlining, interlining, and lining before applying it to another or before joining back to front at the shoulders and side seams.

And it's so much easier:

—to topstitch an edge when it has been pressed flat first.

—to insert a zipper when the seam allowance is pressed back first.

—to achieve a smooth and flat hem if the fullness at the raw edge is ease-pressed before finishing and attaching.

—to set a sleeve when the cap has been blocked first.

—to stitch a lapped seam when the seam allowance has been turned under and pressed back first.

Set up your pressing equipment along with your sewing equipment. The rhythm of work is always sew and press, sew and press, sew and press.

"PRESS" VS. "IRON"

Have you noticed that we've used the word "press" rather than "iron"? There's a difference.

To get the wrinkles out of a handkerchief, you push the iron along the surface. That's ironing—a gliding motion. Cotton, linen, silk, and synthetics are all handled in this way. When it comes to wool, however, this method won't do at all. In the damp stage necessary for pressing wool, the fabric is very malleable. Were the iron to be pushed along the wool as in the usual kind of laundry ironing, it would be easily stretched or shrunk, pushed or pulled, molded or straightened, wrinkled or pushed off grain. Only the careful up-and-down motion of pressing can prevent this. Lower the iron, press, lift, and move to a new section of the fabric and lower, press, lift.

Because of the long stroke, ironing is always done on a flat surface. Because it involves only a small area, pressing can be done on a shaped pad, small though that may be, as well as on a flat surface.

Save the ironing for the smooth-surfaced flat work. For shaped garments (which is just about all of them), press on a shaped press pad.

There is this, too: fabrics that can be laundered are ironed smooth.
Garments that require dry cleaning, because of either their fiber, their
texture, or their inner construction, are pressed. Since tailoring generally has all these latter characteristics, tailored garments are always
pressed.

SOME GENERAL HINTS ON PRESSING

Each garment presents an individual pressing problem, but there
are some general rules that apply to all.

Place a chair or table close to the ironing board to support any fabric that may otherwise trail on the floor.

Don't press darts, seams, folds, pleats, or anything else unless you
are absolutely sure they are exactly where you want them. It is often
impossible to press out the sharp crease produced by pressing.

Pressing is directional. Press all woven fabrics with the grain: off-
grain pressing pushes material out of shape or stretches it. Press all
knit fabrics with the lengthwise rib: pressing across the ribs stretches
the fabric. Press all napped materials with the nap.

You may do your ironing on the right side, but for pressing the
wrong side is the correct side. If the right side must be pressed, protect it with a suitable press cloth. Direct contact with the iron is a sure
way to produce a shine.

Don't press over pins or bastings: both leave marks. If basting is
absolutely necessary, use silk thread, which is less apt to leave marks.

With seam allowances closed, press the seams along the stitching
line in the same direction as stitched. This distributes the thread
evenly along the seam and blends it into the fabric.

Avoid overdampening and overpressing. Do not use too hot an
iron, too much moisture, too much pressure, too many times.

Keep trimming scissors handy. Clip or notch where needed to make
a seam or dart lie flat. Slash and grade to reduce bulk.

When seam allowances are pressed in one direction, press in the direction that produces the least bulk.

Hang up each pressed section as soon as the pressing is complete. If you must store your work in progress, don't fold any more than necessary, or fold over tissue paper as if for packing.

Settle for the best results you can get. Don't attempt the impossible for the fabric. Quit while you're ahead.

EVERY GARMENT PRESENTS AN INDIVIDUAL PRESSING PROBLEM

Every fabric has a character, structure, and surface appearance of its own. Every design has style lines and shaping of its own. Just as the fabric and design determine how each garment is to be sewn, so they determine how it is to be pressed.

One cannot press a gauzy mohair coat as one would a cotton blouse: the gliding motion of the iron would stretch it and crush it. One cannot iron a worsted suit as one would a soft woolen fabric: the kind of pressure needed to produce the crisp edges of the worsted would be completely inappropriate for the soft woolen. A velvet or corduroy jacket cannot be pressed like a smooth silk dress: the pile, which is its beauty, would be flattened and destroyed. The kind of fiber and the character of the fabric must be considered in choosing an appropriate method of pressing.

There is this, too: darts and control seams produce all manner of curves in a garment—subtle ones, deep ones, in-between ones. One cannot press a shirt jacket like a traditionally tailored suit jacket: the former has no shaping while the latter has. Even within the garment itself there are variations of contour that must be handled differently. The gentle curve that fits over the shoulder blades presents a decidedly different pressing problem than does the pronounced curve that fits over the bust. The curve of the collar around the neck and the curve of the sleeve cap need different shaping. Each of the many varied curves in a garment must be pressed and blocked in an individual manner. (See section on Contour Pressing later in this chapter.)

To meet all the contingencies of design, shape, and fabric, a variety of pressing equipment is essential. In fact, a large proportion of all sewing equipment is used for pressing (see page 56).

Assemble all the material you will need for the garment under construction.

Test the Fabric Before You Begin

Don't begin your pressing until you are sure how your fabric will react to heat, moisture, and pressure.

Experiment with a test seam or dart to determine:

    a. the best heat setting on the iron;

    b. the correct amount of moisture;

    c. the best method for flattening seams and edges;

    d. some way in which the surface texture can be preserved;

    e. how to prevent seam imprints or iron marks.

HEAT, MOISTURE, PRESSURE, PROTECTION

Both pressing and ironing are accomplished by heat, moisture, pressure, and some protection.

Heat: Use the heat setting on the iron suitable for the fiber:

High heat for the *vegetable fibers*—cotton, linen. (The vegetables can take it.)

Moderate heat for the *animal fibers*—silk, wool. (The only kind of heat an animal can take—moderate.)

Low heat for the *man-made fibers*—all synthetics. (Heat melts the chemicals of which the synthetics are made.)

In *combinations of fibers,* use the heat setting for the most delicate fiber present. For instance, handle polyester and cotton as if it were all-polyester.

Holding the iron on one spot for any length of time intensifies the heat. For slow work, reduce the heat of the iron.

A moist press cloth tends to reduce the heat. When used on some fabrics, it may be necessary to increase the heat.

Moisture: Most fabrics press better with some degree of moisture. Whether you apply it by hand, by eye dropper, or by press cloth, or whether you sprinkle, spray, sponge, or steam it, depends on the fabric.

Dampened cottons and linens are ironed until they are dry. They wrinkle and muss when limp.

Woolens, however, must *never* be pressed dry. Allow them to dry naturally. Handle them very carefully while damp, since they are easily manipulated out of shape.

No moisture should be used for silks and synthetics: press them dry.

Pressure: All fabrics require some pressure to smooth them. The very word "press" implies this. In tailoring, pressure may be anything from a loving pat to the 1,600 pounds per square inch applied to the edge of a man's coat in a clothing factory.

For some fabrics, the pressure of the iron is sufficient. Others are pressed, then patted with a press mitt. Heavy or firmly woven woolens are pounded with a pounding block. The latter is the home sewer's answer to the pressure exerted by the factory pressing machines.

Protection: One certainly wouldn't want to flatten the raised surface that is a fabric's main attraction by pounding. Remember that many materials require protection rather than pressure in pressing.

A *press cloth of self fabric* is about as good a protection as one can get. When the raised surface of the fashion fabric is pressed against the raised surface of the self-fabric strip, the naps interlock, thereby preserving each other. Moreover, naps so pressed tend to adhere. As the two layers of fabric are separated, the naps are lifted.

In the event that you don't have enough self fabric for a press cloth, use a strip of terry cloth or any other raised-surface material.

When the right side of a fabric is turned to the wrong side for a hem or a facing, that, too, needs protection. (One never knows when one may be needing the underlayer for an upper layer.) Use a self-fabric press cloth both under and over the two thicknesses for *double protection.*

A *garment needs to be protected from itself*—from its seam allowances, pockets, welts, flaps, hems, pleats, lapels, collar, cuffs, buttonholes—indeed, from any applied, folded over, or more-than-single thickness. The damage comes in pressing when the outlines of these details are imprinted on the garment, unless they are prevented from doing so.

The simplest and best protection is a strip of brown wrapping paper to cushion the pressure. The strip should be of sufficient length and width so that it can be folded into thirds lengthwise.

If, inadvertently, an imprint has been made, lift the offending thickness and press out the mark.

NO PRESS—NO PROBLEM

You could limit your wardrobe to no-iron stuff if you wish to avoid the whole pressing problem. But who would want to? It's a safe bet that the fabrics you like require special handling in pressing. They're hard-surfaced, firmly woven, fleeced, furry, raised, napped, nubby, slubbed, looped, ribbed, crinkled, blistered, puckered, or embossed. They're either so tough that they require force to subdue them or so touchy you hardly dare lay a finger on them. Don't the difficult ones somehow always turn out to be the most interesting? Better learn how to handle them.

ON PRESSING WOOL

Wool is a living fiber. It must be treated so. Like any other living thing, it does not like being doused or dunked, scorched, broiled, or beaten within an inch of its life. Don't subject wool to excesses of anything—heat, moisture, or pressure, all of which in some degree are necessary to press it.

Heat: Wool takes a moderate setting on the iron—350° to 375° F. Excessive heat directly applied causes the overlapping scales of the wool fiber to lock, reducing its flexibility and producing a shine. It also damages the fibers and makes them feel harsh.

Moisture: Wool is pressed and shaped with moist heat. The degree of moisture and heat varies with the kind of wool. Some wools require little and some require more. The use of the steam iron for a first pressing is limited to fabrics that respond to a short, light steaming. Most woolens for tailoring require the kind and amount of steam produced when a moderately hot, dry iron is pressed against a damp press cloth.

Though water cannot hurt wool (imagine sheep that weren't waterproof!), it is the press cloth rather than the wool that is dampened. The cloth should be damp, not wet. Wetness plus heat can shrink or felt (mat) wool. Furthermore, the cloth must be uniformly damp so that no part of the fabric will be subjected to more moisture than any other, hence shrinking or felting one part and not another.

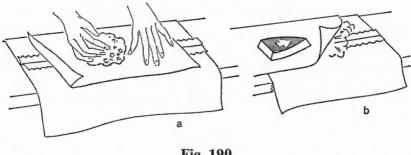

Fig. 190

A press cloth may be dampened by either of the following methods:

1. Dip about one third of the cloth in water and wring it out. Roll or fold the rest of it around the damp third until the entire cloth is uniformly damp.

2. Rub a wet sponge or dampening cloth over the press cloth until it is moist (Fig. 190a). The advantage of this method over the first is that the press cloth is less likely to get too wet.

Place the damp press cloth against the wrong side of the garment. Apply the dry iron to it with a lower-and-lift motion. Press lightly until the moisture changes to steam, then apply more pressure. From time to time allow the steam to escape by raising the press cloth (Fig. 190b). Stop pressing while the fabric is still steaming.

The use of a dampened press cloth both above and below the fabric creates steam that penetrates it. The upper steaming flattens where necessary, the lower steaming freshens and restores the wool. Wrinkles, creases, and folds in the fabric are better smoothed out by this treatment.

Allow wool to dry naturally. Hang the garment on a dress form or a tissue-paper-padded hanger so it will not lose its shaping.

Pressure: For lightweight woolens, the pressure of the iron is sufficient. For the hard-surfaced woolens and worsteds, use the pounding block (Fig. 28d) to achieve that clean, crisp, flat look associated with fine tailoring. See directions below.

Protection: Whatever the degree of heat, the iron should never be brought into direct contact with wool fabric, either on the right or on the wrong side. Use a press cloth for protection. A slip cover or protective plate cover (Fig. 28h) are convenient substitutes for a press cloth. They permit you to see just what part of the seam or dart you are working on.

All raised and novelty surfaces need particular protection (see page 271).

How to Press a Straight, Flat Seam or Crisp Edge in Worsted, Hard-surfaced, or Firmly Woven Woolens

1. Assemble all the equipment you will need: the ironing board and iron, the press board and pounding block, a press cloth and a small bowl of water, plus two folded strips of wrapping paper. Place everything within easy reach, for this is a very quick and deft operation.

2. Place the press board on the ironing board, or on a sturdy table. Place the right side of the garment against the press board. The wrong side is up for pressing.

3. Open the seam allowances with finger-pressing.* Slip the strips of wrapping paper under them.

Finger-pressing: Run the thumb or forefinger along the well of the seam. Use gentle pressure.

4. Dampen the press cloth. Place the damp press cloth over the opened seam.

5. Use a dry iron set on WOOL. Press it onto the damp press cloth. Keep the iron on just long enough to create a good head of steam. Lift the iron and set it aside.

6. Then quickly whisk the press cloth off with one hand while the fabric is still steaming. Almost simultaneously, slap the pounding block (clapper) on the seam with the other hand.

Bring it down with considerable force. Let the clapper rest there a minute before removing it. Presto! Your magically flattened seam.

One forceful blow should work. If the fabric proves stubborn (some are hard to flatten) or you enjoy the pounding, repeat the performance.

Are you curious to know why and how this works? The clapper forces the steam into the porous surface of the press board, which obligingly absorbs it, drying the fabric naturally in the process. The seam is held in place by the pounding block just long enough to train it flat while it is drying. This is why so much of the pressing equipment is of wood—press boards, clapper, shaping blocks, and point presser. The rest—the assorted seam rolls, press pads, and tailor's ham—are best when stuffed with sawdust.

7. Move on to the next section and repeat the operation.

This pounding method of pressing may also be effective on heavy or firmly woven cottons or raw silks.

Whenever the fabric can take it, use the press board and clapper to achieve the very flattest seams and the sharpest edges. This is particularly desirable in lapels, the front closing, facings, hems, pleats, cuffs, collars, welts, pockets, belts, buttonholes—just about anywhere on the garment where a thin, crisp edge is called for.

HOW TO PRESS THE SHORT-PILE FABRICS

There are two methods of "pressing" such fabrics to preserve the pile.

METHOD I

Place the pile of the fabric against the needles of a needle board. Steam-press the wrong side, using very little pressure (Fig. 191a). Let the steam do the work. Press over the center of the needle board: pressing too close to the edge may leave an imprint. Press with the nap.

If a needle board is not available, use a strip of self fabric or any other raised surface, like terry cloth.

When pile fabric is turned back to the wrong side in seam allowances, hems, and facings, they, too, need protection. Use a top needle board or a second strip of self fabric (Fig. 191b).

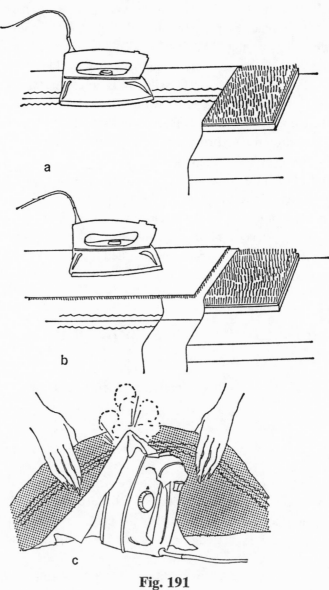

Fig. 191

Stand a hot, dry iron on end. Cover it with a damp cloth. This creates steam. Draw the wrong side of the velvet against the steaming iron (Fig. 191c). Handle lightly to prevent finger marks. (If necessary, these can be steamed out and brushed up.)

Both methods work well. Hang the garment on a hanger or dress form while drying.

HOW TO PRESS A STRAIGHT, FLAT-AS-POSSIBLE SEAM IN FABRICS WITH NAP

1. Assemble the needed equipment: the ironing board and iron, press mitt, press cloth, small bowl of water, the folded strips of wrapping paper, and self-fabric press cloth.

2. Place the self-fabric press cloth on the ironing board with its raised surface up. Place the right side of the garment against it.

3. Open the seam allowances with finger-pressing. Slip the strips of wrapping paper under them.

4. Dampen the press cloth as previously directed and place it over the opened seam.

5. Lower the dry iron (set at moderate heat) onto the damp press cloth. Press lightly and briefly.

6. Whisk off the press cloth with one hand and, with the other hand slipped into the press mitt, pat gently.

If, by chance, you have flattened the surface of the fabric, brush it up while damp to restore it.

Don't attempt the impossible with raised-surface fabrics. They can never be pressed as flat as the worsteds—nor should they be. That would destroy their very special quality.

Deep Fleece, Deep Furry Naps, and Raised Surfaces of All Kinds: These are all pressed in the same way. Use a light touch. Let the steam do the work.

HOW TO PRESS THE FAKE FURS

Fur fabric requires very little or no pressing. Finger-pressing does for most. Should you choose to press lightly, press on the wrong side, using a cool, dry iron. Press over a needle board (best of all), a strip of self fabric, or a Turkish towel. Brush up the nap after pressing.

You may use a steam iron for flattening edges. Hold it a few inches *above* the fur, merely steaming it. Pound the edge with a mallet or the tip of your clapper.

Should you be tempted to use the above technique, better test your "fur" first. Steam will mat some piles and, of course, the pounding will flatten the fluff.

HOW TO PRESS THE SIMULATED SUEDES

The simulated suedes require steam for pressing but neither in the same amount nor to the same degree of heat as for the woolens. Use all the usual pressing equipment, such as point presser and pounding block. Use all the usual precautions, too: press cloth, folded strips of wrapping paper to prevent seam imprints. Should imprints occur, restore the nap by a light brushing with a toothbrush. (Even a light brushing with the fingertips works well.) To seal pin or needle holes, steam-press and lightly brush up the nap.

PRESSING SILK

The most difficult fabric to press is silk. It requires great care to protect its delicate, frequently high luster.

Heat: Like wool, silk deteriorates under excessive heat. Always use a moderately warm iron. Do not keep the iron too long on any one spot.

Moisture: Some silks are washable (and are so labeled) and may be pressed while damp. Most are damaged by water and should never come in direct contact with it. Some silks tend to water-spot. Don't use a sputtering or drippy steam iron on them.

Protection: Most silks are dry-pressed and should always be protected with a dry press cloth or tissue paper. An iron applied directly to silk fabric produces a shine.

Crinkled, blistered, puckered, embossed, and similar surfaces are best left unpressed by the iron lest the raised surfaces be flattened. To open seam allowances on such fabrics, merely finger-press. If the fabric can take it (this requires testing), hold the steam iron about 1 inch above the fabric and move it slowly over the area. Some of these fabrics may be pressed lightly over well-padded terry cloth or a Turkish towel.

Fabrics made of tightly twisted yarns, like crepe, must be pressed very carefully, to prevent pressing out the crinkly surface.

Press satins and brocades with a light touch on the wrong side. With many silks it is impossible to get flat seams or sharp, crisp edges. Don't force the issue. Settle for a reasonable pressing and the soft look the fabrics cry out for.

PRESSING COTTONS

The easiest fabric to press is cotton. It doesn't demand the tender, loving care lavished on wool or silk. It may be pressed either damp or dry, with a steam iron or a dry iron. It depends on the weight and texture of the cotton.

There are a few precautions, however. While white and light colors may be pressed on the right side, the dark colors and dull finishes must be pressed on the wrong side to prevent shine.

Crinkled, embossed, puckered, and like surfaces are either left unpressed or steam-pressed above the surface, as suggested for similar silk fabrics. Embroidered cottons are pressed with the right side against a Turkish towel to prevent flattening the raised surface. Sheer cottons take slightly lower heat; too hot an iron will scorch them.

A tailored cotton garment cannot be treated as an ordinary laundry ironing problem. You would hardly want to sprinkle your good suit, roll it up—linings, interfacings, and all—and allow it to set until evenly damp, like a simple wash dress. Treat it like the tailored garment it is.

PRESSING LINEN

Linen takes a little more effort than cotton but responds easily and beautifully to pressing. The linen should be well dampened; the iron, hot. Press until dry or the linen may muss before you get a chance to hang it up. Right-side pressing is always done over a press cloth to prevent shine.

Embroidered linen is pressed with the right side against a Turkish towel to prevent the flattening of its raised surface.

COOL RULE—PRESSING THE MAN-MADE FIBERS

In general, the man-made fibers are very sensitive to heat. They take very little ironing, if any. (Hurray, hurray! One of the great joys in using them.) Iron on the wrong side with a *cool* iron. It is best to check the label that comes with the fabric for the proper degree of coolness.

The exception to the cool rule is Qiana. Use a hot iron. Pull the stitching line as you press the iron along it.

SHAPE WELL BEFORE USING: CONTOUR PRESSING

However flat they may look on the cutting board, clothes are meant to fit contoured figures. The style lines indicate the three-dimensional quality; the pattern is cut to produce it; the fabric is stitched to achieve it; the interfacing is designed to buttress it. Now it is the turn of the pressing to guarantee that the shape is blocked in forever.

With or without darts or shaping seams, clothes will eventually take on some of the shape of the wearer: witness your favorite sweaters. That's because the body's 98-degree temperature does a bit of blocking on its own. (This is sufficient for some of the no-shape clothes.) However, for classic tailoring, one can't rely on nature alone to do the garment shaping. Here not only the outer fabric but each layer of supporting material must be blocked separately before they can be put together.

All areas of a garment that go over and around some part of the body (which is just about everywhere) are blocked over an appropriately rounded press pad. Come to think of it, it really doesn't make sense to press curves on a flat ironing board. You find yourself pressing out of a garment all the shape you so painstakingly stitched into it.

The seams and darts of worsteds and other hard-surfaced fabrics may be pressed open with the board and clapper first, then shaped and blocked over a curved press pad. The darts and seams of the softer woolens may be both pressed and shaped at the same time.

Think of wool as hair that needs setting. When you set your own hair you use a setting fluid and anything from bobby pins to large rollers to produce the contour you want. Wool, too, needs a setting agent and some shaping device—water for the setting and any or all of the curved press pads for the shaping. As with your own hair, if its setting is unsatisfactory, it can be reset.

Assorted Rolls and Boards

There is an assortment of rolls and boards, pads and cushions, that duplicate practically every curve of the body. However, the most all-purpose shaping device is the tailor's ham. Somewhere on its rounded surface there is a curve that will match a shaped section of the garment. The other pads and boards are fun to have as extras, but the tailor's ham will see you through most of your blocking needs.

HOW TO PRESS A SHAPING SEAM

1. Place the right side of the garment over an appropriate curve of the tailor's ham. This produces a reverse curve—temporarily. When the pressed garment is returned to its right-side-out position, it will assume its correct contour.

2. Insert folded wrapping-paper strips under the seam allowances when necessary.

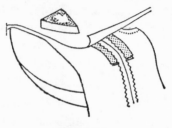

Fig. 192

3. Cover with a dampened press cloth.

4. Press with the lengthwise grain or with the nap (Fig. 192).

5. Lift the press cloth and allow the steam to escape.

6. Remove the **wrapping-paper** strips. Allow the garment to dry on the tailor's ham. If you remove it while it is still damp, you may lose the shaping.

HOW TO PRESS A DART

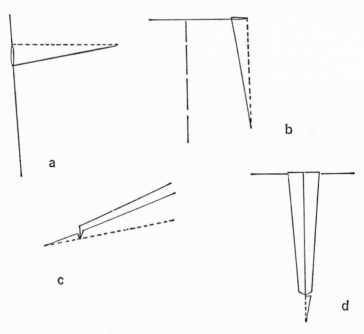

Fig. 193

Very narrow darts and darts in lightweight fabrics are pressed to one side: horizontal darts are pressed down (Fig. 193a), vertical darts are pressed toward the center (Fig. 193b).

Wide darts and darts in medium-to-heavy fabrics are slashed open to within ¼ inch of the dart point. Snip across the unslashed end of the dart almost to the seam line (Fig. 193c). Press the dart open where slashed; press to one side where unslashed (Fig. 193d). Trim the rest of the dart to ½ to ⅝ inch.

1. Place the opened dart over a corresponding curve of the tailor's ham.

2. Slip wrapping-paper strips under the seam allowances.

3. Cover with a dampened press cloth.

4. Press the dart. Start at the wide end and press to the dart point (Fig. 194). Use a slight rotary motion to smooth out the dart point. Try for a perfect blend. It is often necessary to pull the fabric taut while trying to achieve this.

5. Round out the area adjacent to the dart.

6. Remove the wrapping-paper strips. Allow the garment to dry on the tailor's ham.

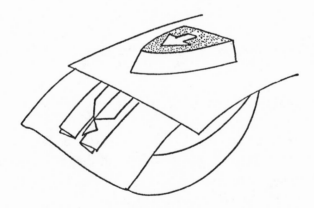

Fig. 194

A double-pointed waistline dart is always clipped at the waistline. Otherwise the dart won't do the shaping for which it was intended. Treat the remainder of the dart above and below the clip as if it were a regulation dart.

Shape the Substructure, Too: Interfacing, underlining, and interlining materials are blocked to shape in the same way, except that pressing may be done with a steam iron directly on the material without a press cloth.

Shape for the Unshaped: Contour pressing is the means of creating shape in any flat surface—a collar, a lapel, sleeve caps, or even a "no-shape" garment: that is, one without darts or shaping seams.

HOW TO BLOCK A "NO-DART, NO-SEAM" GARMENT

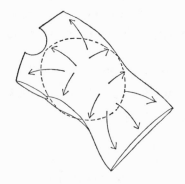

Fig. 195

1. Place the garment on an appropriate curve of the tailor's ham, wrong side up.

2. Press to shape. Start at the center front (or back) and press toward the outer edges—neck, shoulders, armholes, underarm, bust, waist, hips (Fig. 195).

3. Reverse to right side.

HOW TO PRESS A COLLAR INTO A NECK SHAPE

Construct the collar as directed in Chapter 18.

Pressing the Collar in Construction

1. Fold the *undercollar* along the roll line (Fig. 196a).

2. Place the folded collar over an appropriate curve of the tailor's ham (Fig. 196b) or a Turkish towel rolled and curled into a neck shape (Fig. 196c).

3. Steam the fall of the collar (see Fig. 287b) to shape. Do not press a crease in the roll line—the collar must really roll along this line.

4. Allow the collar to dry in position. A few pins will help to hold the collar in place on the blocking pad.

5. Remove the collar from the press pad when dry.

6. Steam the stand of the collar in an inside curve (Fig. 196d).

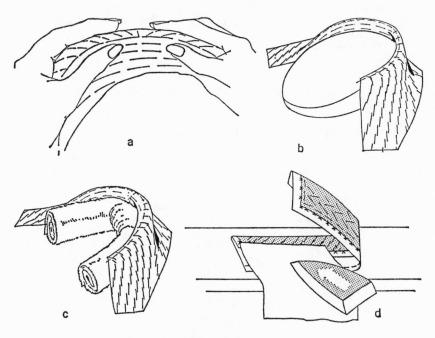

Fig. 196

When the upper collar has been stitched to the undercollar, press the seam allowances open, using the point presser. It is easier to do this pressing without a press cloth, particularly since all the seam allowances are permanently hidden.

Grade the seam allowances and free the corners of bulk. Turn the collar to the right side. Press the edges as thin and flat as the pressing technique for your fabric will permit. Be sure to roll the joining seam to the underside.

Pressing the Completed Collar

1. Fold the completed collar on the roll line.

2. Mold it over a suitable press pad into the shape it will assume when worn. Pin to position if necessary.

3. Steam-press over a protective press cloth. Do not press a crease in the roll line. Remove from the press pad.

4. Steam-press the inside curve of the collar stand to eliminate the rippling that tends to form because of the shorter measurement of the inside curve.

5. Pin to position, once more, over a suitable press pad and allow to dry before finally removing.

HOW TO PRESS THE LAPEL TO SHAPE

A beautiful lapel is distinguished by its thin, flat edges and its natural roll.

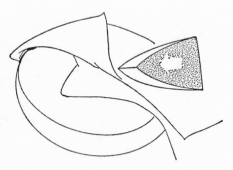

Fig. 197

With right side up, place the entire front, including the lapel, over a suitable curve of the tailor's ham. Steam-press over a protective cloth (Fig. 197). The reverse curve of the lapel is restored to its true contour when the lapel is turned back to its rightful position.

Do not press a crease in the roll line. The lapel must roll to position.

HOW TO SHAPE THE CAP OF A SET-IN SLEEVE

The following method is recommended only for such fabrics as can take steam. For a press pad, use any of these: the narrow end of the tailor's ham, the broad end of a sleeve board or sleeve roll, the press mitt, or any other similarly shaped pad or board.

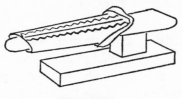

Fig. 198

1. Slip the sleeve over a suitable press pad or board and press the seam allowance open in the technique best suited for the fabric (Fig. 198).

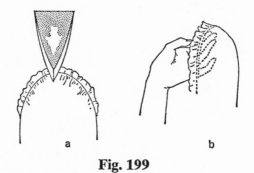

Fig. 199

2. Draw up the gathering at the sleeve cap into a cap shape. Distribute the fullness evenly.

3. Slip the sleeve over the press pad, wrong side up. Fit the cap over the pad.

4. Shrink out the ease in the cap with the point of the steam iron (Fig. 199a). Don't worry about shrinking out too much. One can always spread the sleeve cap to fit the armhole.

It is unnecessary to shrink out all the rippling of the seam allowance at the cut edge, but the ease should be removed at the seam line. With that disposed of, the seam line of the sleeve now matches that of the armhole—all of which makes the setting of the sleeve relatively easy.

5. Block a softly rounded cap ⅜ to ½ inch into the sleeve.

6. When dry, gently push the blocked cap to the right side. You should be able to hold the cap with your hooked fingers (Fig. 199b).

OTHER PRESSING PROBLEMS

Cuffs: Construct and press in the same way as the collar.

Welts and Flaps: Construct and press like cuffs.

For a right-side touch-up on the finished garment of cuffs, welts, flaps: insert wrapping paper under the cuff, welt, or flap to prevent an imprint (Fig. 200a).

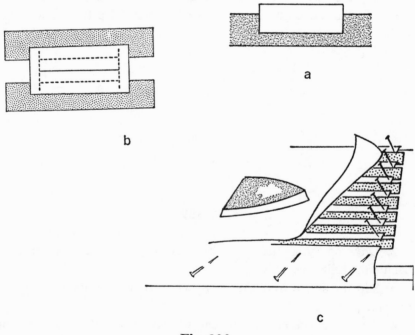

Fig. 200

Bound Buttonholes and Bound Pockets: Insert wrapping-paper strips under the edges of the binding (Fig. 200b). Use the pressing technique best suited for the fabric. Press the area between the buttonholes and around the pocket.

Pleats: To achieve sharp pleats, each side of both upper and under folds should be pressed thoroughly.

Sometimes it is easier to *press each fold separately*. Place the fold of the pleat near the edge of the ironing board and press, using the pressing technique deemed best for the fabric.

Often pleats are *pressed in a series*. Insert wrapping-paper strips between pleats to prevent imprints. Pin the top and bottom of the pleats in place on the ironing board over a damp press cloth. Pin along the sides of the fabric so that its weight will not pull the pleats out of place (Fig. 200c). Remove the pins as you reach the area to be pressed. (Replace them after pressing.) Place a dampened press cloth over the pleats. (In this way both the underside and the right side are against damp press cloths.) Press with the grain, using lengthwise strokes in the direction of the pleats. Press to within six inches of the lower edge. When the hem has been finished and pressed, fold the pleats into position again and press once more. When the right side is completed, turn to the underside and repeat the procedure.

Unpressed Pleats: Lay in soft folds on the ironing board. Steam, holding the iron 2 to 3 inches above the fabric. Allow the pleats to dry in place.

Gathering: Press with lengthwise strokes on the wrong side, working the tip of the iron into the gathers (Fig. 201a).

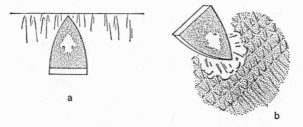

Fig. 201

Shirring and Smocking: Place the shirred or smocked area on the ironing board, right side up. Steam the fabric, holding the iron 1 to 2 inches above it and moving slowly over the area. This preserves the raised effect of the shirring and the honeycomb surface of the smocking. *Do not touch the surface with the iron,* however lightly: let the steam do the work (Fig. 201b).

HOW TO PRESS A HEM

The depth of a hem should be only as much as will lie flat when the fullness is steamed out. Press all inside seam allowances open before marking and turning up the hem. Grade the hem seam allowances (Fig. 202a).

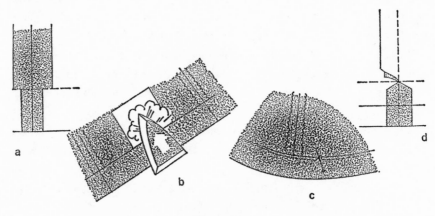

Fig. 202

Straight Hems

1. When the hem is turned up, press it with short strokes from the lower edge up, removing any bastings as you do a small section at a time. (Pressing parallel to the fold stretches the edge.)

2. For a very sharp hem edge in fabric that can take it, "spank" with the clapper. For a soft edge, steam the fabric, holding the iron 2 to 3 inches above it.

3. To shrink out the hem without shrinking the fabric beneath, as well as to prevent a hem imprint, insert a wrapping-paper strip as a shield between the hem and the garment (Fig. 202b).

4. Rebaste or pin hem to position when dry.

Circular Hems

When there is too much fullness at the upper edge of the turned-up hem, run a line of gathering at the hem edge. Pull up the thread until the hem fits the garment (Fig. 202c). Distribute the fullness as evenly as possible. Proceed as for straight hems.

Pleated Hems

1. Clip the pleat seam at the top of the hem.

2. Press the seam allowance open in the hem area and to one side above the hem (Fig. 202d).

ZIPPERED AREA

This is best pressed before the zipper installation. If pressing is necessary after the zipper has been installed, place the right side down over a heavy press cloth or Turkish towel. Press with the tip of the iron beside the metal or plastic. Use folded wrapping-paper strips as a cushion under the placket lap to prevent an imprint.

TAPE SHAPE

When tape is used to reinforce a straight edge, it is preshrunk and pressed in a straight line. When tape is used to reinforce a curved edge, it must be shaped to correspond to the curved seam line. Dampen the tape. Place the dampened tape over the pattern with the outer edge of the tape along the seam line. Set the iron on STEAM and press slowly into shape. Use one hand to swirl the tape into a curve while the other guides the iron. Pull the outer or longer edge of the tape slightly; ease in the shorter or inner edge (Fig. 203a).

If the garment itself rather than the pattern is used as a guide for

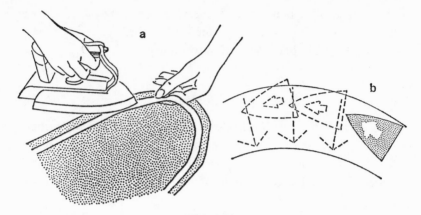

Fig. 203

the shape, place the tape beside it, parallel to the seam line to be taped. This avoids the wet imprint of tape on fabric.

Grosgrain ribbon or bias strips of fabric used as collar, binding, waistband, or facing may be shaped in a similar manner. The side of the iron is parallel to the edge of the ribbon or strip. Push the iron from the outer or longer edge to the inner or shorter edge, easing in the fullness while shaping (Fig. 203b).

THE FINAL PRESSING

If the garment has been carefully and properly pressed during construction it should not need very much of a pressing now. One final hand pressing is advisable, however, before inserting the lining. This is your last chance to get at any part of the inside of the garment before it is covered by the lining.

Of course, if it is an unlined garment you will want to make sure that the exposed underside looks beautiful.

Remove all basting and tailor's tacks, any stray threads or other matter picked up while in construction.

Press both the inside and outside of the garment, using the technique best suited to the fabric. Use the steam iron and press cloths. Be very careful to maintain the shaping of the garment. Use the same press pads as were used for the construction pressing.

BEFORE THE LINING IS INSERTED

This is the order in which the garment is pressed.

On the Underside: Press flat the outer edges of the collar lapels, facings, and hems. Press the facing first, making sure that any joining seam is rolled to the underside.

On the Inside: Press one front, starting at the lower edge, and press as far as the shoulder area but *do not* press the shoulder area. Press the other front and the back in the same way. Be sure to insert folded strips of wrapping paper in any seam allowances, pockets, or welts to avoid imprints.

Place one shoulder area over the tailor's ham or over the narrow end of the ironing board. Press the front, then the back. Do the same on the other shoulder.

Slip the sleeve over the sleeve board, sleeve roll, or sleeve pad and press. Start at the undersleeves and rotate until you have pressed the entire sleeve except the cap.

Press the sleeve cap over a suitable press pad. Take special care not to flatten it.

On the Right Side: Turn the garment to the right side. Lightly steam-press the body of the garment in the same order as the underside. Steam-press the sleeve and cap.

Press the collar and lapels. Place a folded strip of wrapping paper between the collar, lapels, and garment to prevent an imprint. Press the collar from the outer edge to the roll line over a suitable press pad. Make sure that the lower edge of the collar covers the neckline seam by at least ½ inch. "Press" a soft roll (not a sharp crease!) into the collar and continue for several inches down on the lapel.

With the facing up, place the lapel and front edge over the ham and steam-press. Be careful not to press out the roll line.

Place the newly pressed garment on a dress form. Lacking that, stuff the shoulders, sleeve cap, collar, and bust area with tissue paper and place on a sturdy hanger. Pin the garment closed. Allow it to settle and dry thoroughly for a few hours before inserting the lining.

If the garment is unlined, your pressing chores are over. When a lining is involved, proceed as follows.

Before inserting the lining in the garment, press all its seams open. Since the lining is generally of some silky fabric, follow the general directions for pressing these fibers on page 272.

After the lining has been attached to the garment, place the garment over the ironing board, lining side up. Use a moderately warm, dry iron and a dry press cloth to prevent scorching and shine.

Press one front and back from the lower edge to the shoulder area.

Press the other front and back to the shoulder area. Press so that a soft fold of the lining covers the stitching line all along the facings and hem. Press a sharp pleat at the center back.

Place the shoulder area, lining side up, over a suitable press pad or the narrow end of the ironing board. Press the front lining, then the back lining. Repeat the procedure for the other shoulder area.

With the lining side up, slip the sleeve over the sleeve board or sleeve roll with the cap over the broad end. Press a soft fold along the hem edge. Press the sleeve upward toward the cap. Press the cap carefully.

PRESSING THE SKIRT

Use the pressing technique best suited to the fabric. If the skirt has a free-hanging lining, press each separately. Slip the skirt over the ironing board, wrong side up. Press from the hem up.

Slip the tailor's ham under the hip area and press all darts and curved seams.

Press the placket with the zipper closed.

Press the waistband.

Press the skirt with the lengthwise grain, the iron parallel to the seam lines of the skirt and waistband.

PRESSING PANTS

In Construction: Press all seams and darts, using the technique best suited to the fabric.

On Completion: Turn the pants to the right side. Fold each leg in half lengthwise, matching the inseam and side seam at the crotch and hem edges.

Press the back crease. In men's trousers or narrow women's pants, pull the calf area outward in a slight curve and press (Fig. 204). Pants so pressed fall gracefully over the calf.

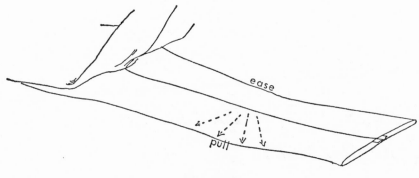

Fig. 204

Press the front creases to about 6 inches from the waist. Shrink out the ripples caused by the outward pull at the calf (when this is done). Press the back creases even with the crotch.

In flared-leg pants, press the areas above and below the knee separately.

RIGHT-SIDE TOUCH-UP

When the garment is completely finished, you may want to give it a right-side touch-up. This is a very light steam pressing.

A good way to simulate the kind of steam pressing currently done in cleaning and tailoring establishments is to steam the garment on a dress form. Use any steaming device (there are several on the market) or the steam iron. Pat lovingly in place. Allow to dry thoroughly on the dress form or hanger before wearing.

This chapter should give you some idea why the pressers in clothing factories are often more highly paid than the sewers. Pressing is a specialized skill. But by following the rules, you can learn to do a very creditable job. There is no doubt that pressing makes the difference between a half-done look and a precise, trim, tailored look. It is worth the effort.

Chapter 16

Tricky Trio — Buttonhole, Pocket, Zipper

Timid about the tricky trio? Otherwise brave, hardy souls have their moments of apprehension when confronted with the necessity of making a buttonhole, applying a pocket, and inserting a zipper.

There is the winter coat that needs buttonholes. You can't put them off much longer or the first robin will appear before your last stitch. Cut that buttonhole? But it's so final! And there it is, good result or bad, plunk out front for all the world to see!

This time you'd really love to put pockets in that suit. You've been making suits without pockets for years. There is a limit to the number of fake pockets or pocketless suits a wardrobe can contain.

And then there is that nifty new skirt with its mauled closing. You've put the zipper in and taken it out so many times, it has become a way of life. But you always end with that same miserable, wobbly line of machine stitching.

Little wonder that beginners and experienced sewers alike put off the awful moment of attempting any of these three until it is literally impossible to proceed without them.

While zippers, buttonholes, and pockets generally serve practical purposes, they often become THE decorative elements of a design (Fig. 205). Anyone who aspires to be a tailor must therefore master the techniques for making them.

Fig. 205

BEST BY HAND: THE STANDARD ZIPPER CLOSINGS

Let me tell you the easiest, fastest, most foolproof way to sew a standard zipper closing. Do it by hand! Hand stitching holds as well as and looks prettier than machine stitching.

Pin the zipper to position. Use a tiny half backstitch* or prick stitch** to secure it. There! In the time it would take to locate your zipper foot in that jumble of sewing tools (not to mention attaching it, stitching, and ripping out that esthetically jarring line of wavering machine stitching) your zipper can be happily in place.

Despite their delicate appearance, the half backstitch (Fig. 206a) and the prick stitch (Fig. 206b) are strong stitches.

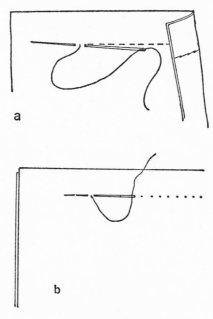

Fig. 206

*HALF BACKSTITCH

Fasten the thread on the underside of the material at the right end. Bring the needle to the right side one small stitch toward the left. Working back to the right, insert the needle half the distance of the first stitch, slide it along the underside, and once more bring the needle out one stitch ahead. Repeat for the length of the seam.

**The *prick stitch* is done in the same way, except that the surface stitch is a tiny one.

REGULATION OR SLOT-SEAM INSTALLATION: WHICH?

If the design is "dressy" and the fabric delicate, looped, or the kind that may catch in the teeth of the zipper when it is closed, use the regulation closing (Fig. 207a). In the regulation closing, the zipper is hidden by a lapped fold. The lap may be to the right or to the left, depending on which is easier for you to use and which is more consistent with the design. If you're right-handed, choose a lap to the right. If you're left-handed, choose a lap to the left. Only one line of stitching is visible in this type of zipper insertion.

Fig. 207

If the design is geometric or the fabric is heavy or pile, use the slot-seam setting for your zipper (Fig. 207b). This is also a suitable method for faced or slashed openings, wrist openings, or openings concealed in box or inverted pleats.

In the slot-seam closing, the zipper is concealed by two folds of material centered over it. There are two visible lines of stitching, one on each side of the closing.

PREPARE THE PLACKET

"Placket" is another name for an opening in a garment used for convenience in putting it on. When a zipper is the placket closing, the placket must be prepared to receive it.

1. With right sides together, stitch the garment below the placket.

2. Press the seam allowances open.

For a slot-seam closing, continue to press the opening along both seam lines.

For a regulation closing, a little more preparation is necessary.

1. Turn and press the upper seam allowance. This becomes the overlap. Mark the under (back) seam line with guide basting (Fig. 208a).

2. Now clip the under seam allowance at the end of the placket to the seam line (Fig. 208b).

3. Fold the under seam allowance to make a ⅛ inch extension (Fig. 208c). This becomes the underlap. Press.

HOW TO INSTALL THE REGULATION ZIPPER

1. Working from the right side, place the folded edge of the extension over the right side of the zipper tape, allowing enough room to work the slider. The top stop of the zipper is placed ⅞ inch below the raw edge of the garment (¼ inch below a cross seam)—a little more if the fabric is heavy. Pin to position.

2. Starting at the top, backstitch the extension (underlap) to the zipper.

3. Bring the fold of the overlap to the seam line (guide basting) of the underlap. Pin to position. This placement of the overlap will completely conceal the zipper.

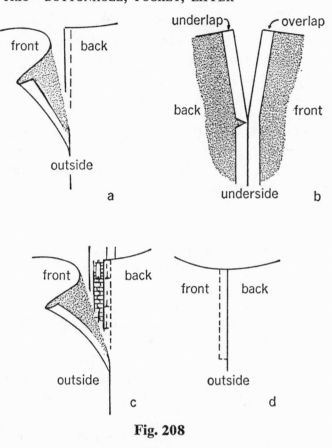

Fig. 208

4. Hand-stitch the overlap in place. Start at the bottom of the zipper. Stitch across the end below the bottom stop and continue to the top. Keep the welt even all the way up. As you approach the top stop, pull the tab down. This makes it easier to preserve a narrow welt in the slider area. Complete the stitching (Fig. 208d). When installing a zipper in a curved seam—as in the hip-fitting side seam of a skirt or pants—hold the seam in a curve over the hand.

HOW TO INSTALL THE SLOT-SEAM ZIPPER

1. Place the fold of one edge *slightly beyond the center* of the closed zipper. This small correction is necessary to offset the tendency

of the stitching to pull the fold away from the center, thereby exposing the zipper teeth. The top stop of the zipper is placed ⅞ inch
below the raw edge of the garment (¼ inch below a cross seam). Pin
the zipper to position.

2. Start the hand stitching at the top of one side and work down
the length of the zipper.

3. Pin the second side of the zipper in the same way as the first—
that is, the folded edge slightly beyond the center of the zipper.

4. Stitch across the bottom below the bottom stop and continue up
the second side. Make the welts even on both sides.

BY HAND (IF YOU CHOOSE)—
BY MACHINE (IF YOU INSIST)

Just because you have the latest sewing machine, don't make the
mistake of thinking that every operation must be done on it. Some are
best accomplished by hand sewing. No worries about pulling the material off-grain, matching cross seams and stripes, stretching the fabric, ragged stitching. After one zipper successfully put in by hand,
you'll understand why it is the method used in expensive and custom
clothes.

If you still insist on a machine-made product, go ahead and find
that zipper foot. Use the same placement for the zipper. Make your
machine stitching directional: that is, stitch both sides from the top of
the zipper to the bottom. Secure the top with back-and-forth stitching;
break the thread at the end of the line of stitching, pull it through to
the wrong side, and tie in a square knot.

HOW TO SET AND STITCH AN EXPOSED ZIPPER

For a Zipper Set in a Slash

1. Mark the center line of the opening on the garment.

2. Measure the width of the zipper teeth. Add a tiny bit to the
measurement for slide-fastener clearance.

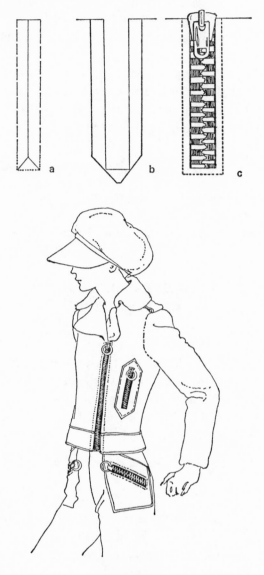

Fig. 209

3. From the center line of the closure, measure over on each side half the amount determined in step 2 for the entire length of the zipper. Mark with basting thread.

4. Continue the marking across the end of the opening (Fig. 209a).

5. Reinforce the corners with small machine stitching (Fig. 209a).

6. Slash the center line of the opening. Slash diagonally to each corner (Fig. 209a).

7. Working from the right side, turn under the seam allowance along the line of guide basting. Press (Fig. 209b).

8. Pin the folded edge of the closing to the zipper tape.

9. Topstitch close to the folds (Fig. 209c).

For a Zipper Set in a Seam

Exposed zippers may be set into seams with only slight variations of the above method.

When the zipper is set above or below a stitched seam, omit step 1.

HOW TO SET AND STITCH A SEPARATING ZIPPER

Separating zippers are a favorite form of closing for casual jackets. They come in several weights, in both nylon and metal. They may be inserted so the zipper teeth are hidden or exposed. In either case, the zipper is sandwiched between the outer fabric and the facing.

The installation of this zipper is a variation of the slot-seam construction.

1. Turn under the seam allowances along the opening edges and press.

2. Place the closed zipper, face up, under one opening edge with the tab ⅛ to ¼ inch below the neck seam. When the teeth are to be exposed, place the folded edge beside them (Fig. 210a). When the teeth are to be concealed, place the folded edges at the center of the zipper.

3. Turn under the tape ends at the top above the pull tab (Fig. 210b).

4. Baste to position.

5. On the underside, turn under the seam allowances of the facings and press (Fig. 210c). Baste to position.

6. Topstitch through all the layers from either side. Keep the stitching an even distance in from the folds.

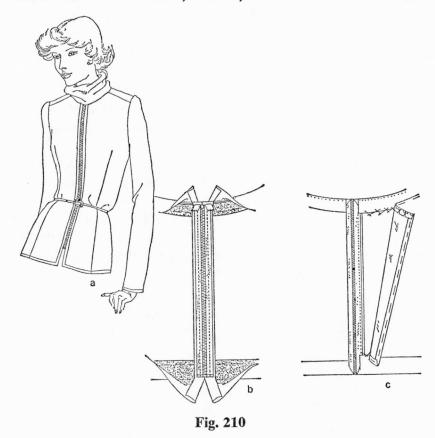

Fig. 210

IT ONLY "SEAMS" THAT WAY:
THE HIDDEN-ZIPPER CLOSING

It's not only the exposed zipper that is decorative. In its own sneaky way the hidden zipper is, too. With this type of installation, the only break in the continuity of the fabric design is that of a normal seam.

There are two types of invisible zippers. One is a featherweight nylon coil for lightweight fabrics. The other is a metal-tooth chain for heavier-weight fabrics. They are both installed in the same way. They may be stitched by hand or—what is more usual—by machine.

The Machine-stitched Invisible Zipper

A special zipper foot must be used for the machine-stitched invisible zipper installation. It has two small grooves to hold the right and left sides of the zipper in place and to guide the stitching in a straight line. A smaller-grooved foot is for the nylon coil; a larger-grooved foot, for the metal zipper.

Before setting, flatten the nylon coil, which has a tendency to curl up. Press it flat with your finger or with an iron. Only the tape should be visible when the zipper is being set.

In all other installations, the seam in which a zipper is set is stitched first, leaving an opening for the zipper. One does just the opposite with the invisible zipper. The zipper is installed first; then the seam below it is stitched.

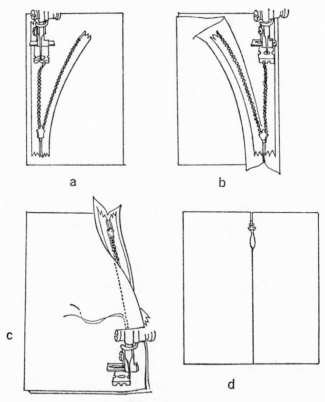

Fig. 211

1. Place the opened zipper face down on the right side of the fabric. The coil or teeth are placed on the seam line, while the zipper tape is in the seam allowance. The top stop of the zipper is placed ½ inch below the cross seam line.

2. Slide the zipper foot into position so the coil or metal fits into the appropriate groove and the needle can be lowered into the center of the hole. Insert the needle. Lower the presser foot. Stitch from the top of the tape until the foot touches the slider at the bottom (Fig. 211a). Lock with backstitching.

3. Pin the second side of the zipper to the second side of the opening on the right side of the fabric. The tape is set the same distance from the top as in step 1.

4. Set the groove of the zipper foot over the coil or metal. Bring the needle down into the tape through the hole. Lower the presser foot. Stitch the second side as in step 2 (Fig. 211b). So far, so good. It's easy. It's fast. The next part, however, is a little more difficult.

5. Close the zipper. Place the right sides of the fabric together below the zipper, with seam lines matching. Pin.

6. Slide the zipper foot to the left of the zipper so it clears it, making it operate like an ordinary zipper foot. Insert the needle through the outside notch, ½ inch above the zipper end and ⅟₁₆ inch to the left of it. Lower the foot and stitch to the end of the seam (Fig. 211c).

7. There will be 1 inch of zipper tail extending below the installed zipper. Stitch each side of the tape to the seam allowance. This stitching must not show on the right side.

No stitching shows on the right side. Successfully done, this closing looks just like another seam (Fig. 211d).

Theoretically, steps 5 and 6 should be easy enough to sew. Actually, it is hard to be precise because of the bulk. Some sewers find it easier to stitch the seam *below* the zipper with the regulation presser foot, then come back and backstitch that half-inch length (step 6).

The Hand-stitched Invisible Zipper

Though it may take a little more time, the hand-stitched installation of even this zipper is much easier to manage. The placement is

a

the same. Instead of machine stitching, use backstitching very close to the zipper teeth. This installation also eliminates the problem at the lower end of the zipper.

In fact, a good rule to follow for all your sewing: When a procedure is too difficult for you to do by machine, do it by hand. Hand stitching came first and it still makes up a large part of tailoring.

THE FLY-FRONT ZIPPER INSTALLATION

We gals have taken over not only men's pants but the fly-front closings that come with them. And that not just for our pants but for our skirts, coats, and dresses as well (Fig. 212a).

In women's pants (or skirts), the fly front is a watered-down version of Savile Row artistry—more a matter of design than of con-

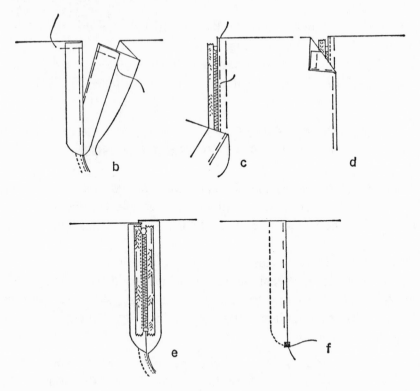

Fig. 212

struction. The feminine version is really a variation of the regulation zipper installation plus fly-shaped topstitching. A truly masculine fly front takes a lot more doing.

1. Mark the center lines, the fold lines, and the topstitching lines on the front extensions.

2. Stitch the pants sections together. Clip the seam allowances at the end of the fly marking.

3. Turn under the front extensions along the fold lines and press.

4. Baste across the upper edges and close to the folds (Fig. 212b).

5. Place the closed zipper, face up, under the left front extension with the folded edge close to the teeth and the pull tab ¼ inch below the cross seam. Pin or baste to position. Stitch close to the edge (Fig. 212c).

6. Overlap the right front opening edge on the left front, matching center lines. Baste to position through all thicknesses close to the edge (Fig. 212d).

7. On the underside, baste the zipper tape to the right front through all the thicknesses (Fig. 212e).

8. On the right side, topstitch the right front along the fly stitching line through all thicknesses, catching in the zipper tape (Fig. 212f).

MATCHING CROSS SEAMS, PLAIDS, STRIPES, OR MOTIFS AT ZIPPER OPENINGS

When a zipper is installed by hand stitching, one has perfect control in matching cross seams, plaids, stripes, checks, and motifs. It takes a little more work when the stitching is done by machine.

1. Machine-stitch the first side of the zipper as usual.

2. Fold under the seam allowance of the second side. Using masking tape, tape the fabric to position on the right side, matching exactly all cross seams, plaids, stripes, or motifs (Fig. 213a).

3. Machine-stitch.

a. *Standard Zipper:* Topstitch; remove the masking tape.

b. *Invisible Zipper:* Turn to the wrong side. Pencil-mark the zipper tape at each seam line or unit (Fig. 213b). Remove the mask-

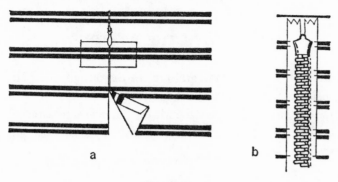

a   b

Fig. 213

ing tape from the right side. Open the zipper. Match the markings on the zipper tape with the seams, lines, or motifs of the fabric. Stitch as usual.

There is no all-purpose zipper or zipper installation. Choose whichever type seems best for the design and the fabric of the garment you are making.

BUTTONHOLES—BOUND TO BE GOOD

Time was when all fine women's clothing sported bound buttonholes, all fine men's wear had hand-worked buttonholes, and the machine-made variety was frowned upon as evidence of cheaper quality. As the cost of labor goes up and the appreciation of fine workmanship goes down (that's not thee or me), more and more machine-made buttonholes make their appearance even on expensive clothes. About all one can say for them is that they are functional—and apparently acceptable. They certainly do not add one whit of beauty to a garment.

While the manufacturers of necessity may have to settle for the machine-made kind, custom tailors and home sewers do not. Beautiful bound and hand-worked buttonholes are still among the hallmarks of fine tailoring. While they do take time and a degree of skill, their presence on a garment lifts it out of the realm of the ordinary and their attractiveness amply repays the sewer for the time and effort.

BEGIN WITH THE BUTTONS

Since the buttons are an integral part of the design, their choice is a prime consideration along with the fabric.

The size of the buttonhole depends on the size and type of button. It will be slightly larger than the button for easy slide through. This is the rule:

Fig. 214

For a flat button: the width of the button plus ⅛ inch ease (Fig. 214a).

For a bumpy button: the width of the button plus its height. An easy way to determine this is to wrap a tape measure completely around the button (Fig. 214b) and note the total length. Half this amount is the size the buttonhole should be.

In heavy coat or suit fabric, the buttonholes have a tendency to end up a little smaller than anticipated. Allow a tiny bit of extra ease to compensate.

Make a test slash in the material to see if the button can slide through easily. Better yet, make a test buttonhole to discover unforeseen problems in size and handling of the material. It is a tragic discovery to find that several painstakingly made buttonholes are too small for the buttons.

In order to ensure that the garment buttons directly on the closing line, a slight correction must be made for the shank of the button. The shank may be built into the button (Fig. 215a) or be created by thread (Fig. 215b). The patternmaker allows ⅛ inch for its width. Therefore the buttonhole begins, not at the closing line where you would expect it to begin, but ⅛ inch beyond the closing line toward the outer edge in a horizontal buttonhole—⅛ inch beyond the marking toward the neck edge in a vertical buttonhole (Fig. 215c). You

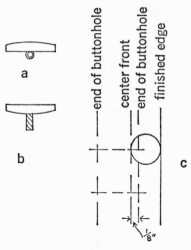

Fig. 215

have undoubtedly noticed this placement on your patterns and perhaps even wondered why. The button itself is stitched *on* the closing line.

THINGS TO REMEMBER BEFORE YOU BEGIN

Bound buttonholes are made on the right side of the garment and turned to the inside. The guide markings must therefore be made on the right side.

Bound buttonholes are always made on the garment before the facing is turned back or attached. The facing is finished separately much later in the construction of the garment.

When making a series of buttonholes, the work is quicker and more accurate if you do the same operation on each buttonhole before going on to the next step, rather than completing one buttonhole at a time.

Guide Markings for Buttonholes

One of the secrets of successful buttonholes is very accurate marking.

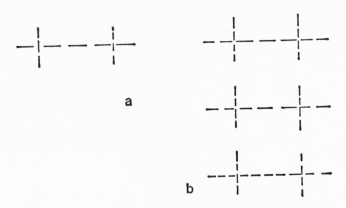

Fig. 216

1. Using a double thread of contrasting color, mark the position of the opening of the buttonhole (slash line). Place cross markings to indicate the beginning and the end of each buttonhole (Fig. 216a).

2. In making a series of buttonholes, make certain that they line up, and that they are identical in size and evenly spaced (Fig. 216b).

Reinforce the Slash Line

Any area that is to be slashed should be reinforced before a cut is made in the material. With the exception of hair canvas, the interfacing or underlining can be that reinforcement. Hair canvas is too tough, too resilient, and too bulky to be incorporated into the buttonhole. When hair canvas is to be the interfacing, make the buttonholes in the reinforced outer fabric first before applying it. Use a patch of iron-on material, organza, muslin, or any other lightweight material as a reinforcement. (An iron-on material is particularly good, not only because it saves time in application but because it hold the yarns in place—a boon in loosely woven or ravelly fabrics.)

METHOD I—*the One-strip Method for Making a Bound Buttonhole*

Prepare the Binding: The following method works well on lightweight to medium-weight fabrics. For heavy or sheer fabrics, use Method II.

1. Cut a strip of garment fabric 1 inch wide by the length of the buttonhole plus 1 inch.

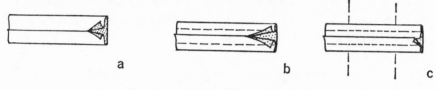

a   b   c

Fig. 217

OPTIONAL:

To make a sturdier buttonhole, reinforce the buttonhole strip by pressing on a strip of iron-on material. Or place a length of cording, heavy yarn, or string in each of the lengthwise folds of Step 3.

2. Fold the strip in half lengthwise, right side outside. Crease or press along the fold. Open out.

3. Fold each lengthwise raw edge to meet the center line, or crease (Fig. 217a). This now makes the strip ½ inch wide.

4. Place a line of hand or machine basting ⅛ inch in from each folded edge (Fig. 217b). When cording, yarn, or string is used for reinforcement, it is enclosed by this stitching. Use matching thread.

5. Place the binding on the right side of the garment, centering the strip on the slash line. Baste to position through the center of the strip (Fig. 217c).

Attach the Binding to the Garment

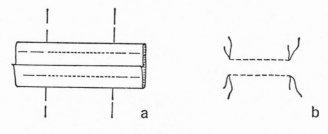

a   b

Fig. 218

1. Starting a stitch or two beyond the cross markings, machine-stitch the binding to the garment directly over the basting of Fig. 217b (Fig. 218a). Do not stitch across the ends. Do not lock-stitch at the beginning and end of the stitching.

2. Turn to the wrong side. You will see two parallel lines of machine stitching and the unsecured thread at each corner. Pull all four sets of thread ends through to the wrong side. Pull them back to the cross markings (Fig. 218b). For perfect corners, each pair of threads must end at the markings and directly opposite another pair. Tie each pair in a square knot (right over left, left over right) and trim the thread close to the knots.

Slash the Opening

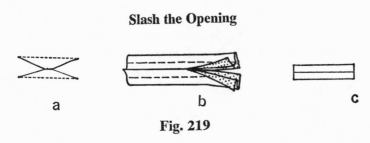

a   b   c

Fig. 219

1. Working from the underside, make a *tiny snip* in the material at the center of the space between the parallel rows of stitching. Use a very sharp pair of trimming or embroidery scissors.

2. From the small opening, slash diagonally to all four corners, coming as close to the stitching as you safely can (Fig. 219a). Be careful not to cut the binding on the other side. Note the long triangular flaps that form at each end.

3. Turn to the right side. Slash through the center of the binding strip without cutting the garment (Fig. 219b).

4. Grasp the pair of strips at each end (one pair at a time) and very gently push them through the opening to the wrong side. The binding will assume its rightful position (Fig. 219c). Behold your beautiful bound buttonhole!

Well, almost. There are a few finishing details that must be attended to.

Stitch the Ends of the Buttonhole

Adjust the strips so the folds just meet at the center without any overlapping. You may have to do a little coaxing to get them into position.

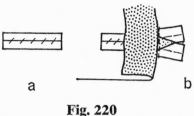

Fig. 220

1. On the right side of the garment, close the lips of the buttonhole with diagonal basting (Fig. 220a). This is very important because the basting holds the binding in place for securing the ends. Omit the basting and you end up with gaping buttonholes.

2. Once again, turn to the underside. Fold back the garment against itself so you can see the long, triangular flaps as they lie against the end of the binding.

3. Stitch each triangle to the strip across each end of the buttonhole. Stitch close to the fold but not over it (Fig. 220b). Were you to stitch over the fold, you would get a tuck on the right side. Stitch too far away from it and you will find a hole at each end.

4. Trim the excess binding to about ¼ inch from the stitching.

Bound to Be Good: This one-strip method of making a bound buttonhole is basic, easy, and practically foolproof. The preparation of the binding guarantees the evenness of the lips of the buttonhole. Centering the binding on the slash line automatically puts the stitching lines in the right position. The buttonhole is bound to be good.

In all honesty, however, one must admit that in very heavy or very sheer materials it is very difficult to handle the tiny strips produced by Method I. For such fabrics, the two-strip method of making a bound buttonhole is preferable.

METHOD II—*the Two-strip Method for Making a Bound Buttonhole*

1. Two separate strips are necessary for each buttonhole. Make them 2 inches wide by the length of the buttonhole plus 1 inch.

OPTIONAL:

To make a sturdier buttonhole, reinforce the binding area of each strip by pressing on a ½-inch strip of iron-on material, centered

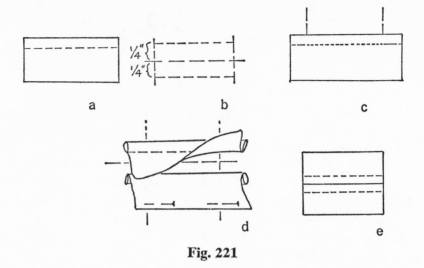

Fig. 221

lengthwise. Or enclose a length of cording, string, or yarn in each of the lengthwise folds of Step 2.

2. With the right side outside, fold each strip in half lengthwise.

3. Using matching thread, make a line of guide basting ⅛ inch from the folded edge (Fig. 221a). This will make the ideal buttonhole ¼ inch wide when finished. In heavy or bulky fabric, however, make the binding a little wider: place the guide basting ³⁄₁₆ inch from the folded edge. This will make the finished buttonhole ⅜ inch wide. It should not be any wider than that, even in heavy fabric.

4. Additional guidelines are necessary to place the larger strips in the same relative position for stitching as in Method I.

Make a line of guide basting above and below the slash line equal to the total width of the finished buttonhole (Fig. 221b). That is, for a ¼-inch-wide buttonhole, ¼ inch above and ¼ inch below the slash line; for a ⅜-inch-wide buttonhole, ⅜ inch above and ⅜ inch below the slash line.

5. Because of the size of the strips, only one at a time is basted and stitched to the right side of the garment. Place strip no. 1 in such a position that the folded edge is against the upper marking. Pin or baste in place.

6. Stitch directly over the basting, starting and ending a stitch or two beyond the cross markings (Fig. 221c).

7. Fold back the strip over itself. Pin it securely in this position (Fig. 221d). This reveals the rest of the buttonhole marking.

8. Position and stitch strip no. 2 in the same way.

9. The rest of the construction of the Method II buttonhole is the same as that of the Method I buttonhole.

10. Note the wide extensions of each strip of binding on the underside of the buttonhole (Fig. 221e). Grade the thicknesses, making the inner thickness narrower than the outer one. Trim the ends.

The use of the zipper foot rather than the regulation presser foot makes it easier to stitch corded strips or strips of very heavy fabric.

You'll be pleased with the no-bulk, no-ridge buttonhole you have so masterfully crafted.

FINISH THROUGH THE FACING

Whatever method you choose to make the bound buttonhole on the right side of the garment, a finish is required for the underside, through the facing. There are several ways to do this. The first two methods are quick and easy. The third takes more time and care but rewards you with twin buttonholes on outer fabric and facing. It is a particularly good method for a convertible-collar style where both sides of the closing extension must look identical.

Mark the Position of the Buttonhole Opening on the Facing

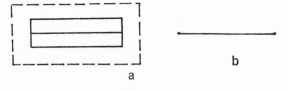

a   b

Fig. 222

1. After the facing has been turned to the inside, pin or baste around each buttonhole through all thicknesses (Fig. 222a).

2. From the upper side, push a straight pin through each end of the buttonhole at the line of the opening.

3. On the facing side, draw a line for the opening with pencil, tailor's chalk, or a line of basting (Fig. 222b).

Make certain that the opening is the same distance in from the edge on both the outside and the facing. Make sure that the length of the buttonhole is the same on both sides. Make sure there is the same distance between buttonholes. Measure!

METHOD I—*Easiest of All Methods*

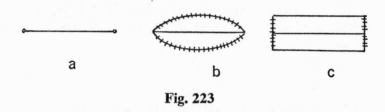

a   b   c

Fig. 223

1. Slash from one end of the marking to the other (Fig. 223a).

2. Turn under the raw edges of the facing to form an ellipse (Fig. 223b). Hem to position.

3. In loosely woven fabrics, it is even possible to push the opening into the shape of a rectangle with the point of the needle (Fig. 223c). Hem quickly to prevent fraying.

METHOD II—*a Little More Work*

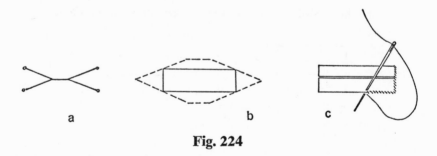

a   b   c

Fig. 224

1. Slash through the center of the marking and clip diagonally to each corner to a depth equal to the width of the binding (Fig. 224a).

2. Turn under each of the four little flaps to form a rectangle exposing the binding (Fig. 224b).

3. With hemming stitches, fasten the rectangular opening to the stitching lines of the binding (Fig. 224c). Take several tiny reinforcing stitches at each corner.

METHOD III—*Face the Facing*

By this method, a faced "windowpane" becomes the opening that reveals the buttonhole binding.

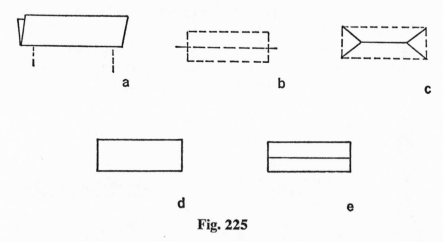

Fig. 225

1. Cut a patch of organza or any other sheer fabric. (Organza is an ideal material for this purpose since it is practically weightless.) Any color will do, since it won't be seen if properly done, but a matching color is a safeguard and a nice touch. Make the patch 1½ inches wide by the length of the buttonhole plus 1 inch.

2. Open out the facing. Center the organza over the buttonhole marking on the facing (Fig. 225a). Pin it to position.

3. Stitch the organza to the facing in a rectangle equal to the length and width of the finished buttonhole (Fig. 225b). Count the stitches if this will help you to get it accurate. Or make a stitching guide by marking the rectangle on the organza.

4. Slash through the center of the rectangle. Clip diagonally to each corner (Fig. 225c).

5. Turn the organza to the wrong side of the facing through the slash. Press or baste to position so no organza shows (Fig. 225d).

6. Place the faced rectangular opening against the underside of the bound buttonhole. Slip-stitch to the stitching lines (Fig. 225e).

HAND-WORKED BUTTONHOLES

Hand-worked buttonholes are classic but less frequently seen on women's clothing than bound buttonholes. They may be made either horizontally or vertically and are much easier to work if they are on straight grain. This buttonhole is made *after* the facing is attached to the garment and is worked through both garment and facing.

In women's tailoring, the vertical buttonhole is made with a bar at each end as a reinforcement (Fig. 226a). The horizontal buttonhole is reinforced with a bar at the left end and a fan at the right end, the end nearest the finished edge of the garment (Fig. 226b).

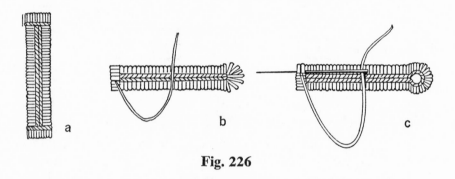

Fig. 226

The *tailor's buttonhole* is usually found on men's suits and coats but it is also used on women's tailored clothing. The buttonhole is made with an "eyelet" nearest the finished edge of the garment (Fig. 226c) to reinforce the point of stress. The shank of the button pulls against this end.

How to Make the Hand-worked Buttonhole

1. Mark the exact placement and length of the buttonhole. Mark the slash with tailor's chalk, the ends with basting thread.

2. Stay-stitch the length of the buttonhole with machine stitching placed close to the slash line and directly over the ends (Fig. 227a).

3. Starting in the center, slash the opening. To ensure that no in-

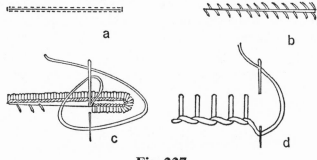

Fig. 227

terfacing or underlining material will show in the opening of the buttonhole, trim away a very narrow rectangle of it.[1]

4. With matching mercerized thread, overcast the slashed edges (Fig. 227b) to prevent raveling. Make the overcasting stitches $\frac{1}{16}$ inch deep.

5. For the buttonhole thread, use a single strand of silk buttonhole twist (used in all fine tailoring) or heavy-duty cotton thread of matching color. Another possibility is a double strand of matching mercerized thread run through beeswax to keep the strands from separating.

Work buttonhole stitches* over the overcast edges. Fan the stitches around the end against which the button will rest (Fig. 227c). Make a bar for a finish on the opposite end by covering two or three straight stitches with small overhand stitches (Fig. 226c).

*THE BUTTONHOLE STITCH

Work from right to left. The needle is held vertically and goes through a loop of thread. Form the loop by placing the thread behind the eye of the needle and under its point. Each purl (the knot that is formed by pulling up the intertwisting thread) should be on the edge of the slit. Make the stitches close together and even in depth (Fig. 227c).

The buttonhole stitch is similar to the blanket stitch. The difference

---

[1] This procedure is applicable to machine-made buttonholes, also, with this exception: the interfacing is trimmed before the buttonhole is made and slashed. Should you wish to reinforce the trimmed area, substitute a rectangle of organza or lining material in the same color as the outer fabric.

is that the blanket stitch has a single purl while the buttonhole stitch has a double purl. The double purl affords better protection.

To Make the Blanket Stitch: Work from left to right. The needle is held vertically with the thread, which forms the loop under its point (Fig. 227d). The stitches are even in depth and an even distance apart.

How to Make the Tailor's Buttonhole

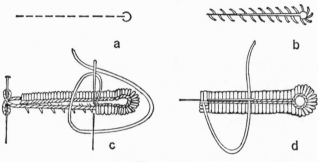

Fig. 228

1. Mark the length of the buttonhole and the position of the eyelet. Center the eyelet at the outer end of the buttonhole (Fig. 228a).

2. Slash the opening. Make the eyelet in any of the following ways: punch it out with an embroidery stiletto or an awl, or make several $\frac{1}{16}$-inch diagonal clips to form a circle with sharp-pointed trimming or cuticle scissors. Trim away the excess fabric to form a perfect circlet about $\frac{1}{8}$ inch in diameter (Fig. 228a).

3. With matching mercerized thread, overcast the cut edges with $\frac{1}{16}$-inch overcasting stitches to prevent raveling (Fig. 228b). Slip the knotted end of the thread between the outer fabric and the facing at the bar end of the buttonhole.

4. Pad the slit with a strand of gimp, linen, or cotton thread (No. 10 pearl), or with buttonhole twist of the same color as the garment fabric. Use a length of thread twice the length of the buttonhole plus several inches. Fasten the strand at the bar end of the buttonhole on a pin. Carry it across each side of the slash and around the eyelet as you work the buttonhole (Fig. 228c).

5. Use a 30-inch length of buttonhole thread knotted at one end.

Slip the knotted end between the outer fabric and the facing at the bar end of the buttonhole.

6. Work the buttonhole stitch over the padding.

7. Fan the stitches around the eyelet. Finish with a bar at the other end. Trim away the excess padding thread (Fig. 228d).

8. Bring the buttonhole thread through to the underside and fasten.

A MACHINE-MADE BUTTONHOLE

If beautiful machine-made buttonholes lured you into buying that new sewing machine with its built-in buttonhole mechanism, this is the time to try it out. Follow the manual for instructions.

There are several possibilities of kinds of thread, depending on the weight of the fabric and the degree of heaviness you wish for the buttonhole.

You may use:

1. buttonhole twist for the upper thread and a regular size 50 thread for the bobbin.

2. a double strand of mercerized thread for the upper bobbin and a single thread for the bobbin.

3. single or double strands of silk thread for both upper and bobbin threads.

It is a good idea to do a bit of experimenting on a scrap of your fabric to arrive at the best possible combination of needle, thread, and stitch.

BUTTONHOLES IN THE LEATHER-LIKE FABRICS

If your leather-like garment has been constructed by the standard regulation method, bound buttonholes are in order.

In garments made by the flat or overlap method, the buttonholes may be simply reinforced slashes.

1. Mark the position of the buttonhole.

2. Stitch a rectangle around and close to the slash line.

3. Slash the buttonhole opening.

PRECISION CLOSING

If you've ever made a jacket or coat with a parade of buttonholes down the front, you've undoubtedly wondered why you didn't settle for that poncho instead. Separating zippers notwithstanding, the complete separation of right and left sides of most jackets or coats makes the buttonhole and button the most satisfactory type of closing to use.

Anything that opens like the front of a tailored garment must close precisely in order to maintain the design and the fitting. For this reason, the correct location and the proper sewing on of the buttons become very important.

TO LOCATE THE BUTTONS

In an unfitted garment, the location of the buttons can be done on a flat surface.

To preserve the shaping of a fitted garment, the button placement is best done over a curved surface—over you, a dress form, a tailor's ham, or a rolled-up towel.

Pin the garment closed, matching the closing lines. Match the cross lines of the design at neck, break of lapel, waistline, and hem. Match any cross lines of the fabric design.

Using a safety pin (this won't fall out as a straight pin may), pin through the buttonhole opening. Close the safety pin. This locates the position for the button.

In *horizontal buttonholes,* the button is placed at the end of the

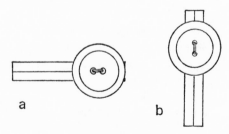

a   b

Fig. 229

buttonhole opening on the closing line (Fig. 229a). In *vertical buttonholes,* the button is placed ⅛ inch below the top end of the buttonhole on the closing line (Fig. 229b).

Mark and sew the first button. Button the garment. Locate the next button. Sew it on. This locate-and-sew procedure assures an accurate placement of each button, thereby a perfect closing for the garment.

HOW TO SEW ON A BUTTON

Fig. 230

There are two types of buttons: those with holes, called sew-through buttons (Fig. 230a); and those with stems or shanks of either self material or metal loops (Fig. 230b).

The shank (or stem) is the bridge between the upper and under parts of a closing. It floats the button on the surface of the garment. Without it, the garment would bunch rather than button. So important is this bridge that when a button doesn't have a shank or stem, one must be created. The most commonly created shank is one made with the thread by which the button is sewn to the garment.

The length of the shank depends on the several thicknesses of the opening edges—outer fabric, interfacing, facing. The thicker the area through which the button is to pass, the longer the shank must be; the thinner the area, the shorter the shank.

The Sew-through Button

1. Use a not-too-long single thread. Double threads tend to pull up unevenly. Use buttonhole twist; heavy-duty thread; a waxed buttonhole thread, size 24; or mercerized thread that has been drawn through beeswax to strengthen it and prevent knotting.

2. Fasten the thread with several tiny backstitches on the right side at the position indicated for the button.

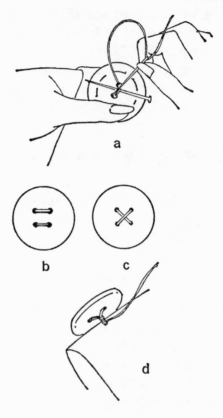

Fig. 231

3. Place a matchstick, toothpick, or thick pin (or any similar object) over the button (Fig. 231a). All sewing is done over the object to provide enough thread for the stem. This is also an easy way to keep all the threads equal in length. The length of the stem will determine what you use for your prop. Make the stem as long as the several layers of fabric are thick—outer fabric, interfacing, facing, plus a tiny bit for ease.

4. Bring the needle up through one hole and down through a second hole. Catch a little of the fabric at the base of the button but do not go through to the underside. Bring the needle up through the third hole and down through the fourth (when there is a third and a fourth). Repeat about four times.

In tailored clothes, the thread is so worked as to form parallel bars (Fig. 231b) or a cross (Fig. 231c).

5. Remove the prop and raise the button to the top of the stitches.

6. Wind the thread around the stitches to form the stem (Fig. 231d). Start the winding right under the button and end it near the fabric, where it can be anchored with several tiny backstitches.

The Shank Button

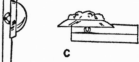

Fig. 232

When the button has a shank, all you need do is sew through the loop, taking enough stitches to fasten it securely (Fig. 232a). In a heavy overcoat, create the needed extra length by adding a stem in addition to the metal shank (Fig. 232b). The shank of the button is always aligned with the direction of the buttonhole (Fig. 232c).

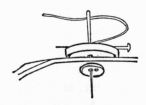

Fig. 233

A Stay Button: When a button is subjected to great strain, the fabric at the base of the shank is apt to tear. To prevent this, a smaller button is used as a reinforcement. Attach this to the underside of the garment directly under the first button (Fig. 233). Both buttons are stitched in one operation.

THOSE OLD FAITHFUL FASTENINGS— SNAPS AND HOOKS AND EYES

Buttons and buttonholes play the star roles. Helpful behind the scenes are those old faithful fastenings—snaps and hooks and eyes.

Snaps and hooks and eyes come in sizes from small to large and in condition from delicate to sturdy. Use snaps where there is not too much strain. Use hooks and eyes in places where there is strain. Use large or heavy-duty hooks and eyes in areas where there is great strain.

How to Sew on Snaps

Snaps are composed of two parts: a ball and a socket.

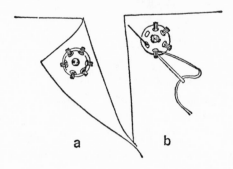

a   b

Fig. 234

1. Mark the exact placement of the snaps.

2. Sew the ball on first on the underside of the overlap (Fig. 234a). Sew with overhand stitches through the small holes at the edge. Carry the thread under the snap from hole to hole. Make sure that the stitches do not come through to the outside. They should never show.

3. Press the ball against the opposite edge to locate the exact position of the center of the socket. Mark with chalk or a pin. On some fabrics, chalking the ball and pressing it against the opposite side works well.

4. Center the socket over the marking and sew with overhand stitches through the small holes at the edge (Fig. 234b).

How to Sew on Hooks and Eyes

Hooks and eyes are composed of two parts: the hook or bill (Fig. 235a) and the eye. There are straight eyes (Fig. 235b) for edges that

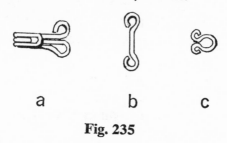

a   b   c

Fig. 235

overlap (like the waistband with extension), and round eyes (Fig. 235c) where the edges meet (as in an inside waistband).

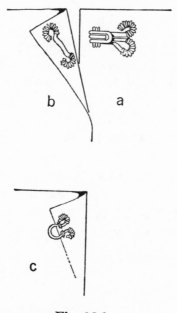

Fig. 236

1. Mark the position for the hooks and eyes carefully.

2. Set the hook close to the edge for a true closing. Sew it first, working the overhand stitches around the first ring.

3. Slip the needle through the fabric and bring it up at the second ring.

4. Sew the second ring, working overhand stitches around it.

5. Slip the needle through the fabric and bring it up at the hook end. Work overhand stitches just under the bill. It is just as important to anchor the bill as to secure the rings (Fig. 236a).

6. Fasten the thread with tiny backstitches. Cut the thread.

7. Stitch the eye with overhand stitches around the rings (Fig. 236b).

A round eye is extended slightly beyond the edge (Fig. 236c).

How to Sew on Heavy-duty Hooks and Eyes

Fig. 237

(Fig. 237) Position them as you would any other hooks and eyes. Using overhand stitches, fasten them through the holes. When necessary, fasten them across any bars in a sufficient number of places to hold securely.

FASTENINGS TAKE OVER

A jarring note in an otherwise beautifully tailored garment is the bare-bones look of metal snaps and hooks and eyes, particularly when they are in exposed positions. A more pleasing and finished appearance results when they are covered in a color to match the garment.

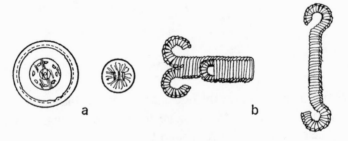

a   b

Fig. 238

Covered Snaps

1. Cut two circles of matching organza, organdy, or thin lining material. Make them twice the diameter of the snap plus a tiny seam allowance (Fig. 238a).

2. Pierce a tiny hole in the center of one circle and force the ball through it.

3. Turn under the seam allowance and gather the outer edges close to the fold.

4. Draw up the gathering until it fits taut over the snap. Use a cross-stitch or several hemming stitches to secure the closing (Fig. 238a).

5. Cover the socket with the second circle of cloth in the same way.

6. Snap the ball and socket together. The exposed ball will create the needed hole in the socket as it is forced into it.

Covered Hooks and Eyes

Using a double strand of matching thread, work blanket stitches over the hooks and eyes until they are completely covered (Fig. 238b). The stitches should be very close together.

You may have to pry the hook open a bit to compensate for the extra thickness of the stitches.

Hide the Hook: You can do a real disappearing act with hooks by hiding them in the weave of the fabric. Instead of the metal eye, use a thread loop.

Fig. 239

1. Mark the position of the bill end of the hook on the facing.

2. Make a small opening in the weave of the fabric by carefully pushing the threads apart with a blunt instrument. In tightly woven fabric, make a tiny slit for this purpose.

3. Gently work the loops of the hook into the opening, one loop at a time, until only the bill of the hook is exposed (Fig. 239).

4. Slip the thread in the opening and fasten the loops with tiny, inconspicuous stitches. Fasten the bill. When the fabric has been slit to make the opening, sew up the ends to prevent tearing or fraying.

The thread loop is made with the bullion stitch, often used in embroidery. Use a short double thread pulled up evenly.

1. Fasten the thread on the underside. Bring the needle up to the surface at the bottom point of the loop (Fig. 240a).

2. Insert the needle at the top point of the loop (about ¼ inch away). Bring the needle out once more at the original point of entry but *do not* pull it through (Fig. 240b).

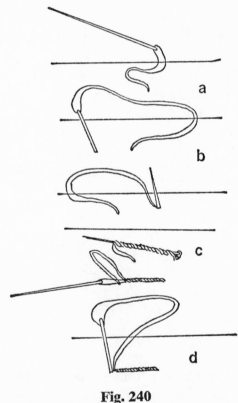

Fig. 240

3. Wind the thread closely but not tightly around the exposed end of the needle to the desired depth of the loop (Fig. 240c).

4. Pull the needle and thread through the winding and draw up tightly (Fig. 240d).

5. Insert the needle at the first point of entry. Fasten the thread securely on the underside.

This thread loop can be used in conjunction with any hook, not merely the hidden hook.

PERFECT POCKETS

From the standpoint of design, there are no limits to size, shape, or placement of pockets. They appear in baffling sizes and in highly improbable places. However well or little they may function as pockets, there's no denying they add dash to a design.

Even if your pattern doesn't have pockets, you can add them. Or you can substitute one type of pocket for another if it is consistent with the pattern design. Many jackets and coats are so simply cut that they offer considerable leeway in the choice of pocket design. In fact, the pockets become the chief design detail.

In designing your own pockets, experiment with paper cutouts or scraps of fabric until you get just the right size, shape, placement, and number of pockets you like. (One good pocket may deserve another and another and another. Chanel did it!) Just remember to keep the lines of the pocket in harmony with the lines of the design of the garment.

Trace the chosen pocket on fresh paper. Add seam allowances and a hem. Decide whether you want it on straight grain, cross grain, or bias. Consider a trimming of braid, ribbon, or topstitching. Let yourself go!

PRACTICAL POCKETS

When a pocket is meant to be used, it should be in such a place and of such size that one can get a hand into it. The general rule for practical pockets is as follows:

For Horizontal and Diagonal Openings: Make them as wide as the fullest part of your hand plus 1 inch for ease.

For Vertical Openings: Make them as wide as the fullest part of your hand plus 2 inches to accommodate the double motion the hand must make to get into the pocket—forward and down.

Do place pockets within easy reach. Change the position of a pocket on a pattern if need be. (Often, coat pockets are placed so low on the garment that one must assume an ape-like posture in order to reach them.)

SURFACE, SEAM, OR SLASH:
THE PLACE FOR POCKETS

There are three basic constructions for pockets.

1. There are those applied to the surface, like the patch pocket (Fig. 241a).

2. There are those stitched into a construction seam (Fig. 241b) or stitched into a slash, like the bound pocket (Fig. 241c).

3. There are those that have elements of both styles—part applied, part set in a seam or slash. This is the case with the welt pocket (Fig. 241d) and the flap pocket (Fig. 241e).

THE POCKET SET ON THE SURFACE:
PATCH POCKET CONSTRUCTION

(Fig. 241a)

1. Mark the position of the pocket carefully on the right side of the garment with guide basting.

2. Cut out the pocket. If striped, checked, plaid, or printed fabric is used, be sure to match the pocket and the garment.

In classic tailoring, the pocket is lined and generally interfaced. If need be, the pocket may be underlined.

1. Cut the pocket lining slightly smaller than the pocket so that the joining seam can be rolled to the underside.

2. Cut the pocket interfacing or underlining. The amount and kind of each will depend on the style effect desired. Trim away all seam allowances.

Fig. 241

3. Apply the interfacing or underlining to the pocket by catch stitching (Fig. 242).

Fig. 242

Attach the Lining to the Pocket

1. Stitch the lining to the hem of the pocket, leaving a small opening at the center of the seam (Fig. 243a). Press the seam allowances open.

2. Fold the pocket along the fold line of the hem. With right sides of pocket and lining together and raw edges matching, pin to position.

3. Stitch around the remaining sides of the pocket (Fig. 243b).

4. Grade the seam allowances, free all corners of bulk, notch all curved edges (Fig. 243c).

5. Turn the pocket to the right side through the opening. Carefully work out all corners. Close the hem opening with slip stitching.

6. Press the pocket, rolling the joining seams to the underside.

A lined square pocket is constructed in the same way.

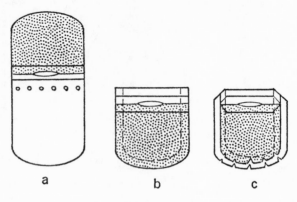

a   b   c

Fig. 243

Position and Slip-stitch the Pocket to the Garment

1. Pin or baste the pocket to position.

If the garment is unfitted, lay it on a flat surface. Place the pocket over it (Fig. 244a).

If the garment is fitted, place the pocket area over a curved pad to simulate the body curve. Position the pocket (Fig. 244b). Pockets so placed will not only lie flat when worn but provide sufficient ease to insert the hand.

The best curved pad over which to work is the tailor's ham. A tightly rolled-up towel is a fair substitute.

2. Slip-stitch the pocket to the garment. Properly done, the slip-stitch method floats the pocket on the surface of the garment.

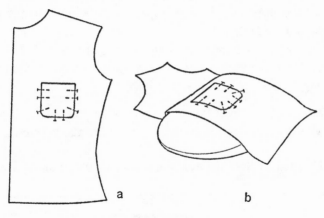

Fig. 244

How to Slip-stitch the Pocket to the Garment

1. Reinforce the starting corner by taking several small over-and-over stitches on the underside of the garment (Fig. 245a). Bring the needle up to the right side.

2. Fold back the pocket against itself, making the fold slightly in from the finished edge of the pocket. Fold back the garment against itself (Fig. 245b).

3. Slip the needle along the folds, alternating between the pocket

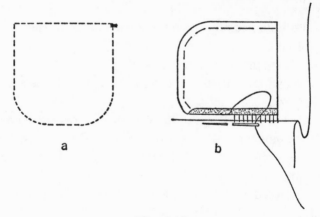

Fig. 245

and the garment (Fig. 245b). The lower stitch starts directly under the end of the upper stitch. The upper stitch begins directly over the end of the lower stitch.

4. Continue slip-stitching around the edge of the pocket.

5. Finish off by making several small over-and-over stitches on the underside.

The Topstitched Lined Patch Pocket: When decorative topstitching is used, it is done before the pocket is applied to the garment.

The Unlined Pocket of Quick-and-Easy Contemporary Tailoring

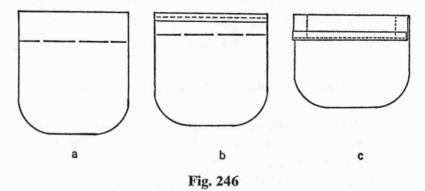

Fig. 246

1. Mark the fold line of the hem (Fig. 246a). It may be helpful to mark the seam allowances, also.

2. Choose an appropriate finish for the hem edge of the pocket (Fig. 246b). Keep it as flat and unobtrusive as possible.

3. Turn the hem of the pocket to the outside (right side) along the fold line. Pin to position and stitch (Fig. 246c). Fasten the stitching securely at the hem edge.

For Rounded Pockets, Continue as Follows

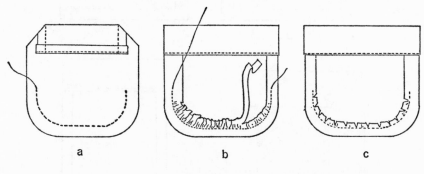

a   b   c

Fig. 247

1. Place a line of gathering stitches around the curve of the pocket about ¼ inch away from the seam line (Fig. 247a).

2. Make a diagonal slash across each corner. Grade the seam allowances (Fig. 247a) and press them open over the point presser.

3. Turn the hem to the inside (wrong side of the pocket), working out the corners carefully (Fig. 247b).

4. Draw up the gathering stitches. Turn the seam allowances evenly to the wrong side (Fig. 247b).

5. Trim the rippling seam allowance to about ⅜ inch (Fig. 247b). Notch sufficiently so the curve lies flat (Fig. 247c). Press.

For Square Pockets, Continue as Follows

1. Make a diagonal slash across each corner of the hem. Clip the seam allowances at the end of the hem. Grade them (Fig. 248a).

2. Press the seam allowances open over the point presser. Turn the hem to the inside, carefully working out the corners (Fig. 248b).

3. Miter the seam allowances of the remaining corners (Fig. 248c).

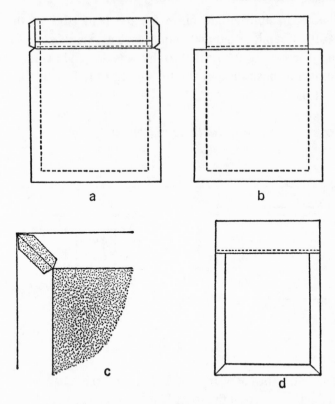

Fig. 248

4. Turn the corners to the inside (wrong side), working them out carefully. Keep the seam allowances even (Fig. 248d).

5. Press the pocket.

The Topstitched Unlined Pocket: When visible stitching is consistent with the design of the garment, attach the pocket to it by top-stitching. This is generally a single line of stitching close to and an even distance in from the edge (Fig. 249a). Begin the stitching at one corner and stitch to the opposite one.

If the pocket will be subjected to much wear, double-topstitch it (Fig. 249b). This is easy on a two-needle sewing machine. On a single-needle sewing machine, start the stitching at the bottom of the pocket rather than at an end. Stitch to one end, and take a few stitches across the end (both to reinforce the end and to place the needle in position for the second row of stitching). Stitch around the

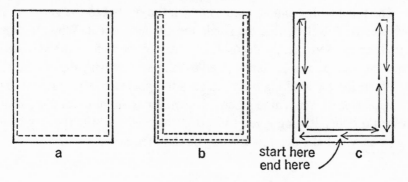

start here
end here

Fig. 249

pocket to the other end; then stitch across the end and down the second side to the start of the stitching (Fig. 249c). Pull the threads through to the underside and tie them in a square knot. Follow the arrows in Fig. 249c. Keep the rows of stitching an even distance from each other throughout. Take the same number of stitches across each end.

For either single or double topstitching, use a regulation stitch size and matching or contrasting thread.

If topstitching is inconsistent with the design, slip-stitch the pocket to the garment.

Topstitching in from the Edge for a Decorative Effect on the Unlined Pocket: A very pretty patch pocket can be made by topstitching in from the edge (Figs. 250a and 250c).

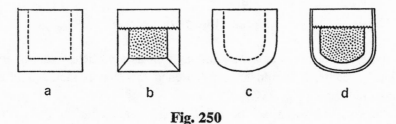

a   b   c   d

Fig. 250

For this effect, a straight-sided pocket needs a much deeper seam allowance (Fig. 250b) and a curved pocket needs a facing (Fig. 250d).

The topstitching can be used to attach the pocket to the garment, in which case it is done like the single-topstitched pocket. When the topstitching is used merely decoratively, it is done before the pocket is applied. The pocket is then applied to the garment with slip stitching.

When the topstitching truly attaches the pocket to the garment, use a regulation-size machine stitch—whichever is suitable for the fabric. When the topstitching is used just decoratively, the stitches may be as large as will make them interesting on the fabric.

THE POCKET SET IN A SEAM

(Fig. 241b)

If the pocket is meant for use, make it large enough to get your hand into it easily and deep enough to let your hand settle comfortably.

You will need a pair of pouch-shaped pieces for each pocket: an upper pocket directly over the top of your hand and a lower pocket resting against the palm of your hand (Fig. 251a).

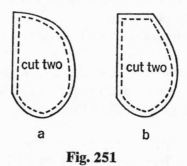

a   b

Fig. 251

When a pocket joins a waistline as well as a vertical seam, as in a skirt or pants, it should have a flattened top that is included in the waistline seam (Fig. 251b).

Pockets like these can be put into any seam whether the pattern calls for it or not.

The opening of the pocket in a seam will reveal the material of which it is made. Anything seen, as this is, becomes a part of the design of the garment. Therefore the material you choose for the pocket should fit in with the total concept of the design.

You could add a splash of color or pattern for drama. The usual treatment of the pocket in a seam of a tailored garment is to preserve the continuity of color and texture. There are several ways in which this can be done.

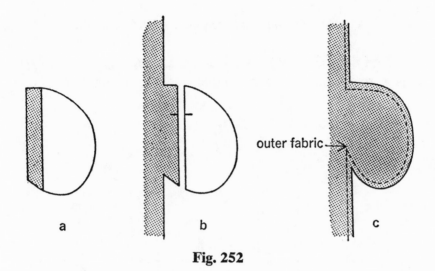

outer fabric

a   b   c

Fig. 252

1. If the fabric of the garment is light- or medium-weight, cut the pockets of the same material.

2. Or cut the underpocket of the outer fabric and the upper pocket of lining material.

3. For heavy material, cut both upper pocket and underpocket of lining material. Face the edges that join the garment with strips of outer fabric deep enough so the lining won't show when the pocket opens (Fig. 252a).

If you enjoy playing with patterns, you might even consider doing one of the following:

1. Scotch-tape a tissue-paper extension to the seam allowance of the pattern at the pocket opening (Fig. 252b). Make it equal in size to the facing of Fig. 252a. Now garment plus pocket facing can be cut as one piece. The pattern for the remainder of the pocket becomes correspondingly smaller.

2. Add the entire underpocket pattern to the garment pattern with

Scotch tape. Cut the two as one pattern (Fig. 252c). Overlap the seam allowances at the joining.

In both cases, cut the garment plus extension of the fashion fabric and the rest of the pocket of lining material.

An Easy Way to Set and Stitch the Pocket into the Seam

1. With right sides together, stitch the straight edges of the pocket to the garment, matching the markings for the opening. Use only ⅜

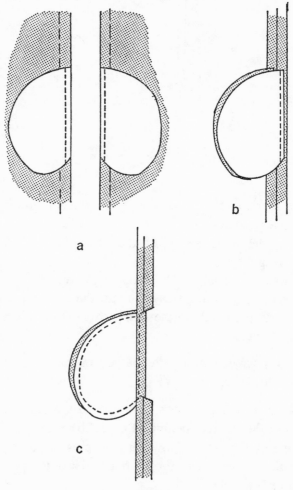

Fig. 253

inch of the usual ⅝-inch seam allowance. This will give ¼ inch for rolling the pocket seam to the inside (Fig. 253a).

2. With right sides together, stitch the seams of the garment below and above the pocket. Take the regulation ⅝-inch seam allowance (Fig. 253b).

3. Clip the seam allowances at the corners where the garment and pocket seams meet. Grade the pocket seam allowances.

4. Press the garment seam allowances open. Press the pocket along the original seam line, with seam allowances pressed toward the front.

5. Stitch the pocket sections together with the standard ⅝-inch seam allowance (Fig. 253c).

When a pocket extends to the waistline, baste and stitch it into the waistline seam.

THE POCKET SET IN A SLASH

(Figs. 241c, 241d, 241e)

In a bound, welt, or flap pocket, the opening of the pocket is slashed right into the garment. You can't change your mind once the fabric has been cut. A little planning beforehand can save a lot of heartache.

The pocket is composed of two parts. One part is seen from the outside as a binding, a welt, or a flap. The other part is the pouch, the pocket proper, which is attached to the underside. The underpocket is just that much longer than the upper pocket to compensate for the depth of the opening. Both are as wide as the opening plus a seam allowance on either side. If you really intend to use the opening as a pocket, make it deep enough to get your hand into it comfortably.

Whenever a slash is made in the garment fabric, the opening should be reinforced with a strip of lightweight interfacing or iron-on material applied to the underside. For the pocket set in a slash, make this reinforcement 2 inches longer than the pocket—1 inch on either side.

The Bound Pocket

Here's a bonus for you: a bound buttonhole (Method II) converted into a bound pocket (Fig. 254a).

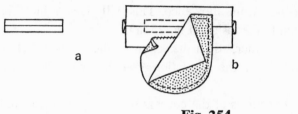

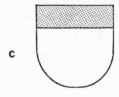

Fig. 254

All you need do is attach an upper pocket to the lower seam allowance with hemming stitches and attach an underpocket to the upper
seam allowance with backstitches (Fig. 254b). Hand stitching is
easier, but you may use machine stitching if you like.

Make the underpocket of fashion fabric so there will be no break in
color or texture at the pocket opening. Or face the lining underpocket
with a strip of fashion fabric in the opening area only (Fig. 254c).
This is a good method for heavy or bulky fabric.

Make the strip wide enough to extend to a safe depth. Use a selvage edge where possible so there will be no need to turn the facing
under for a finished edge. Lap the facing over the lining and stitch.
Another way to solve this problem is to use the garment fabric for the
underpocket and lining for the upper pocket.

Flaps and Welts to Hide the Slash

Whereas the binding of a bound pocket is used to finish and protect
the slash, flaps and welts can be used to hide it.

In order to do this, the welt or flap is placed on the garment in a
position opposite to the way it will look when stitched. When turned
to its rightful position, the opening of the pocket is concealed.

For instance, a welt destined to turn up (Fig. 255a) is placed
"head down" (Fig. 255b), stitched, and turned.

A flap that will eventually hang down when finished (Fig. 255c) is
placed "head up" for stitching (Fig. 255d).

Welts and flaps may appear in other positions (Figs. 255e and
255f) but the rule holds: to hide the opening of the pocket, place the
welt or flap in a position for stitching in a direction opposite to the
way it will appear when finished (Fig. 255g).

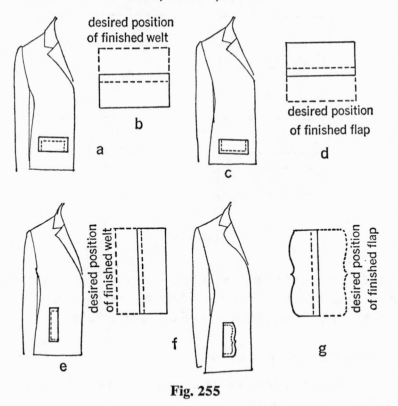

Fig. 255

Welt or Flap Construction

Every bit of sewing skill you possess—stitching, trimming, clipping, notching, grading, and pressing—goes into the making of each welt or flap. The test of your expertise as a sewer is here in microcosm.

Welts and flaps are generally made of the same fabric as the garment, cut on the same grain and same nap. All checks, stripes, or plaids must match the part of the garment where the welt or flap is to be located. The only way to avoid doing so is by cutting them on the bias if the design will permit.

For the One-piece Welt or Flap

1. Cut a strip of fabric the length of the welt or flap by twice its width plus seam allowances on all outside edges.

2. Interface the under half of it (Fig. 256a).

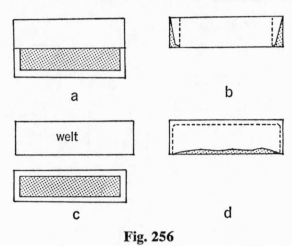

Fig. 256

3. Fold it in half lengthwise, right sides together. Set the raw edges of the upper thickness down a little from the raw edges of the under thickness (Fig. 256b). Stitch across the ends (Fig. 256b).

For the Two-piece Welt or Flap

1. Allow enough fabric on the upper thickness so the joining seam may be rolled to the underside.

2. Interface the facing (Fig. 256c).

3. With raw edges matching, stitch the upper layer to the facing, easing in the fullness. Leave the lower edge open (Fig. 256d).

Complete Both Types as Follows

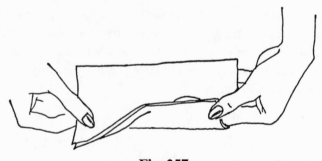

Fig. 257

4. Press all seam allowances open before turning to the right side. Use the point presser.

5. Grade the seam allowances. Free all corners of bulk. Clip and/or notch as necessary.

6. Turn to the right side and press.

With the upper side of the welt on top and the underside against the hand, roll the welt or flap over the fingers, making the needed adjustment in length (Fig. 257). Pin to position. Baste both thicknesses across the lower edge.

How to Make the Welt Pocket

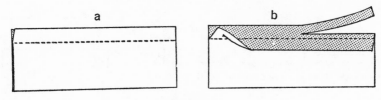

Fig. 258

1. On the right side of the garment, place the seam line of the lower edge of the welt directly on the slash-line guide basting.

2. Stitch through all thicknesses from one end of the welt to the other (Fig. 258a). Do not lock-stitch. It's hard to be so accurate that the lock stitches do not go beyond the welt.

3. Pull the thread ends through to the underside and tie each pair with a square knot.

4. Grade the seam allowances of the welt, trimming them close to the seam line (Fig. 258b).

Then Apply the Pocket

Fig. 259a shows the welt stitched to the garment along the slash line.

1. Cut the pocket of lining material. Make it equal to the width of the pocket by twice its depth plus seam allowances on all outside edges. Mark the slash line in the center.

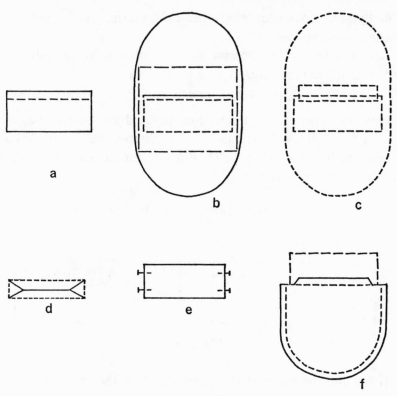

Fig. 259

2. Place the pocket over the welt, right sides together. Set one stitching line of the pocket directly over the stitching line of the welt. Baste to position (Fig. 259b).

3. Stitch a rectangle for the pocket opening (Fig. 259c). This is easier to do if you turn to the wrong side, where the line of stitching that attached the welt to the garment can be used as a guideline. Make the first line of stitching directly over the previous stitching; stitch across one end for ¼ inch; make the third side of the rectangle parallel to the first; stitch across the second end, making it parallel to the other end.

Turn the last corner and continue the stitching ½ to 1 inch directly over the first side of the rectangle to secure the stitching.

CAUTION: Be sure to start and stop the stitching two or three stitches in from each end. This makes the opening of the pocket a little smaller than the welt. When the welt is turned to its final position, it will completely conceal the opening. Were you to stitch all the way to the ends of the welt, you would wind up with two conspicuous gaping holes at the ends of the pocket.

4. Slash all thicknesses through the center of the rectangle to within ¼ inch of the ends. Clip diagonally to the corners (Fig. 259d).

5. Turn the pocket to the wrong side by slipping it gently through the opening. Pocket and welt will assume their proper positions.

6. Pin the welt in place and slip-stitch the ends to the garment (Fig. 259e).

7. On the underside, pin the upper pocket and underpocket together. Note that the upper pocket is slightly longer than the underpocket. This is because of the ¼-inch depth of the opening. Trim it to match the underpocket.

8. Machine-stitch the remaining sides of the pocket (Fig. 259f).

This method of construction has three distinct advantages:

1. The complete length of the welt is attached securely without involving the pocket itself.

2. Because the welt has already been attached, the rectangular opening may safely be made smaller.

3. When the pocket lining is stitched to the welt and garment from the underside, using the previous line of stitching as a guide, one can be sure it is correctly done. No guessing and no X-ray eyes necessary as when stitching blindly from the right side of the garment.

Flap Pockets

Unlike the welt pocket, whose ends are fastened to the garment, a flap hangs free—to flap, of course. A flap can hide the opening of any

kind of pocket—patch (Fig. 260a), seam-inserted (Fig. 260b), or
bound (Fig. 260c).

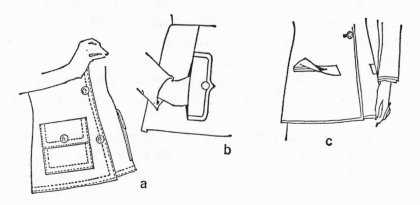

Fig. 260

The Flap over a Patch Pocket

A flap may be attached over a patch pocket in one of two ways:
with a welt seam under the flap, as in Fig. 261, or topstitched over
the flap, as in Fig. 262.

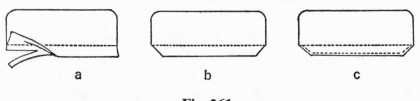

Fig. 261

To Construct Fig. 261

1. Place the flap in position on the designated placement line. Pin
and stitch.

2. Trim the under seam allowance close to the stitching (Fig.
261a).

3. On the upper seam allowance, fold under the ends diagonally
(Fig. 261b).

4. Turn under part of the upper seam allowance as for a welt
seam. Stitch (Fig. 261c).

To Construct Fig. 262

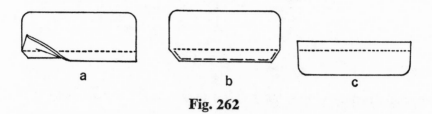

Fig. 262

1. Grade the seam allowances. Clip the ends of the under seam allowance diagonally (Fig. 262a).

2. Fold under the ends of the upper seam allowances diagonally (Fig. 262b). Baste to position.

3. Turn the flap to position. Topstitch an even distance from the fold (Fig. 262c).

A Flap Added to a Bound Pocket

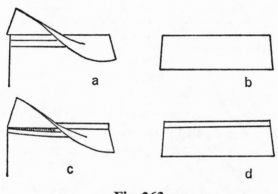

Fig. 263

When a flap is added to a bound pocket, it is included in the upper seam. The flap may be inserted over the binding (Fig. 263a) to cover it (Fig. 263b) or under the binding (Fig. 263c) to reveal it (Fig. 263d). Both methods are acceptable. It is merely a matter of design.

To Construct Fig. 263a—the Flap over the Binding
1. Make the flap and stitch it to the garment ⅛ inch above the

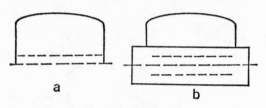

Fig. 264

pocket opening (Fig. 264a). Trim the seam allowances close to the stitching.

2. Place the binding over the flap so that the stitching line of the upper binding is directly over the stitching line that fastened the flap to the garment (Fig. 264b).

3. Construct the bound pocket.

To Construct Fig. 263c—the Flap Under the Binding

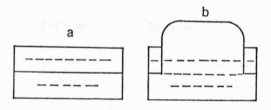

Fig. 265

1. Place and stitch the upper binding the full length of the opening. Stitch the lower binding parallel to the first, but tapering in ⅛ to ¼ inch at each end (Fig. 265a). If you do so, the flap will cover the opening of the pocket.

2. Make the flap and stitch it in place directly over the stitching line of the upper binding (Fig. 265b).

3. Construct the bound pocket.

Fake Flaps and Would-be Welts

They look real enough, but they're only fake flaps and would-be welts. Their function is purely decorative. There are two ways in which you can apply these great pretenders.

1. Complete the three sides of the welt or flap. Attach the fourth side to the garment as directed in this section.

2. Complete all four sides first. (Machine-stitch three sides, turn to the right side, and tuck in and slip-stitch the fourth side.) Slip-stitch the finished welt or flap to position.

The second method makes a flatter application by avoiding the turnover essential to the first method. In some fabrics this is a decided advantage.

Inevitably, anything that appears on the surface of a garment and can be seen, like a pocket or a buttonhole or a zipper, becomes an important element of the total design of the garment. As such, each demands your best effort and your expertise—nothing short of terrific for the tricky trio.

Part IV
PUTTING IT ALL TOGETHER

Chapter 17

Sew the Shell

After considerable pondering, you have chosen the pattern and altered it to fit. After careful deliberation, you have selected, prepared, cut, marked, and stay-stitched the fashion fabric. With due consideration for the design and the fabric, the appropriate interfacing and/or underlining have been decided, cut, and marked. All the equipment and findings needed to assemble and press the garment are ready and handy. The techniques for stitching and pressing this particular garment have been studied and determined. Now is the time when all the previous bits of disjointed information are put together for the final, speedy, and (we hope) satisfactory conclusion.

With all the preliminaries out of the way, the work of putting it all together will proceed quickly.

FIRST—A PIN FITTING

Before any stitching is done, it is wise to make sure that the darts and seams are in the right places. This should be just a simple matter of checking, since the trial muslin presumably took care of all major changes.

Pin-fit the shell of the garment only. Do not include set-in sleeves, collars, or facings or any other double thicknesses of material.

Do all fitting from the right side. Right-side adjustments are transferred to the wrong side with tailor's chalk or basting thread. These marks become the new stitching lines. Be sure to make similar adjustments in everything that goes underneath the outer fabric—the interfacing, underlining, lining, and interlining when used.

You'll get a better idea of how the completed garment will look if the darts and seams are pinned on the wrong side. However, it is easier to make the needed changes if the pins are on the right side. Perhaps some of each?

Try on the garment. Pin it on the closing line. When shoulder pads are to be used, set them in place. If necessary for a better judgment of fit, slip the pinned or basted interfacing or underlining into position.

Check the position of the darts and shaping seams. Check the ease and the fullness. Keep in mind that the garment will look quite different after pressing, blocking, and the addition of the completed interfacing or underlining. This fitting is not so much for appearance as for size and shaping.

Determine the exact location of the buttonholes—especially if there have been pattern alterations. Decide the best placement of the pockets. (When the design depends on a particular location for the pocket, you may not have much choice about placement.)

A PLAN FOR ACTION: THE UNIT METHOD

You'll get farther faster if you have a plan for action.

The simplest plan for sewing is *unit construction*. By this system, all that it is possible to do on one section of a garment is completed before going on to the next or before joining it to another. Keeping the work flat as long as possible increases the speed of construction. It is easier to handle the separate units.

A unit of work consists of all the parts that go to make a complete front, a complete back, the complete sleeves, the complete collar, and so on. Most pattern directions, particularly for simple designs, follow a unit work plan.

SO SEW!

Using all the sewing techniques outlined in Chapter 13, join all darts, seams, sections, insets, and so on, that complete each unit of jacket, skirt, pants, or coat. This goes for outer fabric, interfacing, and underlining. (A great deal of work is disposed of in these two short sentences.)

Do all of one kind of stitching at a time. Stitch all darts, stitch all similar seams, make all the pockets, work all the buttonholes, before going on to another kind of operation. Getting into the swing of a particular action makes it more uniform, more perfect, easier, faster. Changeover to a new operation makes for loss of rhythm, momentum, and efficiency. Anyone knows that it is easier and faster to wash all the dishes before drying them than to wash and dry each dish separately.

When there is considerable shaping via hair canvas, make the buttonholes and pockets in the outer fabric *before* the hair canvas is applied.

When a soft or lightweight underlining is used, the bound buttonholes and applied pockets can be made *after* the underlining has been applied, using it as a reinforcement for the openings. *Heavier* or *stiffer* underlinings are treated in the same way as hair canvas.

When there is minimal shaping with hair canvas, the canvas can be joined with the outer fabric *first.* Then remove a "window" of the canvas in the buttonhole or pocket area and substitute a lighter-weight reinforcing fabric. Directions for doing so follow.

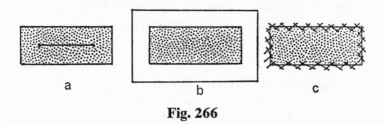

a   b   c

Fig. 266

1. Transfer the buttonhole or pocket markings from the right side to the hair canvas on the underside.

2. Draw a rectangle ⅜ inch away from the markings on all sides (Fig. 266a). Don't make the opening any larger than this or you will lose the benefit of the canvas interfacing. It should be just large enough to take the binding comfortably.

3. Cut out the interfacing rectangle.

4. Place the cut-out rectangle on the new backing material as a guide. Trace around it. Draw a new, larger rectangle around the tracing, making it at least ¼ inch larger all around for an overlap (Fig. 266b).

5. Cut out the replacement material.

6. Either insert the new backing in the opening of the interfacing or place it on top of it. You may use the markings of the original rectangle in step 2 as a placement guide.

7. Fasten with catch stitching (Fig. 266c). An iron-on replacement need only be pressed on.

In the Classic Tailored Jacket or Coat: Each unit of the outer fabric is completed separately from every other. Each unit of the interfacing and/or underlining is separate from every other. The outer fabric and understructure are separate from each other. Trim, clip, notch, and grade where necessary. Using all the pressing techniques outlined in Chapter 15, press each unit of the garment, interfacing, and/or underlining. Using suitable press pads, shape all areas of the garment and underpinning that require it.

Only now can these disparate elements be joined as one.

HOW TO JOIN THE FASHION FABRIC AND THE UNDERSTRUCTURE

The interfacings and fashion fabrics of all garments, shaped or unshaped, are best joined in the same relative position in which they will be worn (fashion fabric topping foundation fabric) and over a tailor's ham to simulate the body contour. This is the order: the tailor's ham representing the body, then the supporting fabric, and lastly the outer fabric, right side up. Because an inside curve is smaller than an outside curve, some of the foundation fabric will extend slightly beyond the edges of the fashion fabric. This positioning automatically adjusts the necessary length and width of the supporting material. The excess can be trimmed away after the layers are joined.

HOW TO HANDLE THE UNFITTED, MINIMALLY INTERFACED JACKET OR COAT

1. Place the front interfacing on a flat surface.

2. Place the completed front unit of the fashion fabric over it, matching the front edges. Pin to position.

3. Make a line of basting 1 inch in from and along the front edges (Fig. 267a).

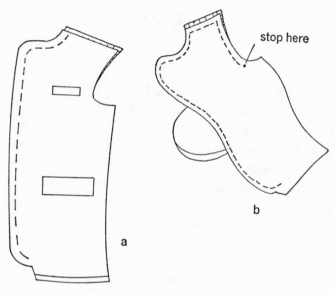

stop here

b

a

Fig. 267

4. Place the two joined layers over the tailor's ham, fashion fabric right side up over the interfacing. Smooth the fabric toward all the outer edges. Pin to position.

5. Make a line of basting 1 inch in from and along all other outer edges that are interfaced (Fig. 267b).

HOW TO HANDLE THE SHAPED JACKET OR COAT

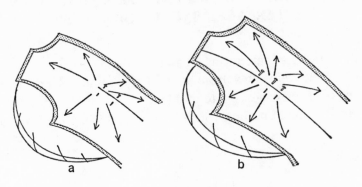

Fig. 268

Front

1. In matching the front outer and supporting fabrics, start at the dart (Fig. 268a) and work toward the outer edges. Pin. When matching shaping seams, start at the crest of each curve and work toward the outer edges (Fig. 268b). Pin to position. You can see how this procedure makes for exact shaping.

2. Tailor-baste the two thicknesses. The first line of tailor basting goes over the dart or shaping seam—up toward the shoulder, down toward the hem, stopping several inches short of each (Fig. 269a). This line of tailor basting may also run through an upper and lower pocket when they are present.

3. When there are pockets involved, turn back the side-front outer fabric section against itself to expose the seam allowances of any welt or bound pockets (Fig. 269b). Fasten them to the interfacing with hemming stitches.

Replace the side-front fabric. Turn back the front outer fabric against itself exposing the second side of any welt or bound pockets. Fasten the seam allowances to the interfacing with hemming stitches. Return the fabric to position.

In the same way, you may fasten the seam allowances of any waistline darts.

4. Locate the exact position of the buttonhole and pocket openings

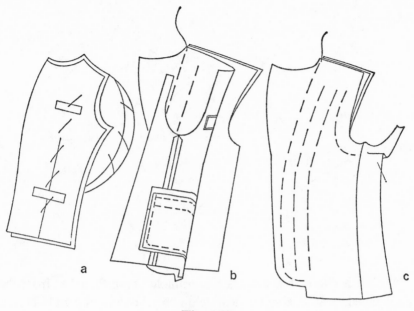

a   b   c

Fig. 269

on the interfacing. Cut out rectangles of the hair canvas just large enough to expose the openings. Slip the canvas under the seam allowances of pocket and buttonholes. Fasten the seam allowances to the interfacing with catch stitching.

5. Working from the right side, continue the tailor basting, making several lines of it several inches apart toward the side and toward the front. Smooth the fabric toward the outer edges as you work. Make the last rows of tailor basting 1 inch in from the front and side edges (Fig. 269c).

How to Join the Back Interfacing and Outer Fabric

1. Place the supporting fabric on the tailor's ham.

2. Place the fashion fabric over the supporting fabric, right side up, matching the center backs.

3. Join the center backs with tailor basting, ending about 1 inch down from the neck (Fig. 270a).

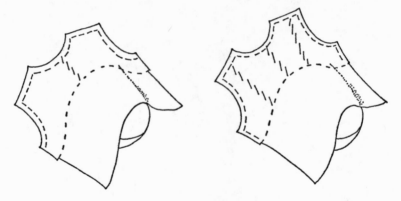

Fig. 270

4. Run a line of basting at each armhole about 2 inches from the armhole edge. Start about 1 inch below the shoulder and end about 1 inch from the side seam (Fig. 270a).

5. Run a line of basting 1 inch in from and along the shoulder and neck edges (Fig. 270a).

6. OPTIONAL: If it will hold your fabric more securely, you may run another line of tailor basting between the center and armhole edge (Fig. 270b).

If both underlining and interfacing are used, first join them to each other with stay stitching, then join them to the garment fabric with tailor basting. The underlining is placed directly against the wrong side of the outer fabric. The interfacing is placed against the underlining. This method of joining ensures that the shaping of both fabric and understructure correspond.

CAUTION: If needles and pins leave permanent marks or bruises on the fashion fabric (velvets, brocades, satins, and so on) *do not join the units with tailor basting.* Baste the sections together in the seam allowances of all outside edges. Work over the tailor's ham, of course.

Now hold up the interfaced fronts and back (with their stitched-in, blocked-in contour) against you. Behold the transformation from those limp unit "rags" to the "riches" of your truly tailored coat or jacket.

THE SECOND FITTING

The second fitting locates the position of the shoulder and side or underarm seams. It is also a time to refine and perfect the fitting of the interfaced or underlined sections. Often the addition of the understructure does make a difference in the ease and fit.

True, it is much simpler if you have someone to do the fitting for you. However, by careful observation (and enough time) you can do a surprisingly good job yourself even though it be trial and error.

1. Using your fitted trial muslin as a guide, pin the shoulders and the side (or underarm) seams on the right side of the garment. (Remember that all fitting is done from the right side.)

2. Try on the garment over the dress, blouse, sweater, skirt, pants —whatever—with which your jacket or coat is to be worn.

3. When shoulder pads are to be used, slip them into position.

4. Pin the garment closed from the top button to the bottom of the garment, matching the center markings.

5. Perfect the fit following all the guides set forth in Chapter 6.

6. Remove (reluctantly?) the jacket or coat.

7. Transfer the markings to the wrong side of the garment for stitching.

STITCHING CONSTRUCTION SEAMS

While stitching a dart through many thicknesses is hazardous, it is fairly safe to include most supporting materials in the major construction seams—*but not hair canvas*. It is too springy and too resilient to be pressed flat. The following methods produce seams that are trim and flat without involving the hair canvas interfacing.

How to Remove the Hair Canvas from the Construction Seams

The Cut-away Method

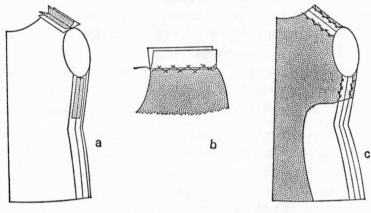

Fig. 271

1. Open the seam allowances between the outer fabric and the back interfacing of shoulder and side or underarm seams. Using tailor's chalk, mark the seam line as pinned on both the hair canvas and the outer fabric (Fig. 271a).

2. Do the same for the front seam lines.

3. Unpin the seams.

4. Trim away the seam allowances of the hair canvas, as marked.

5. Catch-stitch the cut edge of the interfacing to the seam line of the fashion fabric (Fig. 271b). Use a matching single thread, and pick up only one thread of the outer fabric so the hand stitches do not show on the right side. Do not pull up the thread too tightly—just enough to secure the interfacing.

6. With the right sides of the outer fabric together, pin and stitch the shoulder and side or underarm seams. Stitch *beside* the interfacing, not through it.

7. Press the seam allowances open as flat as possible, using the pressing technique determined best for your fabric.

8. OPTIONAL: If you'll feel more secure about it, catch-stitch the seam allowances to the interfacing (Fig. 271c).

This cut-away method can be used wherever on the garment one would wish to eliminate the hair canvas from a seam (Fig. 272).

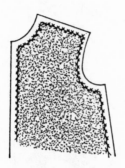

Fig. 272

The Taping Method

Taping is done after the sections of the garment are joined. This method not only eliminates the bulk of the interfacing from the seam line but stays the length and shape of the outside edges. It is used by professional tailors around the neck, lapels, and closing edges of a jacket or coat and under the roll line of the lapel. In classic tailoring, it may also be used at the fold line of a vent, and along the hemline of a soft fabric like cashmere. Often, too, it is used around the armhole.

Tape is applied in a number of ways, depending on where it is used in the garment.

On Outside Seams

1. Trim away ¾ inch of the hair canvas interfacing at the neck, lapel, and front edges.

2. Preshrink a length of ⅜-inch twill or cotton tape to cover all your needs. When you grow very proficient in its use, you may use the narrower ¼-inch tape.

3. Cut a length of tape to fit the entire neckline from the tip of one lapel to the other (Fig. 273a).

Cut a length of tape to fit each lapel-and-front edge. In a curved-bottom style line, bring the tape to the end of the interfacing (Fig.

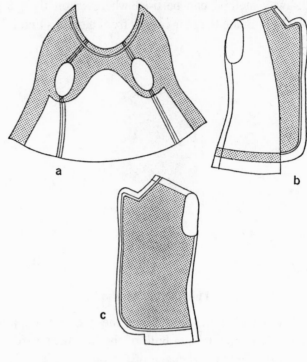

Fig. 273

273b). When the entire front section is interfaced, bring the tape to the side or underarm seam (Fig. 273c).

In general, tape is cut to the *actual measurement* of the edge to be taped, neither more nor less. However, there are two exceptions:

a. Pull the tape taut between the top and bottom buttons and around any lower curved style line (Fig. 274a). This tends to hold the garment against the body.

b. Pull the tape taut under the roll line (Fig. 274b). This tends to throw the lapel back into a soft roll.

Taut means that the tape is cut about ¼ to ½ inch shorter than the actual measurement.

4. The tape is swirled to fit any curved edges—neck, lapel, or style line at the lower edge of the garment (see page 285). It is pressed smooth on all straight edges.

5. Apply the front tape so the outer edge clears the seam line and rests on the outer fabric. The inner edge of the tape lies on the inter-

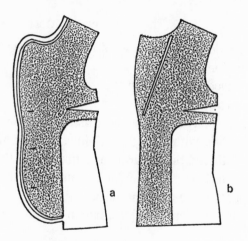

Fig. 274

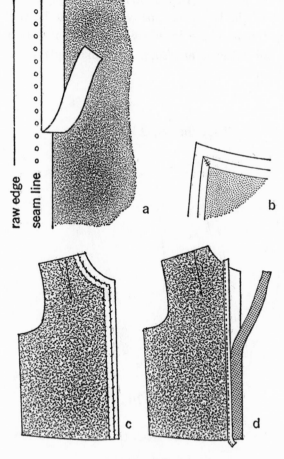

raw edge

seam line

Fig. 275

facing. The tape straddles the cut edge of the interfacing (Fig. 275a).
Pin or baste to position.

6. Apply the curved neck tape in the same way. Miter the tape at
the corners (Fig. 275b).

7. Using a single matching thread, hem the outside edge of the
tape to the outer fabric with tiny, "easy," invisible hemming stitches,
lifting only a single thread of the fabric at a time. Hem the inner edge
of the tape to the interfacing (Fig. 275c). Catch only the interfacing.
Do not come through to the garment fabric.

8. When joining garment sections, stitch *beside* the tape, not
through it.

In some cases, it is possible to stitch the inner edge of the tape to
the interfacing by machine (Fig. 275d) before applying the interfacing to the outer fabric. However, one would have to be very sure that
all needed adjustments (occasioned by the precise matching of seams
and darts of fashion fabric and supporting material) were made before the tape is set.

Tape the Lapel Roll Line

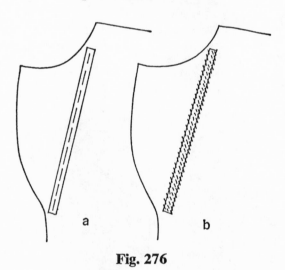

a   b

Fig. 276

1. Measure the lapel roll line from the neckline to the front seam
line.

2. Cut a length of preshrunk tape to this measurement minus ¼ to ½ inch. (Some schools of tailoring end the taping one-third of the way up from the front edge.)

3. Align the outer edge of the tape with the roll line of the lapel. This setting stays the roll line but does not interfere with the roll.

4. Starting at the neckline seam, pin or baste the tape flat for a distance of about 4 inches.

5. Pull the remainder of the tape taut. Pin or baste to position (Fig. 276a).

6. Pad-stitch* both edges of the tape and, after removing the pins or basting, down the middle of the tape (Fig. 276b).

*PAD STITCHING

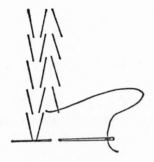

Fig. 277

Pad stitches permanently join layers of fabric so they perform as one piece (Fig. 277). They add firmness and some stiffness to the area. Apply them to any part of the garment that must maintain a permanent roll as in the collar, cuffs, and lapel.

The stitch is a small tailor basting except that the needle picks up only one thread from the underside (Fig. 277).

Generally, the stitches follow the grain of the fabric. They are about ¼ to ½ inch in length. Pad stitching is only done on an undersurface where the stitches will never show.

Tape to Stay the Hemline or Vent

1. Cut the necessary length of preshrunk tape.

2. Align one edge of the tape with the fold line of the vent (Fig.

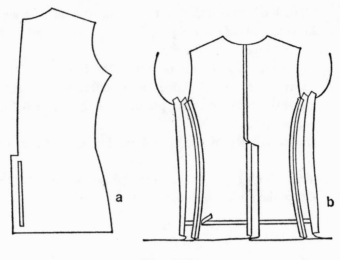

Fig. 278

278a) or with the hemline of the jacket (Fig. 278b). Pin or baste to position.

3. Fasten both edges of the tape to the garment with small, invisible slant hemming stitches.* Use a single length of matching thread. Lift only one thread of the outer fabric. Keep the stitches "easy."

*SLANT HEMMING STITCHES

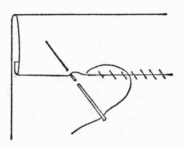

Fig. 279

Slant hemming stitches (Fig. 279) are a series of fast, strong, small diagonal stitches that go through two thicknesses of fabric—one is generally an edge. Both the needle and the stitch are slanted.

The Armhole May Be Stayed with Tape

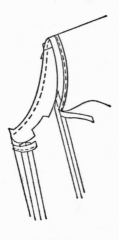

Fig. 280

1. Place a length of preshrunk tape around the armhole, starting and ending at the underarm with a slight overlap. Place one edge of the tape slightly over the seam line and the other edge in the seam allowance. Pin or baste to position.

2. Machine-stitch through the tape (Fig. 280).

Tape Where Necessary

Any seam, dart, or fold line that needs staying to avoid stretching may be taped. The tape may be stitched *into the seam* (if this does not produce too much thickness) or *beside the seam* (if it does).

Don't get carried away by the usefulness of tape. There are times when not to use it is the better part of wisdom.

Don't use tape in any place that needs to be eased or stretched, since the taping would obviously prevent this. For example: A collar neckline is stretched slightly to fit the neckline of the garment. Many collars are cut on the bias to facilitate this stretching. Taping would make this needed stretch impossible.

The Fold-back Method of Eliminating Hair Canvas
from Construction Seams

The fold-back method of eliminating hair canvas from the seams is used when one wishes to retain the hair canvas yet does not wish to involve it in a seam. A good example of this treatment is stitching the sleeve into an interfaced armhole.

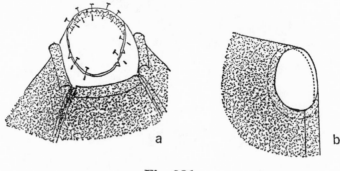

Fig. 281

1. Fold back the hair canvas from the armhole seam. Pin it out of the way (Fig. 281a).

2. Stitch the sleeve into the armhole in the usual way.

3. Bring the hair canvas back to position. Permanently baste it to the seam allowances just beyond the seam line (Fig. 281b).

4. Trim away the underarm seam allowance close to the stitching.

Having put together the basic shell of the garment, we are ready now to proceed with the all-important setting of the collar and the sleeves.

Chapter 18

Portrait Area — Set of Collar, Set of Sleeves

You might get away with a little less than perfection in other parts of the garment, but it's that *portrait area* of you—set of collar, set of sleeves—that people see head on. And judge your workmanship by.

TIPS FOR TAILORS—TAKE YOUR TIME

The real test of your tailoring is how you handle the classic tailored collar and lapels. It isn't that the techniques are so difficult, it's just that they take time: time to put in those hundreds of tiny hand stitches—all invisible, all important; time to test and shape and mold. You may go full speed ahead on other tailoring techniques, but the perfection of collar and lapels takes time. Even in this age of machines and mass production, the construction of collar and lapels is still largely done by hand, even in factories.

THE COLLAR AND LAPEL: A UNIT

The two collars traditionally associated with tailoring are the classic notched collar (Fig. 282a) and the shawl collar (Fig. 282c).

In the classic notched collar, part of the garment rolls back to form lapels. A separate collar is set on the neckline and lapels a little dis-

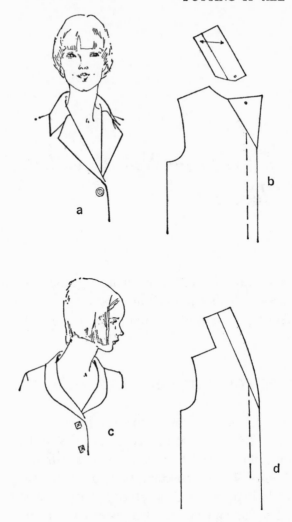

Fig. 282

tance in from the ends to form a notch (Fig. 282b). In the shawl collar, the entire collar is part of the garment front (Fig. 282d).

In the shawl collar, the seam that joins right and left collars is at the center back (Fig. 283a). No seaming is visible from the front.

In the classic notched collar, the seam line that joins collar to lapels is visible from the front (Fig. 283b). The collar may or may not have a center-back seam.

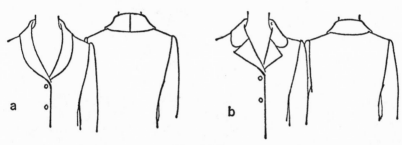

Fig. 283

Whether the collar is all in one piece or in two pieces and whether the joining seam is visible or invisible does not matter. The collar is thought of as a unit that extends from the center back to the break— the point at which the collar rolls back to form the lapel.

Cut-on and Try-on

Since the shawl collar is generally part of the front it must be cut when the front is cut. This leaves only one place where an adjustment can be made if needed—the center-back seam.

Presumably all gross changes have been taken care of in the trial muslin. Just in case further changes are needed in the fashion fabric, it is wise to cut-on (add) a seam allowance. It can always be trimmed away if not needed.

There is more opportunity for fitting in the classic notched collar. It is a separate collar; one can therefore test it in the interfacing material before cutting the collar in the fabric. When a shawl collar has a separate undercollar, it, too, can be treated like the notched collar.

HOW TO ADJUST THE CLASSIC NOTCHED-COLLAR PATTERN

After the jacket or coat has been carefully fitted at the shoulders, neck, and body seams, and after the garment has been joined at the construction seams and pressed, proceed as follows:

1. Place a line of guide basting at the neck seam line of the garment (Fig. 284a). This is placed just above the neckline tape.

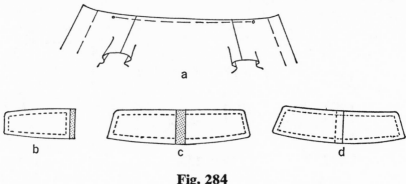

Fig. 284

2. Measure the length of the neck seam line from the center back to the point at which the collar joins the lapel.

3. Measure the neck seam line of the undercollar pattern from the center back to the point where the collar joins the lapel.

4. Compare the pattern measurement with the garment measurement. The undercollar pattern (half the total collar) should measure ¼ inch less in length than the garment neckline. (A whole collar measures ½ inch less in length than the garment neckline.) Stretching the collar to fit the jacket or coat neckline produces a better roll and a slightly deeper stand. When a collar neckline just fits the garment neckline, there is less stand.

5. Make any necessary adjustments to the collar pattern. Up to a seam allowance may be added or subtracted at the center back. If the pattern is cut with a center-back seam, this is easy enough. Add at the seam line (Fig. 284b). When the collar is cut in one piece, slash the pattern at the center back, spread the slashed sections, and insert the needed amount (Fig. 284c). To reduce the length of the one-piece collar, slash the center back and overlap the necessary amount (Fig. 284d).

Do not make too large an alteration in any one place. This distorts the shape of the style line. When more than a seam allowance adjustment is needed, slash and spread in several places, or slash and overlap in several places. This is necessary to preserve the over-all shape of the collar.

TEST THE UNDERCOLLAR INTERFACING

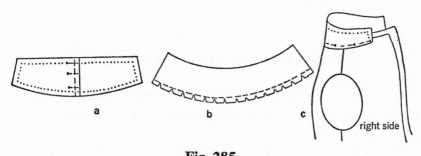

right side

Fig. 285

1. Cut the undercollar interfacing from the corrected undercollar pattern. Mark all seam lines with pencil or dressmaker's carbon.

2. When there is a center-back seam, overlap the seam lines of the interfacing and pin. Place the pins at right angles to the seam for easy fitting (Fig. 285a).

3. Clip the seam allowance at the neck edge in a sufficient number of places to provide the necessary spread for the fitting (Fig. 285b).

4. Overlap the collar interfacing on the garment, matching neck seam lines. Pin. Place the pins directly on the seam line (Fig. 285c).

NOTE: It is impossible to get a true fitting unless the collar is overlapped on the garment.

Match the center backs. On the classic notched collar, match each point on the lapel where the collar joins it. On the all-in-one shawl collar, clip the seam allowance at the corner where shoulder and collar meet. Stretch the collar neckline between these fixed points to fit the garment neckline.

5. Try on the garment. If you plan to use shoulder pads, slip them into position. Pin the center front closed from the top button down. Examine the collar for fit. Adjust as necessary.

HOW THE UNDERCOLLAR SHOULD FIT

The real burden of fine fit falls upon the undercollar. The upper collar is just so much decoration.

The collar should fit in length (at the neckline, the roll line, and the style line) and in depth (the stand and the fall). These two dimensions are so interrelated that to change one often means an automatic change in the other.

FITTING THE LENGTH OF THE COLLAR

The *neckline* of the collar should fit without straining or rippling. When a change is indicated, unpin the neckline seam and make the needed adjustment.

To Relieve Strain: Add length by using some of the back-seam allowance in a two-piece undercollar. Slash, spread, and insert additional interfacing in a one-piece undercollar.

To Reduce Rippling: Reduce the length of the undercollar by overlapping more seam allowance at the center back of a two-piece undercollar. Or, create a back seam in a one-piece undercollar by slashing the interfacing and overlapping.

The roll line should fit without any strain. Nor should it stand away from the neck unless it is designed that way. Adjust the length of the collar interfacing at the roll line by using the center-back-seam allowance (when there is one) to add or subtract. When there is no center-back seam, create one.

The style line should lie smoothly around the shoulders without pulling, rippling, or poking out at the center back. Add or subtract to the length of the interfacing style line at an existing or a created back seam.

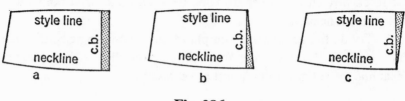

Fig. 286

Adjustments may be balanced: that is, the same amount at the neckline as at the style line (Fig. 286a). Or they may be made in one place only: that is, change at the neckline but not at the style line

(Fig. 286b). Or retain the neckline measurement but change the style line (Fig. 286c).

FITTING THE DEPTH OF THE COLLAR

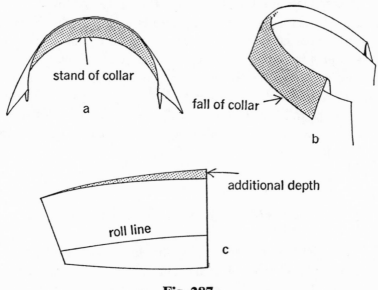

stand of collar

a

fall of collar

b

additional depth

roll line

c

Fig. 287

The stand of the collar is the amount of the rise from the neckline to the roll line (Fig. 287a). It should be neither too high nor too low for your neck. When a change is indicated, unpin the neckline seam.

If the stand is too high, lower it by adding length to the collar neckline. If the stand is too low, raise it by shortening the length of the collar neckline. Adjustments are made at the center back.

The fall of the collar is the depth of the collar from the roll line to the style line (Fig. 287b). It should completely cover the neckline seam plus at least ½ inch. When the stand of the collar fits well around the neck yet discloses the neckline seam, add depth at the style line (Fig. 287c).

MOMENT OF DECISION

This is your big chance to get a collar that really fits your neck.

Stand before a mirror. Decide whether the neckline is too tight, too loose, or just right. Decide whether the stand of the collar looks and feels comfortable. Would it be improved if it were made higher or lower? Examine the fall of the collar. Does it safely cover the neckline seam? Does the style line ease comfortably around the shoulders?

When you are satisfied with the fit of the undercollar, mark the roll line with pins from the center back to the break of the collar at the front closing. Work on one side—the one easiest for you to reach. Remove the garment. Substitute a chalk or pencil marking for the pins along the roll line. Unpin the collar. Transfer the roll-line marking to the other half of the collar and the other lapel. This will make both sides identical.

PREPARE THE COLLAR

1. Using the adjusted undercollar interfacing as a guide, trace the alterations on the undercollar and upper collar patterns. Remember to add the roll ease to all outside edges of the upper collar.

2. Cut out both upper collar and undercollar in fabric.

3. Overlap and stitch the center-back seam of the interfacing. Trim the seam allowances close to the stitching line.

4. Stitch the fabric undercollar at the center-back seam. Press the seam allowances open. Trim when necessary.

COLLAR CONTOUR

In a jacket or skirt, it is the darts and shaping seams that produce the garment contour. In a collar, it is those hundreds of tiny hand stitches and the blocking that give it shape.

From the moment the collar interfacing is positioned on the undercollar, one must stop thinking of the two as flat lengths of cloth. Think of them in the round. After all, they are destined to fit *around* the neck.

Pad-stitch for Shape

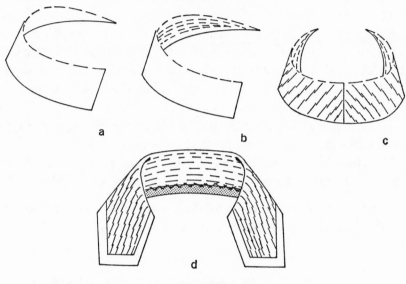

Fig. 288

1. Place the collar interfacing over the wrong side of the under-collar. Pin to position.

2. Using matching thread, make a row of uneven horizontal basting stitches along the roll line. Make the stitches ¼ inch in length on the interfacing. Catch only a thread or two of the undercollar fabric.

3. When the entire row of stitching along the roll line is completed, tug the thread slightly until the collar begins to curve into a neck shape (Fig. 288a).

4. Fill the stand with parallel rows of similar uneven horizontal basting to the *neck seam line*. Tug the thread slightly at the end of each row (Fig. 288b).

5. Hold the collar over the hand in a neck shape while pad-stitching. Starting at the center back and following the grain of the interfacing, pad-stitch the fall of the collar *from the roll line to the seam line* (Fig. 288c).

The smaller the stitches and the closer the rows, the stiffer the pad-stitched area becomes. Many sewers like to pad-stitch the stand heavily (¼-inch stitches, rows ¼ inch apart) and to pad-stitch the fall lightly (⅜- to ½-inch stitches, rows ⅜ to ½ inch apart). To ensure that the points of the collar and lapel lie flat against the body, the pad stitches may be made even smaller and the rows even closer together as they near the point.

NOTE: It is the way the collar is held while pad-stitching (in a curve) and the direction of the stitching that produce the collar contour. The horizontal stitching of the stand determines the neck shape; the bias pad stitching of the fall guarantees the easing around the shoulders.

6. Trim away all the seam allowances of the interfacing. In the standard method of collar application, continue as follows.

7. Trim, clip, and turn up the neck-edge seam allowance of the undercollar over the interfacing. Catch-stitch in place (Fig. 288d).

From this point on, never store the collar flat. Drape it around the tailor's ham, a rolled-up towel, or the neck of a dress form.

COMPLETE THE COLLAR: CHOICE OF METHODS

The upper collar is applied to the undercollar in one of several ways.

METHOD I—*the Most Frequently Used Method in Women's Tailoring*

1. Machine-stitch the upper collar to the interfaced undercollar around all but the finished neck edge. That must be left open (Fig. 289a). Use all the tailoring techniques previously learned for easing, stitching, trimming, grading, and pressing.

2. Decide whether to topstitch (and when) or understitch the enclosed seam.

In general, curved style lines are easier to stitch by machine than are those that call for sharp corners. Often when dealing with men's-wear worsteds or heavy coatings, turning corners while allowing enough fullness for the roll ease can present a stitching problem. With

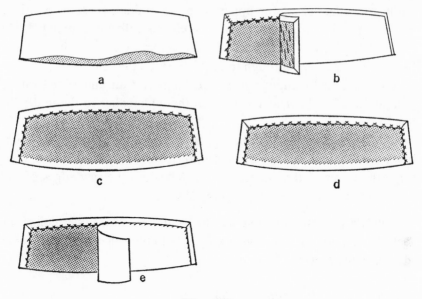

Fig. 289

such fabrics, it is wiser to attach the upper collar successfully by hand than to botch the collar with imperfect machine stitching.

METHOD II—*a Hand-stitch Method*

1. Trim all the undercollar seam allowances to ⅜ to ½ inch.

2. Turn *all* the undercollar seam allowances over the interfacing and catch-stitch to position, clipping as necessary.

3. Miter the seam allowances of the undercollar at the corners.

4. Turn under and baste the seam allowances of the upper collar, allowing enough for the roll ease.

5. Miter the corners of the seam allowances of the upper collar.

6. Pin the undercollar to position over the upper collar. Slip-stitch all edges but the neck edge (Fig. 289b).

METHOD III—*an Excellent Method for Heavy or Pile Fabrics*

1. Trim all undercollar seam allowances—fabric as well as interfacing.

2. Pin the trimmed interfaced undercollar to the upper collar, placing its raw edges along the upper collar seam lines. Baste to position, the basting stitches to be removed when the collar is completed. Or permanently catch-stitch lightly to the upper collar, making certain that no stitches come through to the right side (Fig. 289c).

If you are lucky enough to be working with an underlined rather than an interfaced collar, catch-stitch the undercollar to the underlining.

3. Miter the corners of the upper collar seam allowances. Trim, press the seam allowances open, and turn them to the right side, covering the edges of the undercollar. Catch-stitch the raw edges of the upper collar to the undercollar (Fig. 289d).

This is a particularly good way to handle a velvet upper collar. In fact, this method produces such a neat, flat collar that it is a desirable one for many fabrics.

METHOD IV—*the Flattest Collar of All*

1. Underline or interface the *upper collar* but do not pad-stitch.

2. Miter the seam allowances at the corners of the upper collar. Trim, press open, and turn to the right side.

3. Catch-stitch all raw edges to the underlining or interfacing.

4. Cut an undercollar of felt or melton cloth. Trim away ⅜ inch of all seam allowances, leaving ¼ inch for an overlap.

5. Place the undercollar against the seam allowance of the upper collar. Attach with slant hemming stitches (Fig. 289e).

By whichever method you choose to complete the collar, press all outside edges as flat as possible. Use the pressing technique determined best for the fabric.

Steam and shape the completed collar over an appropriate press pad.

PREPARE THE LAPEL

Pad-stitch the Lapel

Holding the lapel over the hand in the position in which it will be worn, pad-stitch from the roll line to the outer edge or to the tape

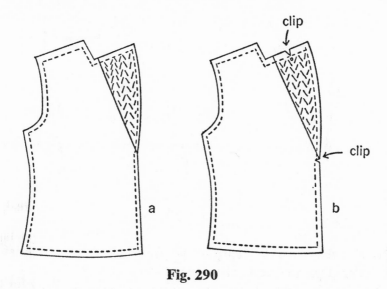

Fig. 290

when used (Fig. 290a). The stitches follow the grain of the interfacing. The size of the stitches and the space between the rows follow the same rule as for the collar.

ATTACH THE FACING TO THE GARMENT

By Machine Stitching

Stitch the facing to the front edge of the garment from the hem to the point at which the collar joins the lapel. Clip the seam allowance at this point and at the break of the collar (Fig. 290b). The former clip is necessary for the collar setting; the latter, for the change of direction at the turnback of the lapel.

Use all the tailoring techniques previously described for easing, trimming, grading, pressing, and the handling of the enclosed seams.

Or by Hand Stitching

As with the collar, it is advisable in some fabrics to attach the lapel facing by hand rather than by machine.

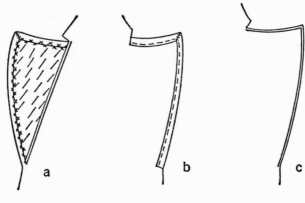

Fig. 291

1. Machine-stitch the facing to the garment as far as the break of the collar. Treat the seam as an encased seam.

2. Trim, clip, and fold the *garment* seam allowances over the lapel interfacing. Miter the corners. Fasten with catch stitching (Fig. 291a).

3. Turn under the seam allowances of the *facing,* allowing for the roll ease. Miter the corners. Baste to position (Fig. 291b).

4. Position the facing over the lapel and fasten with slip stitches (Fig. 291c).

ATTACH THE COLLAR TO THE GARMENT

It's easier, quicker, more accurate, flatter, neater to join the collar to the garment with hand stitching.

Work from the Right Side

1. Overlap the finished edge of the undercollar on the seam line of the garment neck edge. The garment seam allowance will slip into the opening of the collar.

2. Pin at each point where the collar joins the lapel. Pin the center back. Stretch the collar neckline to fit the garment neckline. Do not include the front facing or the upper collar in either the pinning or the stitching.

3. Make sure that both ends of the collar are the same size. Make sure that both lapels are the same size.

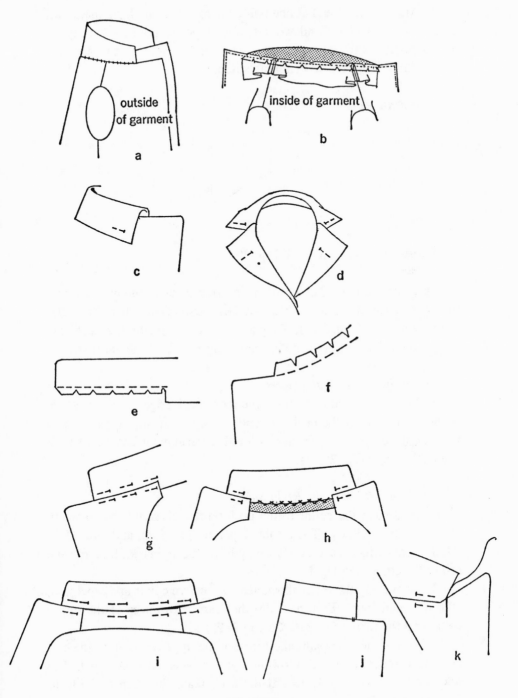

outside of garment

inside of garment

a

b

c

d

e

f

g

h

i

j

k

Fig. 292

4. Anchor the thread at one point where collar and lapel meet with over-and-over stitches and work to the opposite point, securing the thread in the same manner. Attach the undercollar to the garment (Fig. 292a) with vertical hemming stitches.*

*VERTICAL HEMMING STITCH

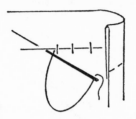

Fig. 293

Use a single thread. The needle is inserted through the garment and the collar edge at an angle. The stitches are vertical—at right angles to the seam line (Fig. 293). They are tiny, close together, and strong. They are meant to hold the collar intact for the life of the garment.

Turn to the Inside of the Garment

5. Trim, clip, and turn down the loose neck-edge seam allowance of the garment over the neckline tape or the interfacing. Press it open with the tip of the iron. Fasten with either permanent basting or with catch stitching (Fig. 292b).

Once More, Back to the Right Side

6. Fold back the collar to the position it will assume when worn, and pin (Fig. 292c). Turn each lapel to position, and pin (Fig. 292d). This will ensure enough length on the upper surface for the roll of the collar and lapel.

7. Trim away the seam allowance bulk where collar and lapel join, with diagonal snips. Trim and clip the seam allowances of the upper collar and the facing (Figs. 292e and 292f).

8. Turn under the seam allowance of the upper collar into the collar. Turn under the seam allowance of the lapel into the lapel. The folds of collar and lapel meet at the neck seam line. Pin or baste to position (Fig. 292g).

When There Is No Back-neck Facing: Clip the collar seam allowance at the shoulder (the end of the front facing). Bring it down over the neckline tape or the interfacing from one shoulder to the other, clipping as necessary to make it lie flat. Fasten with either permanent basting or with catch stitching (Fig. 292h). The lining will cover this.

When There Is a Back-neck facing: Attach it to the front facing at the shoulder seams, making any needed adjustments. Press the seam allowances open. Trim, clip, and turn under the entire collar seam allowances into the collar and the entire front-and-back-facing seam allowances into the facing. Pin to position (Fig. 292i).

9. Remove the pins that are holding the collar and lapels in their rolled-back positions.

10. Using matching thread, secure the end with several strong over-and-over stitches on the underside of the collar where it joins the lapel (Fig. 292j). Bring the needle through to the right side at the seam line between the folds of the collar and facing (Fig. 292k).

11. Slip-stitch the collar to the facing through the folds. Don't draw up the stitches too tightly. When the stitching is completed, secure the end of the thread with several strong over-and-over stitches on the underside.

Fig. 294

12. To make sure that the upper collar and facing will always stay in place, anchor them by either of the two following methods:

(a) Catch some of the undercollar seam allowance while slip-stitching the upper collar to the facing.

(b) Gently lift the joined upper collar and facing, separating them from the undercollar and garment. Fasten the seam allowances of the former to the seam allowances of the latter with permanent basting (Fig. 294).

13. Remove all pins and basting threads. Press carefully.

SEW EASY

The foregoing standard method of constructing and applying the regulation tailored collar is so easy and produces such spectacular results that you will probably never go back to the strictly machine-stitching methods suggested in most pattern directions. What's more you'll soon discover its possibilities for other types of collars as well.

THE SHAWL COLLAR

While the upper layer of a shawl collar is always cut all in one with the front facing, the undercollar is often a separate section. The cut and amount of undercollar is determined by the designer.

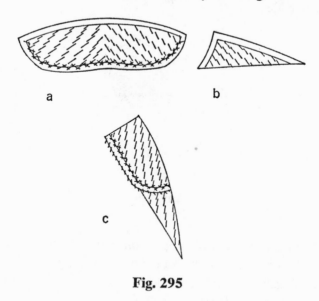

a   b

c

Fig. 295

1. Test and adjust the undercollar interfacing in the same way as for the regulation tailored collar.

2. Transfer any changes to the under and upper collars.

3. Cut the under and upper collars from the adjusted patterns.

4. Apply the undercollar interfacing to the undercollar fabric and pad-stitch to the seam lines, following the grain.

5. Trim away all interfacing seam allowances.

6. Trim, clip, and turn the fabric seam allowance over the interfacing at the neck and any other seam that joins the front facing (Fig. 295a).

7. Pad-stitch the lapel (Fig. 295b).

8. Attach the undercollar to the garment with vertical hemming stitches in the same way as for the regulation tailored collar (Fig. 295c).

9. Machine-stitch the upper collar at the center-back seam. Press the seam allowances open.

10. Stitch the front-facing-upper-collar to the garment. Use all the tailoring techniques previously described for stitching, trimming, clipping, grading, pressing, and handling of encased seams.

THE STANDING COLLAR

While the standing collar is not, strictly speaking, a tailored collar, it appears so frequently in otherwise tailored garments that we must include it in our discussion.

There are several ways to make a standing collar really stand.

The Iron-on Method

1. Cut the iron-on material from the undercollar pattern, minus the seam allowances.

2. Place the interfacing in position on the wrong side of the undercollar. Press it on (Fig. 296a).

The Stiff-interfacing Method

1. Cut a length of stiff interfacing material from the undercollar pattern, minus seam allowances.

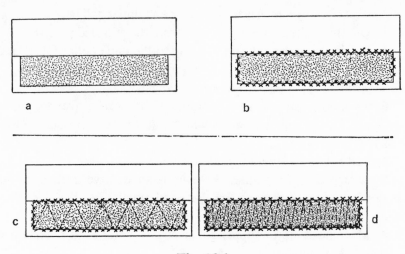

Fig. 296

2. Place the interfacing in position on the wrong side of the under-collar. Lightly catch-stitch all edges (Fig. 296b).

The Stiffened-interfacing Method

1. Cut a length of interfacing material, either single or double thickness, from the undercollar pattern, minus seam allowances.

2. Make diagonal rows of machine stitching until the interfacing is the desired degree of stiffness (Fig. 296c). The smaller the stitches and the more closely spaced the rows of stitching, the stiffer the interfacing will be (Fig. 296d).

3. Place the interfacing in position on the wrong side of the under-collar. Catch-stitch all edges.

4. Join the collar, however stiffened, to the facing. Attach the finished collar to the garment by machine stitching. (Reserve the hand stitching for those places where the seam will not be visible in wearing.)

THE SETTING AND STITCHING OF SLEEVES

Among the last important operations in the construction of a garment is the setting and stitching of the sleeves. Well-set sleeves, like the well-set collar, are a hallmark of fine tailoring.

SLEEVE CAP AND ARMHOLE—
DESIGNED FOR EACH OTHER

Most tailored sleeves are cut generously enough to fit all but problem arms. Unless you have a marked need for adjustment, use the sleeve of the pattern.

The sleeve cap in the pattern is meant to fit not just any armhole but THE armhole of the unaltered pattern. It may be that in the fitting of the shoulder and underarm seams the shape and size of the original armhole have been changed. If that should be so, it is necessary to re-establish the armhole stitching line before the sleeve can be set.

The easiest way to do this is to use the original pattern as a guide. But, before you can do that, it is necessary to establish the point on your shoulder where the sleeve is to be set. It's ideal, of course, to have someone determine this for you, but you can do it yourself if you must.

1. Try on the garment with the shoulder pads in place. Pin the garment closed, with center fronts matching.

2. Slip the sleeve in place to locate its position on the shoulder.

3. Using a safety pin, mark the position of the sleeve cap on the shoulder seam. This gives you a *shoulder point* for the setting.

4. Remove the garment.

RECUT THE ARMHOLE

1. Should it be necessary, pin together as many sections of the pattern as will provide a complete front armhole and a complete back armhole.

2. Pin the shoulder seam of the pattern front on the shoulder seam of the garment front. Set the armhole seam of the pattern at the newly established shoulder point.

3. Pin the side seam of the pattern on the side seam of the garment. Let the underarm of the pattern fall as much below the armhole of the

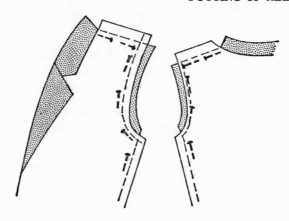

Fig. 297

garment as is necessary for the pattern to lie flat and still touch the side seam.

4. Repeat the procedure for the back. The back shoulder seam must match the front shoulder seam. The back side seam must match the front side seam.

The shaded areas in the illustration (Fig. 297) represent an armhole that needs changing. The broken lines represent the pattern placed in position to make the necessary changes.

5. Using the pattern in its new position as a guide, cut out the armhole.

Another way to correct the armhole is to use the sleeve itself as a pattern. See the directions below (Fig. 300).

The shoulder marking on the sleeve cap should be at the crest of the sleeve cap curve. For instance, if, in fitting, the shoulder seam has been brought forward, then the crest of the cap curve and the shoulder marking should be brought forward a corresponding amount. Redraw the sleeve cap, making the needed adjustment.

STAY THE ARMHOLE

Whether you are working with the original armhole or the newly cut-out one, stay it with tape or with chain stitching.*

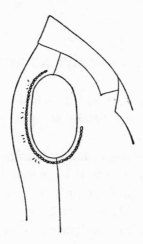

Fig. 298

To Tape: See Fig. 280.

To Chain-stitch (Fig. 298): Start at the front notch and stitch around the underarm to a point 1 inch below the back shoulder. Work in the seam allowance close to the seam line.

*TO MAKE THE CHAIN STITCH

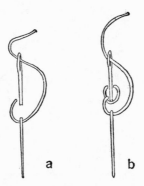

a   b

Fig. 299

Take a ¼-inch stitch. Loop the thread under the needle. Draw it up (Fig. 299a). Make successive links (Fig. 299b), using the thumb to hold the thread in place. Keep the stitches even in tension and in size.

SLEEVE SETTING: START AT THE SHOULDER

In setting the sleeve, start at the shoulder and work down! This may be the reverse of the generally accepted procedure but it works like magic.

When you start the setting at the underarm and work your way up the sleeve cap, you may end up with a handful of fabric at the shoulder that has no place to go except into a leg-of-mutton puff. Whereas, if you start at the sleeve cap and work down, such slight adjustments as still need to be made can be done at the underarm, where there is some room for change.

1. Stitch and press the sleeve. Gather across the sleeve cap and block it so it cups over your hooked fingers (Fig. 300a).

2. With right sides together, insert the sleeve into the armhole.

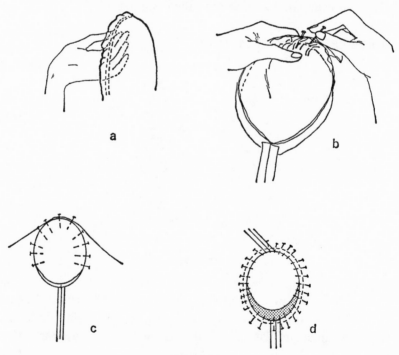

Fig. 300

Work on the wrong side with the sleeve up so you can distribute the fullness evenly across the cap. Hold the sleeve in the outside curve it will assume when worn.

3. Start the setting at the shoulder. Match the shoulder seam of the bodice with the shoulder marking of the sleeve cap. Place a pin at right angles to the seam line (Fig. 300b).

4. Working down on each side, distribute the fullness evenly across the cap. Place the pins at right angles to the seam line (Fig. 300c).

5. Pin the underarm into the armhole, matching the underarm seams (or markings) of both sleeve and garment.

In hard-to-ease fabrics (rigid, firmly woven, or stiff) distribute the fullness so the cap drops slightly below the underarm of the garment. The drop may be as much as a seam allowance but no more (Fig. 300d).

6. Using the underarm of the sleeve as a pattern, cut away the garment to match the sleeve.

7. Baste the sleeve into the armhole for the fitting.

In setting the sleeve by this method, there is often the great temptation to eliminate a good deal of the ease at the cap. Don't! Ease is a must—as necessary in a sleeve as it is in a bodice or a skirt, and for the same reasons: comfort and ease of movement. At least 1½ inches of ease (a bit more in most tailored garments) are absolutely necessary to accommodate the curve of the shoulder and upper arm. Since this part of the sleeve cap is on a near-bias angle, it should not be too difficult to ease this amount into the armhole.

CHECK THE SLEEVE FITTING

1. Try on the garment. Facing the mirror, examine the position of the sleeve on the shoulder, across the chest, across the back. Note any needed changes.

2. Turn so that you can see the entire sleeve setting. Check the cap of the sleeve for just-right fullness. Check the position of the grain. The vertical grain should be at right angles to the floor. The horizontal grain should be parallel to the floor. All horizontal lines, checks,

plaids, stripes, and so on, should match those of the body of the garment. Note any adjustments that need to be made.

3. Remove the garment. Make any necessary changes. Try it on
again. Examine once more. You may have to repeat this procedure
until you are satisfied with the fitting.

With a Little Help from a Friend

When it comes to the following sleeve setting, a little help from a
friend can be a big help, since the sleeve is set on you from the right
side. Or you yourself can set the sleeve over a dress form, if you have
one.

1. Turn under the seam allowance of the gathered cap.

2. Overlap it on the armhole, distributing the fullness. Pin to position.

3. Slip-baste the cap to the bodice.

STITCH THE SLEEVE INTO THE ARMHOLE

In stitching the sleeve into the armhole, you may, if you wish, include the hair canvas in the seam (the only place in the garment
where one would do so). In this instance, the interfacing, pressed into
the sleeve cap, helps prop it up. In heavy or difficult-to-ease fabrics
(like some men's-wear) it is easier to use the fold-back method for
hair canvas described on page 372.

Sure Sewers: Work with the sleeve side up so you can continue to
control the ease. Start the stitching at one notch (or where a notch
would be if there were one) and return to the starting point, *but do
not stop.* Continue the stitching until you get to the opposite notch
position (Fig. 301a). This reinforces the underarm, an area that gets
much wear and tear.

Unsure Sewers: Start at the underarm seam and stitch until you return to the starting point. Examine the stitching line from the garment
side. This time, working with the garment side up (so you can see
what, if anything, needs correction) make a second row of stitching

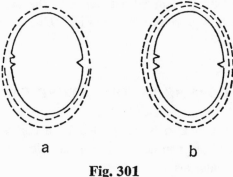

Fig. 301

very close to the first, correcting as necessary (Fig. 301b). This method ensures stitching perfection as well as underarm reinforcement.

Clip and Cut

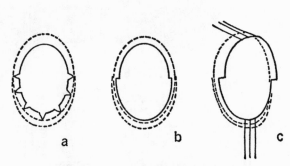

Fig. 302

The sleeve is meant to fit at the *armhole seam* and not at the cut edge, which is shorter. So clip the seam allowances at the notches almost to the stitching. Clip the underarm seam allowances every ½ inch (Fig. 302a). If you skip the clipping, your sleeve will be too tight on the underarm.

Since you have two rows of stitching for strength on the underarm, you can safely trim the seam allowances close to the underarm seam (Fig. 302b).

Press the remaining seam allowances into the cap of the sleeve, where they serve as a prop for the cap (Fig. 302c).

PROPPING UP THE SLEEVE CAP

The sleeve cap can also be supported by a *cap underlining* or a *sleeve head* instead of or in addition to a shoulder pad. See page 201 for patterns and materials.

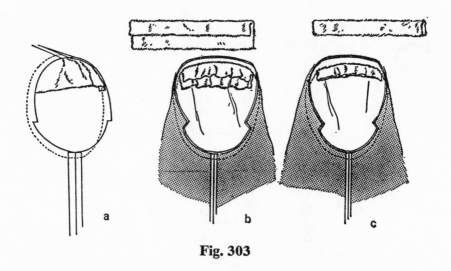

Fig. 303

How to Insert the Cap Underlining

Place the cap underlining of lamb's-wool padding in position and fasten with tiny hand stitches to the armhole seam (Fig. 303a).

How to Attach the Sleeve Head

1. Place the sleeve head into the sleeve cap with one folded edge along the armhole seam—half to the front, half to the back (Figs. 303b and 303c).

2. Fasten with slip stitches to the armhole seam.

HOW TO SET AND STITCH THE SHOULDER PADS IN PLACE

While shoulder pads are always fitted from the outside, they may be fastened to position from either the outside or the inside.

A Set-in Sleeve Shoulder Pad

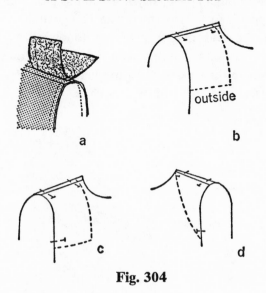

Fig. 304

1. Turn the garment to the inside.

From the inside:

2. Place the pad so that the shoulder line of the pad matches the shoulder seam of the garment and the edge of the pad extends about ½ inch into the sleeve cap (Fig. 304a). This is the positioning of the squared-front shoulder pad. When any other type of commercial pad is used, one third of the pad goes into the front armhole, two thirds go toward the back. Remember that the squared part of the pad is the front.

From the outside:

3. "Pinch" the pad, holding it firmly in place. Reverse the garment to its normal wearing position. Slip the shoulder pad under the neck facing.

4. Pin the pad securely at the shoulder and at the neck (Fig. 304b).

5. Slip your hand under the pad. Smooth the material down from the shoulder. Locate the point at which the tip of the shoulder pad meets the front-armhole seam. Pin (Fig. 304c). Do the same for the back (Fig. 304d). Don't force this. Let the tips of the pad go where they want to go even if this means that they go off the armhole seam somewhat. Sometimes the shape of the garment or the shape of your shoulders makes this happen. If you force the positioning of the pad tips on the armhole seam, you will create a bulge in the shoulder area.

6. Anchor the pad in either of the following ways. For both methods, fasten the end of a matching single thread on the underside at the point where the shoulder pad meets the armhole seam at either the front or back. Use over-and-over stitches.

METHOD I

Fig. 305

Bring the needle up to the right side directly into the armhole seam. Working from the right side, fasten the shoulder pad to the garment along the armhole seam with stab stitches.*

Stab Stitch: To make a stab stitch (Fig. 305), take a tiny stitch on the surface directly into the armhole seam straight through the garment and the shoulder pad. Bring the needle up through all the thicknesses into the armhole seam for the next stitch, about ½ inch away. Do only one stitch at a time. Repeat until you reach the other end of the shoulder pad. Keep the stitches relaxed—not tight. Fasten on the underside with over-and-over stitches.

METHOD II

Working on the underside, sew the pads to the seam allowances close to the armhole seam with permanent basting.

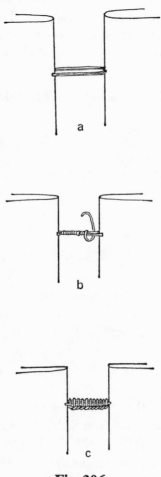

Fig. 306

FOR BOTH METHODS

7. Fasten all loose, unattached points of the shoulder pad at front, back, and neck to the interfacing with swing tacks.*

*A *swing tack* is made of several long, loose stitches that link together any two separate parts of a garment.

Take a tiny stitch on one part, then another directly opposite on the part to be joined. Pull up the thread to the desired length. Repeat, making two to three stitches between the layers (Fig. 306a). Fasten the thread.

When a swing tack is in a hidden position (as in this case), this is sufficient. When a swing tack is in an exposed position, it is protected, strengthened, and beautified by wrapping thread around it (Fig. 306b) or by working blanket stitches over it (Fig. 306c), whereupon it is called a French tack.

The Dropped-shoulder, Kimono, or Raglan-sleeved Shoulder Pad

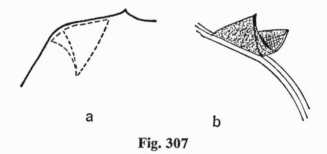

a   b

Fig. 307

In these styles, there is no convenient armhole seam to guide the setting. You will have to try on the garment and slip one shoulder pad into position, cupping the shoulder (Fig. 307a).

1. Pin the pad in place from the outside. Remove the garment. Measure carefully the distance from the neck to the shoulder-point setting.

2. On the inside, set the second shoulder pad in exactly the same position on the other shoulder. The shoulders must balance.

3. Slip the neck end of the shoulder pad under the neck facing.

4. Using a single matching thread, fasten the shoulder pad securely to the shoulder seam with stab stitches (Fig. 307b.)

5. Fasten the tips of the shoulder pads in place with swing tacks, or catch-stitch the entire front and back edges of the pad to the front and back interfacings.

ANOTHER LOOK

Before we get on with the finishing details (yes, we are almost up to that), better have another look at that jacket or coat.

Try on the garment and pin it closed.

Examine it carefully for anything else that could possibly be done to refine or perfect the fit. A smidgen too much fabric here? A mite more ease needed there? This is your last chance to take it in or let it out before turning up the hem and inserting the lining. It's so much easier to make any needed changes now. It's a chore after they have been put in.

Chapter 19

Hemming Ways

When you get to the hems, the end is surely in sight. In fact, if you run true to form, you are probably planning your next project.

Coat hems are generally 2½ inches to 3 inches, jacket hems are 1½ inches to 2 inches, jacket sleeves have 1½-inch hems, coat sleeves have 2-inch hems. Straight skirt hems in tailored garments are generally 2 inches in depth. Flared hems on any of these are less.

REMOVE THE FULLNESS AT THE HEM EDGE

In anything other than a straight hem, the depth of the hem should be no more than can be made to lie flat against the inside of the garment. See page 284 for easing the fullness at the upper edge of a hem.

SOMETIMES FULLNESS IS TAKEN OUT AT EACH SEAM

In Gored or Slightly Flared Designs

1. Turn the hem to the outside of the garment.

2. Pin each seam close to and matching each corresponding seam (Fig. 308a).

3. Stitch. Trim away excess material. Notch the seam allowances at the fold line to prevent bulk when the hem is folded up to its cor-

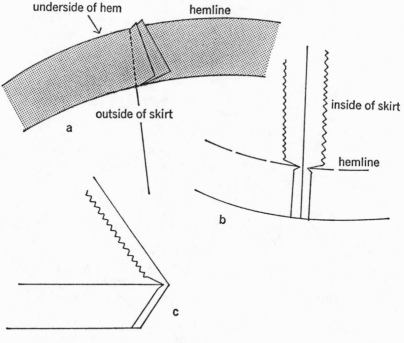

Fig. 308

rect position (Fig. 308b). Grade the seam allowances to the fold line (Fig. 308b). Press open.

4. Note that the shape of the hem is the reverse of the shape of the garment (Fig. 308c).

5. Turn the fitted hem to the underside and finish as one would any other hem.

In Very Flared, Circular Hems or Shaped Hems

Turn up a narrow hem and topstitch (Fig. 309a).

OR

Apply a facing cut in the same shape and on the same grain as the hem edge of the garment (the cut-away hem of the vest and the rounded hem of the jacket in Fig. 309b).

Fig. 309

THE HANG OF THE HEM

To avoid "dippy" hems, let the fabric settle before setting the hem. Overnight will do for most fabrics and styles. Bias-cut, knit, flared, or circular garments take longer—often as much as a week. It's a good idea to hang up the garment when you have finished working on it. Use a tissue-paper-padded hanger or a dress form. Then, by the time you are ready to work on the hem, the fabric will have settled sufficiently.

When you have determined the fold line of the hem, mark it with basting thread or tailor's chalk *on the inside.* For the next operation, we will be working on the hem on the wrong side of the fabric.

Measure and mark the depth of the hem. Using a gauge or a ruler, measure an even distance from the fold line. Mark with chalk, pencil, or pins, depending on the color and texture of the fabric. Trim the excess material.

THE INTERFACED HEM

For a Crisp Edge

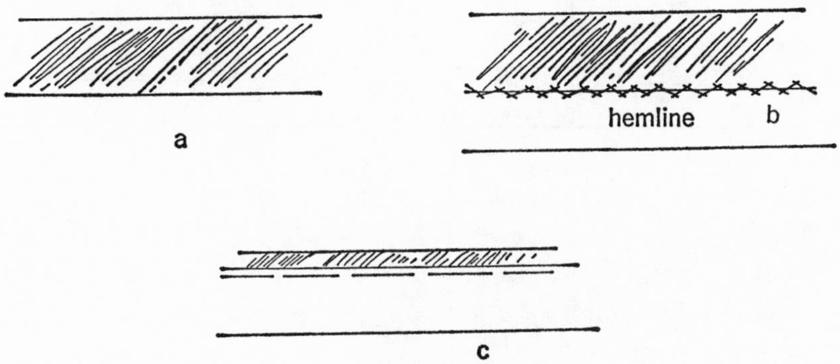

hemline   b

a

c

Fig. 310

1. Cut a bias strip of interfacing the width of the hem plus ½ inch, and as long as needed plus two seam allowances.

2. Overlap the straight-grain ends of the bias strip, stitch, and trim the seam allowances close to the stitching (Fig. 310a).

3. Place the interfacing against the garment with the lower edge along the fold line of the hem. Lightly catch-stitch the lower edge to position (Fig. 310b).

4. Turn up the hem. Fasten the upper edge of it to the interfacing with permanent basting or catch stitching (Fig. 310c).

5. Pin the interfaced hem to the garment at all seams, centers, and suitable intervals between. Place the pins at right angles to the fold. Distribute any fullness evenly between the pins (see Fig. 311c in following section). As far as possible, match the grain of the hem and the grain of the garment fabric. (It often helps to baste the hem close to the fold before pinning.)

6. Fasten the upper edge of the interfacing to the garment in a tailor's hem. See page 411.

For a Soft Edge

1. Cut a bias strip of interfacing the width of the hem plus 1 inch and as long as needed plus two seam allowances.

2. Overlap the straight-grain ends of the bias strip. Stitch. Trim the seam allowances close to the stitching.

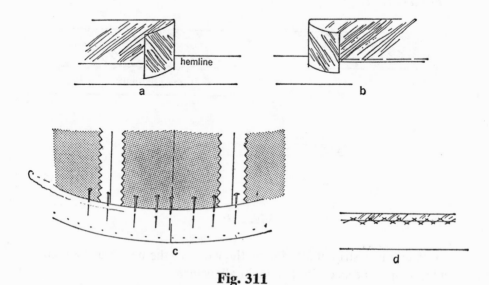

Fig. 311

3. Place the interfacing against the garment with the lower edge ½ inch beyond the fold line into the hem (Fig. 311a).

4. Permanently baste the interfacing strip to the hem slightly in from the fold line toward the hem (Fig. 311b). Pick up only one thread of the hem fabric in loose stitches.

5. Turn up the hem. Pin it to the garment as directed for a crisp edge, step 5 (Fig. 311c).

6. Fasten the hem edge to the interfacing with permanent basting or catch stitching (Fig. 311d).

7. Fasten the upper edge of the interfacing to the garment in a tailor's hem.

Note that in both of the above hems ½ inch of the interfacing extends above the hem in order to grade the thicknesses. It is the method used when a lining is brought down over the hem edge. When there is no lining, the grading is reversed: make the interfacing ½ inch narrower than the hem depth.

THE TAILOR'S HEM

THE hem for tailoring is naturally, a tailor's hem. It is the neatest, flattest, most invisible way of attaching a hem. It is a method that, with variations, can see you through the miles and miles of hems you will be doing in a lifetime.

The true tailor's hem has no edge finish—simply the cut edge of non-ravelly material. Used this way, it is reserved for garments to be lined.

When the tailor's hem is to be exposed—as in an unlined garment—its raw edge must be protected in some way. Any ridgeless finish is good: pinking, a line of machine stitching, overcasting—either by machine or by hand—or binding.

What distinguishes this hem from all others is its bulk-free edge finish and the method of attachment to the garment. There are no telltale marks on the right side to even hint that a hem has been stitched in place. Because of the position of the hem and the garment for hand stitching there is a sufficient length of thread between them to prevent the quilted look so many hems suffer from.

Here is the way it is done.

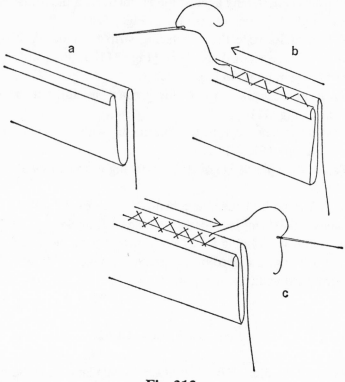

Fig. 312

1. Fold back the edge of the hem toward the hemline to a depth of about ⅛ to ¼ inch. Fold back the garment on itself. This places the folds of hem and garment opposite to each other (Fig. 312a).

2. Using a single strand of matching thread, lift one thread of the garment, then one of the hem, alternating between the two. Use either a *running-hemming stitch* (Fig. 312b) or a *catch stitch* (Fig. 312c).

The *running-hemming stitch* is a series of small, loose basting stitches running from right to left.

The *catch stitch* is a series of small, loose backstitches worked from left to right, though the needle is inserted from right to left.

You'll be happy to learn that it's not only cricket but it's actually preferable to put up a hem with the *least number of stitches* that will do so securely. Since the stitches are never visible (even on the underside), you do not need to perform as if you were in an embroidery contest.

THE HEM IN AN UNDERLINED GARMENT

The problem of weighting the hem is somewhat different in the underlined garment. Use the underlining itself as a reinforcement or add a strip of interfacing material to the underlined hem in the same way as for the interfaced hem.

When the Underlined Garment Is Unlined

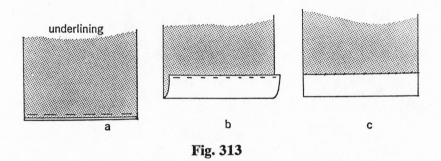

Fig. 313

1. Carry the underlining of the garment down to the very edge of the hem. Baste it to position (Fig. 313a).

2. Turn up the underlined hem and trim it to an even depth (Fig. 313b). There is now a double thickness of underlining to reinforce the hem.

3. Finish the hem edge in any appropriate manner.

4. Using a hemming stitch, fasten the hem to the underlining only (Fig. 313c), making sure that no stitches come through to the right side.

When the Underlined Garment Is Lined: Omit Step 3 above.

THEY ALSO SERVE WHO—WEIGHT

As if all this were not enough, some tailored jackets and coats may need even more weighting to hold the hem in place. A hem may be weighted uniformly with a chain. Stitch the chain every other link

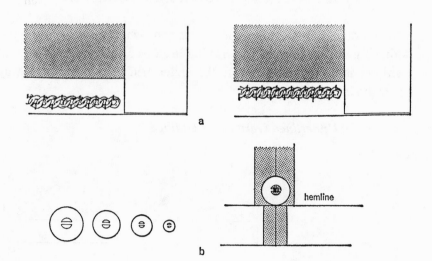

a

b

hemline

Fig. 314

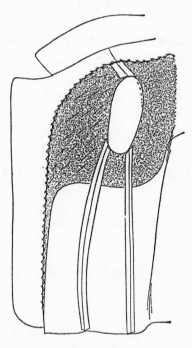

Fig. 315

along the top and bottom from facing to facing at the lower edge or just below the lining (Fig. 314a).

A hem may be weighted in spots by the use of dressmaker's weights. So they will never be seen, they are inserted into the hem at seam lines and are stitched to the seam allowances (Fig. 314b). In circular or very flared garments (a cape, a coat, a skirt), a dressmaker's weight stitched to the hem at each deep fold will guarantee that the ripples will always fall into their planned position.

FASTEN THE FACING

After the hem has been completed, it is the facing's turn. Turn the facing back against the inside of the jacket or coat from the hem all the way around to the opposite hem. Fasten the facing to the interfacings (and shoulder pads when used) with catch stitching (Fig. 315).

Sometimes when the facing is turned to its true position, bulk forms at the hem because of the many (often thick) layers of fabric superimposed one on another. To avoid this, many patterns are cut with a seam allowance rather than a hem at the lower edge of the facing (Fig. 316a). If the pattern doesn't provide this feature, you can draft

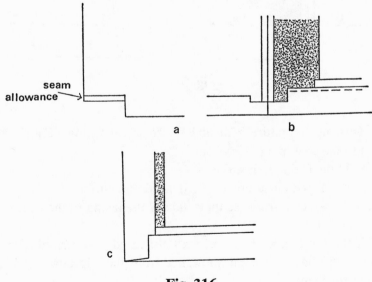

Fig. 316

it yourself. Just be sure to allow enough length for rolling the joining seam to the underside.

Here is another way to eliminate the bulk in the lower corner.

1. Cut away the seam that joins the facing to the garment to within ½ to ¾ inch of the hemline (Fig. 316b).

2. Grade the facing hem (Fig. 316b).

3. Fold the facing to position. Clip the seam allowance of the facing at the top of the hem (Fig. 316c).

4. Fold under the seam allowance of the facing from the clip to the hemline, and along the hemline (Fig. 316c).

5. Slip-stitch the folded edges to the hem.

Bulk or no bulk, coat facings are often treated in the following manner if there is the least possibility that the coat will need lengthening at some future time.

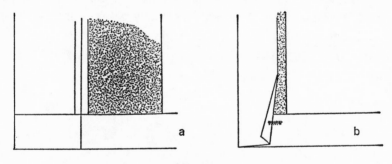

Fig. 317

1. Turn up the entire hem of both coat and facing (Fig. 317a). Fasten to the coat in a tailor's hem.

2. Fold the facing to position.

3. If the fabric does not ravel, it needs no further finish. Simply make a French tack from the underside of the facing to the hem (Fig. 317b).

4. If the fabric does ravel or if a finished edge is desired, clip the facing; turn under the seam allowance from the clip down and slip-stitch to the hem.

IT CAN'T BE LONG NOW!

All that is left to be done now before inserting the lining is to remove all the basting and tailor's tacks and all loose threads or lint accumulated during construction. And give the jacket or coat a final light pressing both inside and out.

Chapter 20

Classic Tailoring Is a Many-layered Thing

Classic tailoring is a many-layered thing in which the last of the layers is the lining. So much loving care and so many thousands of hand stitches (count 'em) have gone into the making of your coat or jacket that your reluctance to cover up your handiwork with a mere lining is quite understandable. It is to be hoped that the lining will be so beautiful that it will compensate for the loss.

In most schools of tailoring, *the lining is made by machine and inserted by hand.*

THE MACHINE CONSTRUCTION

1. Cut, mark, and stitch the lining with the same care and precision as you did the fashion fabric.

2. Stitch all darts and all seams with the exception of the shoulder seams. Leave them open (Fig. 318a). Press.

3. Stitch the sleeve seams and press them open. Make two rows of gathering stitches across the sleeve cap. Draw up the gathering to form a cap shape. Distribute the fullness evenly (Fig. 318b).

4. Lay a soft fold at the front shoulder and pin to position. Fasten through all thicknesses with cross-stitches (Fig. 318c) or with bar tacks* (Fig. 318d).

5. Lay a tentative soft fold at the center back and pin to position (Fig. 318e).

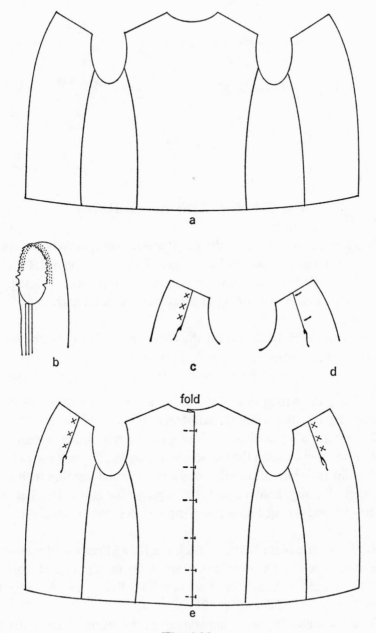

a

b   c   d

fold

e

Fig. 318

Bar tack: Cover two or three straight stitches (Fig. 319a) with small overhand stitches (Fig. 319b).

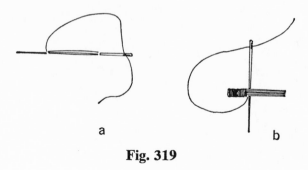

a

b

Fig. 319

INSERT THE LINING BY HAND

Turn the jacket or coat inside out. Place it over a curved surface. A dress form is ideal. A tailor's ham is fine. Don't work on a flat surface or you will eliminate the ease so necessary to prevent drawing and pulling. By inserting the lining in a reverse curve, an extra bit of ease is added.

Work from each front toward the center back. Do the same operation on each side before going on to the next.

1. Place the wrong side of the lining against the wrong side of the garment. By this placement the construction seams will be hidden.

2. Match the open side seams of garment and lining. When there are no side seams, match the side-front or side-back seams instead.

3. Join the seam allowances close to the stitching line with loose permanent basting. Leave a jacket lining free for about 4 inches from the bottom and a coat lining free for about 6 inches from the bottom (Fig. 320a).

4. With permanent basting, stitch the lining firmly to the armhole seam allowance close to the seam. Start at the underarm and work toward the shoulder. Leave the back-armhole lining free for about 2 inches from the shoulder (Fig. 320b).

5. Turn under the seam allowances at the front edges of the lining. Pin in place over the front facings, raw edges matching.

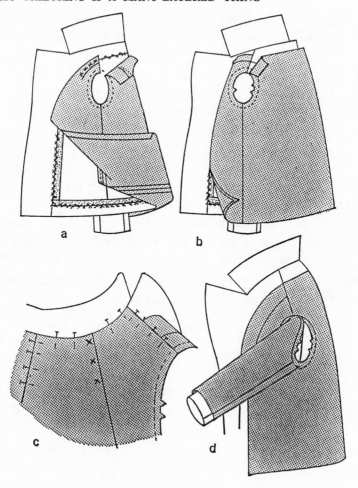

Fig. 320

6. Slip-stitch the front edges of the lining to the facing, leaving the bottom free for a few inches from the hemline (Fig. 320b).

7. Attach the front lining to the back-shoulder seam allowance with permanent basting.

8. Clip the neckline curve of the lining.

9. Turn under the back-lining seam allowance at the shoulders.

10. Lay in the center-back pleat, making any needed adjustments. The fold is directly on center back; the pleat is on the right back. Fasten the pleat at the neck, waist, and lower edge with cross-stitches or bar tacks.

11. Turn under the back-neckline seam allowance.

12. Pin the back lining to position over the front lining at the shoulders and over the back facing, raw edges matching (Fig. 320c).

13. Slip-stitch the lining to position.

14. Clip the sleeve lining on the underarm curve.

15. Turn the sleeve to the wrong side. Slip the sleeve lining over the sleeve, wrong sides together.

16. Adjust the lining cap to fit the sleeve cap, distributing the ease.

17. Turn under the seam allowance of the entire lining sleeve cap. Bring the fold of the sleeve lining to meet the armhole seam line. Match the underarm, shoulder, and sleeve seams (Fig. 320d).

18. Slip-stitch the sleeve lining to the garment lining. Tiny hemming stitches instead of slip stitches are advisable for a garment that is to get hard wear. They may not look as pretty but they're far stronger. Or you might try using buttonhole twist or a heavy-duty thread of matching color for sturdier hand stitches.

HOW TO HANDLE THE HEM OF THE LINING

When this much of the lining has been inserted, let the garment hang out for a while so that the lining settles before finishing the hem.

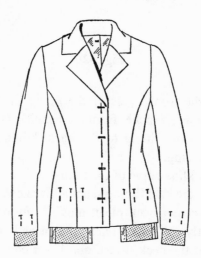

Fig. 321

Then pin or baste the lining to the garment several inches above the hemline (Fig. 321).

THE ATTACHED HEM

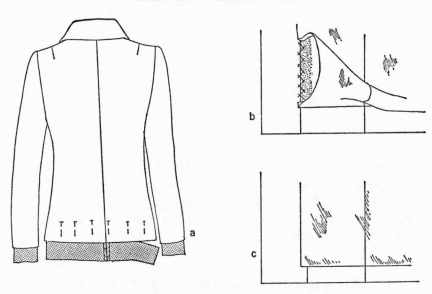

Fig. 322

1. Cut off any lining that shows below the finished hemline (Fig. 322a).

2. Turn under the seam allowance of the lining and pin it over the top of the hem, raw edges matching. Note the small tuck that provides the lengthwise ease (Fig. 322b).

3. Slip-stitch the lining to the garment.

4. Smooth the lining down over the hem so the tuck ease forms a soft fold (Fig. 322c).

5. Close the remaining front edges with slip stitching.

THE FREE-HANGING HEM OF A COAT

1. Trim the lining 1½ inches below the finished hem (Fig. 323a).

2. Turn up the coat lining to make a 2½-inch hem. This makes the coat lining 1 inch shorter than the coat.

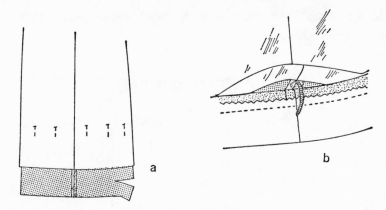

Fig. 323

3. The hem of the garment and the hem of the lining are completed separately with any suitable edge finish.

4. Close the remaining front edge with slip stitching.

5. Attach the lining hem to the garment hem with 1-inch French tacks at all seams (Fig. 323b).

LINING A RAGLAN OR KIMONO-SLEEVED STYLE

Fig. 324

1. Make such adjustments as were made in the garment.

2. Stitch the entire lining together. Clip all curved seams. Press the seam allowances open.

Fig. 324

3. Turn the entire garment inside out.

4. Place the wrong side of the lining against the wrong side of the garment so the construction seams are concealed.

5. Pull the sleeve lining over the sleeve.

6. Match the side and underarm seams. Pin. Fasten to position with permanent basting.

7. Fold under the seam allowances of all outside edges except the hem. Clip where necessary.

8. Place the folded edges over the facings, raw edges matching. Slip-stitch.

9. Finish the hem in the same manner as directed for set-in sleeve styles.

HONG KONG FINISH FOR A LINING

A very decorative touch for a lining is the one that has come to be known as the Hong Kong finish (Fig. 325).

Fig. 325

Insert a length of bias piping or cording of either matching or contrasting color or texture between the lining and the facing.

COPING WITH THE COLD—THE INTERLINING

Want to keep warm in winter? Move to a warm climate. Or get a fur coat. Or pile on layers of anything handy—sweaters, shawls, blankets, ponchos. Or interline your winter coat! If the latter is your only alternative for coping with the cold, see page 192 for suggestions on patterns and materials.

Interlining a fabric adds warmth. It also adds weight and bulk. The trick is to get the coat as warm as possible with as little weight and bulk as possible. There are a number of ways in which this can be done, depending on how much time and patience you have.

METHOD I—*Each Section Separately*

The ultimate in interlining insertion is a complete hand operation where each section of the interlining is set and stitched into position individually. It is trimmed in such a way that the edges of the inter-lining just meet the edges of all seam allowances, all facings, and the top of the hem. All edges are joined by catch stitching (Fig. 326).

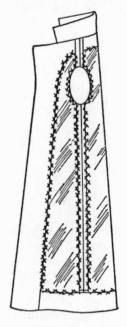

Fig. 326

By this method, there is never any place on the garment that has more than two thicknesses of fabric—not even a small overlap.

Perhaps you are thinking this is carrying the flatness fetish a bit too far. Consider this: in addition to the trimness of this type of insertion, it has another advantage. It is often much easier to handle one piece of interlining at a time than to insert another great coat of wool into what may already be a voluminous garment.

It may be the most work, but Method I is the most precise and the least bulky of the several suggested methods.

METHOD II—*Two Layers, One Fabric*

The opposite extreme is to back the lining with the interlining and treat the two layers as one fabric. (There is a commercial fabric like this on the market.) However, you can see how the four thicknesses of material at each dart and seam, as well as at all turn-unders on outside edges, would create bulk.

While this method is the least amount of work, it produces the most bulk. In a loose-fitting coat, the bulk can be absorbed without too disastrous a result. A fitted coat would, however, be another matter.

Insert Method II interlining like a lining but omit the center-back pleat.

METHOD III—*Compromise*

The following compromise method produces excellent results: not as much work as Method I—not as much bulk as Method II.

1. Cut the interlining from the pattern suggested on page 193. Overlap and stitch all the seams and darts in the same way as for the interfacing. Use a longer straight or zigzag stitch and a looser tension. (Interlining material, being loosely woven, tends to be stretchier.) Trim the seam allowances on both sides close to the stitching (Fig. 327a).

2. Turn the coat inside out. Place the interlining in position. Match the side seams. Match any shaping seams and darts. Smooth the fabric so there is no rippling.

The interlining may go in before the shoulder pads are attached (a preferable method), or may be put in place over the shoulder pads.

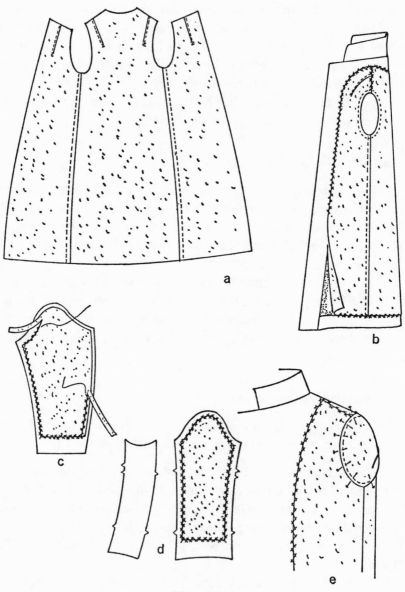

Fig. 327

3. Fasten the side seams with permanent basting. Overlap the shoulder seams and fasten them with catch stitching (Fig. 327b).

4. Trim the seam allowances of all outside edges. Trim the interlining to meet the top of the hem. (Fig. 327b). Fasten all outside edges with catch stitching.

5. Trim the seam allowances of a one-piece sleeve interlining. Apply as an underlining to the underside of the sleeve before stitching the underarm seam. Catch-stitch the interlining edges to the sleeve seam lines (Fig. 327c). Proceed with the usual sleeve construction.

In a two-piece sleeve, generally only the upper sleeve is interlined. Handle the upper sleeve and interlining in the same way as the one-piece sleeve and its interlining (Fig. 327d).

If the underlining is put in as a separate unit after the sleeve has been stitched, overlap it on the armhole seam and catch-stitch (Fig. 327e).

6. Turn up the sleeve hem to meet the interlining. Catch-stitch the edge of the hem to the interlining.

ALL METHODS

Whatever the method of interlining insertion, it is best to work over the dress form or over the tailor's ham. This will provide just the amount of ease necessary to preclude any pulling or buckling of the outer fabric.

In most coats these days, the lining is attached to the hem, thereby covering the interlining. If the lining is to hang free of the coat, cut the interlining sufficiently shorter so that it won't be visible.

Chapter 21

The Stripped-down, Unstructured, Unlined Tailoring

You like the style but not the substance of the classic tailored jacket or coat. Well, then, strip it down to its shell and in no time flat—almost—you can have its lightweight counterpart.

SOME GENERAL SUGGESTIONS

1. Choose a simple style with as few seams and darts as possible. (They'll show on the exposed underside.)

2. Patch pockets are more satisfactory than the more intricate welt or bound variety. (That dangling pouch of a pocket set in a seam or a slash is not a particularly attractive sight even though it is on the inside.)

3. No underlining is necessary. (Obviously the fashion fabric must be firm enough to go it alone.)

4. Interfacings are minimal and cut slightly smaller than the facings so they will be unseen.

5. The only lining is in the sleeves (the easier to slip them on and off). If you must—a half lining across the back.

There is only one hitch to this too-good-to-be-true construction. Since the inside of the garment is exposed when it is taken off, the finish and workmanship must be just about perfect. All of this does take a bit more time than one would think (or wish), but not nearly as much as the classic tailored garment.

Lay out and cut the garment in the same way as the traditional tailored garment. In designs with an upper welt or bound pocket, cut an extra-wide front facing to hide it.

For marking, use tailor's chalk, which can be brushed off, or basting thread, which can be removed. Save your dressmaker's carbon paper for areas where it will not show.

Use a softer or lighter-weight interfacing than one would normally use for a lined garment. This avoids too much difference in thickness or stiffness between the interfaced parts and the rest of the garment.

Use the same stitching and pressing techniques as for the traditional tailored garment.

THE INSIDE MUST BE AS DECORATIVE IN ITS WAY AS THE OUTSIDE

As much to protect them as to make them more attractive, all raw edges of darts, seam allowances, facings, and hems should be finished off in some way. The finish could be hand or machine overcasting, or turned-under-and-stitched edges, or bound edges.

BOUND CAN BE BEAUTIFUL

Make your binding as inconspicuous or as eye-catching as you would like. Use a self color or a contrasting one, either plain or printed. It all depends on how much attention you wish to call to the inside of your garment.

Straight edges are bound with a straight binding. Curved edges require a bias binding. Commercial binding ½ inch wide is available in a range of colors, but the quality is often not as good as the binding you can make for yourself. Make your own of very lightweight silky or cotton material. Cut the strips four times the desired finished width plus ¼ inch for stretching and turning. This is to compensate for the fact that your binding will have raw edges rather than the woven edges of commercial binding, making the application somewhat different. Cut as many lengths as necessary to enclose the edges. Join on the straight grain where needed.

The Machine-stitched Commercial Straight Binding: Fold the bind-ing lengthwise with the bottom half slightly wider than the top to make sure the loose under edge is caught in the machine stitching. Press. Enclose the raw edge with the binding (Fig. 328). Pin or baste to position. Machine-stitch, beside the basting when used.

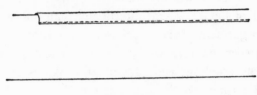

Fig. 328

Made-by-you Binding: Treat straight and bias binding in the same way. Fold ¼ of the full width, bringing the lengthwise raw edges to the center of the underside, and press.

For Machine-topstitched Binding: Fold the binding again length-wise with the bottom half slightly wider than the top. Proceed as for the commercial binding above.

For Combination Machine- and Hand-stitched Binding

1. Open out the binding.
2. Place the right side of binding against the right side of the seam

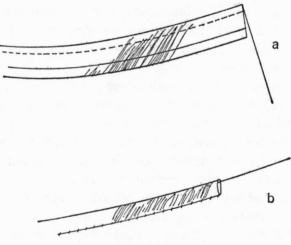

Fig. 329

allowance or hem, raw edges matching, stretching and easing as necessary. Pin to position.

3. Machine-stitch along the fold nearest the edge (Fig. 329a).

4. Fold the binding over the edge, enclosing it. Fasten the remaining fold of the binding to the line of machine stitching with hemming stitches (Fig. 329b). Such a finish may also be used for the tailor's hem, in which case, for some unknown reason, it is called a dressmaker's hem.

SEAMS AND DARTS IN UNLINED GARMENTS

There is another way of handling the seams and darts in unlined garments. By this method, the structure of the garment becomes decorative without the addition of applied decoration like bindings.

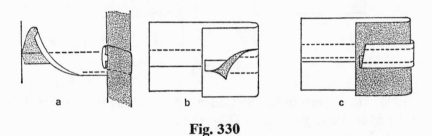

Fig. 330

Use a fell seam (Fig. 330a), a welt seam (Fig. 330b), or a double-stitched welt seam (Fig. 330c). Directions for making these seams will be found on page 215.

Darts may be stitched to match the seams (Figs. 173a and 173b). See page 236 for directions.

NOTE: The above methods of stitching the seams and darts may also be used in the making of an unlined reversible garment.

THE FUSIBLE INTERFACING

If even this streamlined construction appears too much for you, cut corners further with the use of a fusible interfacing. Don't expect the same fine tailored look as you will achieve with traditional tailoring methods, but it will do nicely if time is important to you.

The fusible interfacing is used only for reinforcement and not for shaping. Cut it from the interfacing pattern but eliminate any darts that may fall within the area.

TO ELIMINATE A DART

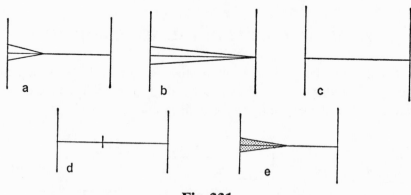

Fig. 331

1. Divide the dart in half and draw a line midway through the dart to the other side of the pattern (Fig. 331a).

2. Draw new lines, starting at each dart end, to the new point at the opposite side of the pattern (Fig. 331b).

3. Crease on one line and bring it to meet the other (Fig. 331c). Pin or Scotch-tape to position.

4. On this elongated closed dart, mark the length of the original dart (Fig. 331d). This will become a slash line.

5. Using this new pattern, cut out the interfacing.

On the Interfacing

6. Trace the slash line determined in Step 4. Slash the interfacing along this line.

7. Slip the open, stitched dart of the outer fabric through the slit in the interfacing, covering the slash (Fig. 331e).

If you plan to use basting thread for any right-side marking, apply the fusible interfacing *before* you mark with the thread. It is too difficult to remove the bastings from the fused material.

Tape the garment in the same way as when using standard interfacing material, though the stitching that fastens it to the garment may be by machine rather than by hand.

Obviously you will not need the pad stitching. To compensate for its omission, firm the stand of the collar (Fig. 332a) and the tip of the lapel (Fig. 322b) with a second layer of fusible material.

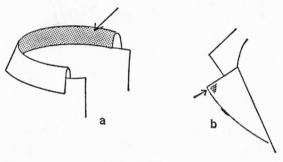

Fig. 332

Remember to trim away all interfacing seam allowances and snip away the interfacing from the points of the lapel and collar to facilitate the turning of the corners.

Are you wondering why anyone would ever bother again with all that time-consuming construction of the classic tailored suit or coat if one can get such good results without it? No one way is ever the answer to all your needs or your moods. Know how to do both. Be free to choose what appears right for the time or the fabric.

Chapter 22

Skirts and Slacks: A Snap

For anyone who has come this far and mastered the art of tailoring a jacket or coat, skirts and slacks should be a snap. Just about the easiest and speediest article of clothing one can make is the straight, slim skirt of the classic tailored suit. With a few more seams (and a few more fitting problems) but exactly the same techniques, you can have your slacks or pants—short, long, or any length between. The only new information necessary concerns the construction and application of the waistband.

THE ANATOMY OF A WAISTBAND

The waistband is the anchor that holds the fit of the skirt or pants in place. (A waistband can do the same for the lower edge of a jacket or blouse.) It may be unabashedly visible—decorative even—or as an inside band, be discreetly hidden from view.

The visible waistband is made of three layers—an outside (upper band), an inside (under band), and one sandwiched between (the interfacing). Any part of a garment that has so many parts has many possibilities for variety in design and fabric.

The upper and under bands can be all of a piece or in two pieces. The interfacing can be firm or rigid. The waistband may be straight or contour, wide or narrow, straight grain or bias. The waistband may be of self fabric or a contrasting texture, the same color as the skirt or slacks or a different color.

The correct placement of the waistband is vital. However well or attractively made, no waistband will serve its purpose unless the waistline seam to which it is attached is *the exact curve of your waist.*

Ready-to-wear clothes and all commercial patterns are built on the presumption that the ideal waistline tilts forward slightly (Fig. 333a).

a   b

Fig. 333

What if your waistline does just the reverse—tilts backward (Fig. 333b)? Many waistlines do.

For a skirt to fit the waistline (whatever the tilt) without wrinkling, pulling, or straining, the exact line of the waistline seam must be located.

HOW TO DETERMINE YOUR WAISTLINE

1. Try on the skirt. It should be large enough to rest comfortably at the waist and hips without riding up. Where necessary, let out or take in the seams and darts to make the skirt fit as it should.

2. Tie a heavy string snugly at the waist (or where you would like your waistline to be).

3. Place a row of pins along the bottom of the string around the entire waist. This is easy enough to do for yourself if you have to, though it's helpful to have someone mark the waistline for you.

4. Remove the skirt. Replace the pin markings with a line of guide basting.

5. Trim the excess to a seam allowance.

Follow the same procedure for the waistline of pants.

SEEING IS DECEIVING

Standard waistlines in ready-to-wear clothes and commercial patterns are symmetrical—that is, right and left sides are balanced. You may discover upon examination of the waistline marking that your waistline is not symmetrical—right and left sides are different.

If the difference is slight, ignore it. It may be the result of inaccurate marking. However, if the difference is pronounced, you must respect it. A waistband attached to your waistline, however unbalanced, will look right, while one attached to the symmetrical pattern waistline will look all wrong on you.

ANY WAY YOU WANT IT!— WAISTBAND CONSTRUCTION

The construction of the waistband may be as simple as the straight, self-fabric bands of many women's skirts or as complicated as the two-piece waistband of men's trousers. It can be any way you want it.

The Skirt or Pants Waistband

It's easier and faster to construct the band if it is cut all in one piece (Fig. 334a). There is much to be said, however, for cutting the upper and under bands separately (Fig. 334b). They can be shaped like a contour belt for the best of fits (Fig. 334c). If the fabric is too heavy or too bulky for a complete waistband, the under band can be made of some lighter-weight material—lining, French belting, or grosgrain ribbon.

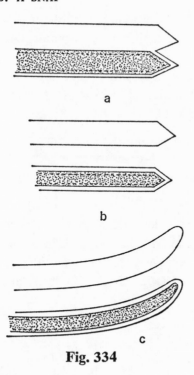

Fig. 334

How to Determine the Width and Length of a Waistband

The width of the all-in-one-piece waistband is equal to twice the finished width of the waistband plus two seam allowances. For instance, the width of a 1-inch waistband will be:

> 2   inches—the doubled band
> 1¼ inches—two ⅝-inch seam allowances
> ⎯⎯⎯⎯⎯⎯⎯⎯
> 3¼ inches—total

The width for separate upper and under bands is equal to the finished width of each band plus two seam allowances. For example, the width of each 1-inch band will be:

> 1   inch —the waistband width
> 1¼ inches—two ⅝-inch seam allowances
> ⎯⎯⎯⎯⎯⎯⎯⎯
> 2¼ inches—total

Straight and narrow waistbands fit without shaping. When a waist-band is more than 1½ inches wide, it requires a shaped side seam to fit the indentation of the waist.

The length of the waistband is equal to the waist measurement, plus ease, plus seam allowances. For example, the length of the waistband for a 26-inch waist will be:

> 26   inches—waist measurement
> ¼ inch   —ease
> 1¼ inches—two ⅝-inch seam allowances
> ───────
> 27½ inches—total

If you plan to use a closing extension, add 1½ inches. The closing extension may be an overlap (Fig. 335a) or an underlay (Fig. 335b). You need not use a closing extension. Simply run the zipper to the top of the band (Fig. 335c). The latter makes a very attractive and effective closure.

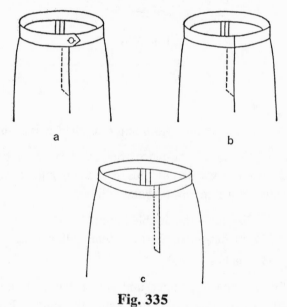

a

b

c

Fig. 335

Bias Is Better

Bias waistbands fit best of all. Their moldability makes them settle comfortably into the natural indentation of the waist.

The length of the bias waistband should be less than your actual waist measurement because the bias will stretch. The heavier the fabric, the fuller the skirt, the more the pull on the waistband and the more the bias will stretch. Generally, subtract 1 inch from the waist measurement to compensate for the stretch. If the fabric is very heavy or the skirt very full, subtract 1½ inches to 2 inches. Because the stretch in length reduces the width, make the bias waistband a little wider than a straight band. Because the bias band will conform beautifully to the shape of the waistline area, its extra width is no problem.

Stiffened-to-stand Band

Most people like a little stiffening in a waistband. Choose an interfacing material of the degree of stiffness you prefer.

1. Cut the interfacing from either the upper or under band pattern. Trim away the seam allowances.

2. Place the interfacing over the wrong side of either of the bands. While it is generally the under band or facing that gets interfaced, it often works better if the upper band is interfaced. Pin or baste the interfacing to position.

3. Catch-stitch around all edges (Fig. 336a).

NOTE: In the one-piece waistband, one long edge rests against the fold line (Fig. 336b).

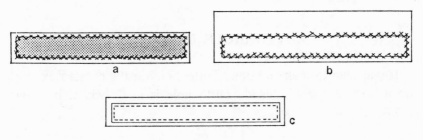

Fig. 336

When *lightweight interfacing* is used in the waistband, it may be included in the seams.

1. Cut the interfacing the same size as the waistband.

2. Apply the interfacing to the waistband like an underlining (which it is).

3. Stitch through both waistband and interfacing (or underlining).

4. Trim the interfacing material close to the seam (Fig. 336c).

VARIATIONS ON A STRAIGHT WAISTBAND

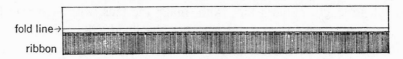

Fig. 337

For heavy or bulky materials or those that need to be stayed because of *stretchability:*

1. Cut the upper waistband of the fashion fabric plus seam allowances.

2. Cut a similar length of grosgrain ribbon of the same width the finished waistband is to be.

3. Overlap and pin the ribbon on the right side of the fashion fabric waistband so one edge is about ¼ inch from the seam line (into the seam allowance). This will provide an allowance for rolling the seam to the underside.

4. Stitch close to the edge of the ribbon (Fig. 337).

BUTTONHOLE FASTENING?

If you plan to make a bound buttonhole on the overlap extension, do it now. A machine-made buttonhole is made when the band is finished.

AN EASY WAY TO ATTACH THE WAISTBAND

There are two ways in which the waistband may be attached to skirt or pants. By one method, the band is machine-stitched to the right side of the material and hand-stitched on the underside. By the second method, the band is machine-stitched to the underside of the waistline and topstitched on the right side. Whichever method you choose, the application is easier if you leave the waistband *open at both ends.*

METHOD I—*Standard Method for a Waistband with an Extension*

Sewing Sequence: Stitch the darts and seams of the garment. Insert the zipper. Attach the band as follows:

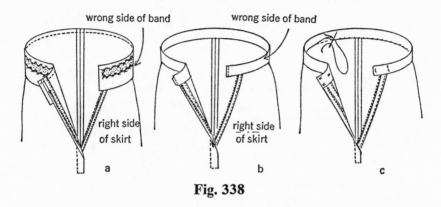

Fig. 338

1. With right sides together, pin the upper band to the skirt (or pants) along the seam line. When there is an extension, it projects beyond the opening (Fig. 338a).

2. Stitch the upper band to the garment. Trim, grade, and clip the seam allowances.

3. Press the seam allowances first open, then into the band.

4. Fold the band lengthwise along the fold line, right sides together. Stitch across the ends (Fig. 338b). When cut separately, stitch the under band to the upper band along the length.

5. Press the seam allowances open over the point presser. Grade the seam allowances and free the corners of bulk.

6. Turn the band to the right side. Fold the all-in-one band lengthwise along the fold line. Make sure that the waistband is even in width from seam to fold along its entire length. Pin or baste to position. When an under band has been stitched to an upper band, roll the joining seams to the underside.

7. Press, then baste to position.

8. Turn under the seam allowance of the loose edge of the under band and hem or slip-stitch it to the garment along the stitching line (Fig. 338c).

9. *For an Overlap Extension:* Make the machine buttonhole. Sew on the button.

For an Underlay Extension: Sew on the hooks and eyes or snaps.

METHOD II—*the Topstitched Waistband*

The procedure for this construction is the reverse of that for the standard waistband.

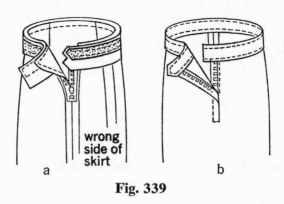

Fig. 339

1. Stitch the right side of the under band to the wrong side of the skirt or pants (Fig. 339a). Trim, grade, and clip the seam allowances. Press them open, then into the band.

2. Fold the all-in-one-piece band or turn the separate band-and-facing waistband so the right sides are together. Stitch across the ends.

3. Press the seam allowances open over the point presser. Grade them. Free the corners of bulk.

4. Turn the band to the right side (outside).

5. Fold the all-in-one band lengthwise along the fold line, keeping it even from seam to fold. Pin or baste to position. When upper and under bands have been joined by a seam, roll it to the underside. Press and baste to position.

6. Turn under the seam allowance of the loose edge. Overlap the folded edge of the band on the right side of the garment, covering the seam line. Pin or baste to position.

7. Topstitch through all thicknesses (Fig. 339b).

8. Sew on the fastenings.

ZIPPERED TO THE TOP OF THE BAND

Sewing Sequence: Stitch the darts and seams of the garment. Attach the upper band to the garment. Insert the zipper to the top of the upper band (Fig. 340a).

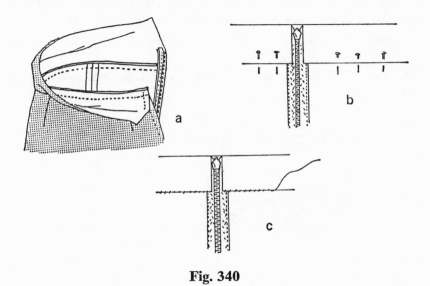

Fig. 340

1. In a one-piece band, fold the band to the inside along the fold line. In a two-piece band, attach the under band and turn it to the inside.

2. Turn under the seam allowances at both ends of the under band along the zipper tape. Pin to position.

3. Turn under the seam allowance of the loose, long edge of the under band. Pin to position along the line of machine stitching that fastened the upper band to the garment (Fig. 340b).

4. Hem or slip-stitch the under band to position (Fig. 340c).

HIDDEN FROM VIEW—THE INSIDE WAISTBAND

1. Use a length of 1-inch to 1½-inch grosgrain ribbon or French belting. Cut it to the waistline measurement plus ease plus two seam allowances—one for each end.

2. Turn under the seam allowances at each end and stitch (Fig. 341a).

3. Swirl the grosgrain ribbon into a slight curve with the steam iron. The waistband will fit better if contoured.

4. With right sides up, overlap and pin the ribbon on the skirt at least ¼ inch above the waistline marking—into the seam allowance (Fig. 341b). This will provide an allowance for rolling the seam to the underside. In heavier fabrics, you may need more than ¼ inch. Use your judgment. Stitch.

5. Trim and clip the seam allowance under the ribbon for a flat and easy turning.

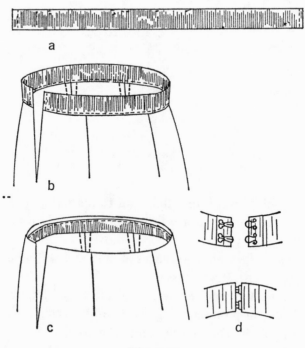

Fig. 341

6. Turn the waistband to the inside of the skirt or pants, rolling the seam to the underside. Press to position (Fig. 341c).

7. Tack the band securely to all seams and darts on the underside.

OPTIONAL: You may topstitch the band to position if it is consistent with the design of the garment.

8. Sew hooks and eyes to the ends of the band for fastening (Fig. 341d).

PANTS PERFECT

Many men and boys go happily on their way untroubled by wrinkles, crinkles, and saggy, baggy seats. But women are pretty finicky about every ridge and wrinkle. It's not the sewing that is the problem in making skirts and slacks. It's the fitting!

The trim fit of both skirts and pants starts with the right size. If the skirts or slacks that complete your outfit came with the jacket pattern, the size was determined by the size of the jacket. You may have to do a little altering to make the skirt or pants fit. So many of us have tops that don't match our bottoms. When you buy a skirt or slacks pattern separately, you have more control. You can choose a size that comes closer to your lower-figure needs. It may even be worth doing this if you have a great disparity in sizes between top and bottom.

That Crucial Waist-to-hip Area

The crucial area in fitting a skirt or pants is the waist to hips (Fig. 342a). The rest of the garment is merely an extension from hips to hem. When there are any fitting problems below the hipline, look for the cause above it.

SUGGESTED SEQUENCE FOR FITTING SKIRTS

1. Pin the waistband in position.

2. Pin the center front and center back of the garment to the center front and center back of the waistband.

3. Pin the side seams at the hips. Make certain that the center-front and center-back vertical grain lines hang at right angles to the

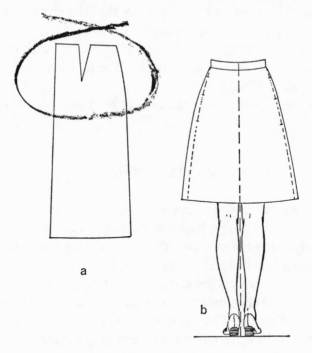

a

b

Fig. 342

floor and that the horizontal grain lines, both front and back, are parallel to the floor (Fig. 342b).

4. Pin the side seams, fitting the curve of the hips.

5. Check the front and back darts or seams for correct shaping. Unsightly bulges indicate the darts are too large. Spanning across the abdomen and buttocks indicates darts that are too long or incorrectly placed. Repin the darts, making the needed corrections. Or more width may be needed.

6. Continue pinning the side seams from hips to hem. Should the side seams tend to swing forward or backward, unpin the seam, check the grain line, check the darts, correct as necessary, and repin.

STYLE LINES STREAMLINE THE SLACKS

Whatever one's problems are in fitting a skirt, they are magnified (literally) when fitting pants. In pants, there are all of the skirt problems PLUS that crucial fitting area—the crotch. What to do?

The first bit of advice about pants is to choose a style that is best for your figure. Try on some slacks or shorts to get an idea of what is most becoming. You'll soon find which styles reveal your bad features and which conceal them. Find a similar pattern.

Fortunately, pants are generally designed to minimize a hippy look. In a skirt, the shaping from waist to hips is accomplished by darts and seams with a considerable amount of the shaping allocated to the curved side seams. In slacks and shorts, the side seams are kept fairly straight while most of the shaping is placed at front and back. This produces an illusion of straightness that is slimming.

While the design of the pants is your first consideration, the second concern is making the standard-size pattern fit your not-so-standard figure. This is even more important in pants than in a skirt. You may salvage a skirt in the seam allowances, but you get no second chance to change a crotch, say, once the pants are cut.

It's a good idea to work from a basic-fitting pattern or a trial muslin. Once you've made either of these two, you will have an excellent guide for cutting and fitting.

Lastly, fit meticulously, manipulating the fabric in any way necessary to make the pants fit the figure.

SUGGESTED SEQUENCE FOR FITTING PANTS

1. Stay-stitch the crotch. Baste the crotch seam. Clip the seam allowance of the crotch *almost* to the stay stitching.

2. Pin or baste the remaining seams and darts.

3. Pin the waistband in place, matching crotch seams at front and back, the side seams, and any other pertinent markings.

4. Check the grain lines, making certain that the grain at center front and center back of each pants leg hangs at right angles to the floor, and that the horizontal grain lines of both front and back are parallel to the floor.

5. Check the front and back darts and/or seams for correct shaping. Release for added width where spanning occurs. Reduce the dart control where unsightly bulges appear.

6. Check the side seams and the inseams (inner leg), making sure they hang at right angles to the floor. Should they swing forward or backward, unpin the seam, check the grain line, reposition the seam, and repin.

7. Check the crotch seam for length and ease, adding or subtracting as necessary. The crotch should not be too tight or too loose, too high or too low, for comfort.

8. Test the pants for ease in sitting. Does the thigh area bind? Is it possible to cross one's legs? Note the position of any pull or strain. Add ease accordingly.

9. Determine the length of the pants.

HINTS ON PANTS CONSTRUCTION

To facilitate stitching the crotch seam, slip one pants leg inside the other.

Because the crotch area takes considerable strain, the crotch seam needs some reinforcement. An easy way to do this is with the machine stitching itself. Use a smaller straight stitch or a very small zigzag stitch for the curved crotch seam. Clip at each end of the curve and press the seam allowances open from the clip to the waistline. Make a second row of stitching close to the first between the clips. Trim the seam allowance to ¼ inch. Overcast this edge with machine or hand stitching.

CHIC, NOT SHOCKING

Despite all the discouraging things about fitting pants to perfection, it appears difficult, if not impossible, to get girls out of them. Whether it's really the comfort (as so many women claim) or the ease of pants dressing, whether it's that they are right for modern life or just that women think themselves more attractive in them, the fact is that pants appear to be an indispensable (and very acceptable) part of our wardrobes. There is hardly a size or an age of person that does not wear them, a place or a function where they are not worn. Better learn how to make them chic, not shocking.

AND SEW ON

It's been long and you have worked hard. It is to be hoped that you are proud of what you have created. When the picture is done, the artist signs it. The final touch is your signature. This could be your initials embroidered on the lining a few inches above the hipline. Or a label that you can make for yourself of your favorite color of ribbon. Embroider your name or initials. Cross-stitch it in place at the center back of your lining 1 to 2 inches below the neckline (Fig. 343). It will write "finish" with a flourish.

Fig. 343

My wish for you is the one with which my family always greeted me when I appeared in something new:

"WEAR IT IN THE BEST OF HEALTH!"

Index

Abdomen, pattern adjustment for, 81, 82, 84
Arm, measuring, 68
  pattern adjustment for, 79, 80
Armhole, 76, 105, 106
  chain-stitch stay, 395
  hair-canvas reinforcement, 196–97
  recutting, 393–94
  and sleeve, 393–95, 398–400
  tape stay, 371, 394

Back, 78, 79
Backstitch, 209, 221, 292
Ball-point needle, 250
Bar tack, 420
Basting, 208–10, 221, 234
  edge, 223
  even, 209
  fabric marking, 160, 163
  tailor's, 234–35
  uneven, 209
Belts, 44, 48, 269
  interfacing, 182, 183, 187
Biceps, measuring, 64
Binding, 431–33
  bias, 225, 431
  combination machine- and
    hand-stitched, 432–33
  fusible interfacing, 433–34
  machine-stitched commercial straight,
    431, 432
  machine-topstitched, 432
  made-by-you, 217, 431, 432
  seam edge, 225
  seams and darts in, 433
  shaping, 286
Blanket stitch, 317–18
Blocking, 58, 274–75
  no-dart, no-seam garment, 278

Blocks, matching, 42, 43, 44, 150
Blouse(s), 20, 48
Bodice, shaping, 22
Bodkin, 56
Bound pockets, 282, 330, 331, 341–42
  flap added to, 349–50
Brocades, 35, 146
  pressing, 273
Bullion stitch, 328
Bust, high, 7, 9
  measuring, 7, 8, 9, 22, 64
Bust line, 108
Buttocks, pattern adjustment for, 82
Buttonhole stitch, 317–18
Buttonholes, 44, 160, 162, 265, 269, 290,
    291, 305–19, 351
  bound, 283, 307, 308–13
  hair canvas shaping, 357–58
  hand-worked, 316–18
  horizontal, 306, 320
  leather-like fabrics, 319
  machine-made, 319
  one-step method, 308–11
  precision closing, 311–13
  size and type of button, 306–7
  tailor's, 316, 318–19
  two-step method, 311–13
  underlining, 357–58
  vertical, 306, 320–21
Buttonhole twist, 219
Buttons, 50–51, 162
  how to sew on, 321–23
  sew-through, 321–23
  shank, 306, 321, 323
  size of, 306–7
  stay, 323

Capes, 10, 20, 131, 408
Catch stitch, 223, 224, 228, 332, 412

Chain stitch, 394, 395
Chanel chain hem weight, 202
Chanel-type jacket interfacing, 173–74
Checks, 14, 16, 89, 101
    dominant stripe placement, 148, 149
    key pattern piece for, 155
    matching, 42, 43, 44, 48, 141, 150,
        158, 213
    style lines for, 47–48
Circumference
    lines, 87, 108, 109
    measurements, 7
Clapper, 56, 57, 268, 269
Closings, pressing, 261, 269
Cloth, double thickness, 131–34, 217–19
Coats, 10, 20, 27, 66, 131
    fitting, 95, 97
    hem, 109, 110–11, 406
    interfacing, 172, 181–82, 184, 188, 359
    interlining, 192, 193, 194
    lining hem, 422–24
    material for, 33
    pressing before stitching, 358
    raglan sleeve, 181–82
    shaped, 360–61
    sleeve hem, 109, 406
    unfitted, 359
    unlined, 184, 236–37
    wrap style, 172
Collar, 20, 44, 50, 286
    applying upper collar to undercollar,
        382–84
    attaching to garment, 386–90
    classic tailored, 188, 189, 190
    contour, 380–82
    cutting, 139
    double thickness of cloth, 131–34,
        217–19
    facing, 71, 377
    fitting depth, 379
    fitting length, 378–79
    fitting undercollar, 377–78, 380
    flat (Peter Pan and cape), 191
    interfacing, 171, 182, 183, 187, 377
    neckline, 378
    notched, 373, 374, 375–76
    pressing, 261, 265, 269, 278–80
    reducing rippling, 378
    relieving strain, 378
    roll lines, 378
    set of, 373
    shawl, 189, 190, 373, 374, 375, 390–91
    standing, 191, 391–92
    style line, 378
    unit with lapel, 373, 375
    unlined garment, 435
Collar press pads, 59–60
Corduroy, 2, 49, 146
    pressing, 263

Corner
    stitching, 237–38
    freeing of bulk, 238–39
    mitering, 240–41
    reinforcing, 242
    stitching style line to, 239–40
Cotton, 15, 16, 17
    polished, 146
    preshrinking, 127–28
    pressing, 264, 269, 273
Crepe, 17, 35
    pressing, 273
    satin-backed, 17
Cross-stitch, 228
Crotch, fitting, 448
    measuring, 8
    pattern adjustment for, 68, 69, 70,
        82–83
Cuffs, 50
    double thickness of cloth, 131, 134
    interfacing, 171, 182, 183, 187, 191
    pressing, 261, 263, 269, 282
Cutting
    bias, 44
    duplicates, 137
    general instructions, 158–59
    in pairs, 137
    on fabric fold, 136, 137–38
    phony fur, 251
Cutting surface, 53

Dart control, 20–27
    and design, 27–30
    divided, 24, 25
    and fabric design, 30–31
    pinwheel patterns, 26–27
Darts, 20–27, 47, 102–3
    abutted seam joining, 231
    double-pointed, 227
    eliminating, 434–35
    in interfacing, 228, 230–31
    in underlining, 232–35
    marking, 160
    moving, 87–88
    overlapped seam joining, 230–31
    pressing, 260, 261, 263, 275, 276–78
    relocating, 102–3
    single-pointed, 226
    stitching, 226–27
    Ultrasuede garments, 253, 255–56
    unlined garments, 236–37, 433
Design
    built into fabric, 32–46
    built into pattern, 27–31
    dart control, 30–31
    layout, 143
    matching, 40–46
    moving in one direction, 147

placement, 147, 148, 158
repeat, 40, 46, 137, 141, 147
Design Your Own Dress Patterns
(Margolis), 28 n
Directional (one-way) fabric, 33
layout, 34, 137, 141, 142
matching, 44
yardage required, 41, 46
Dobby weave, 35, 36
Double knits, 38
Dresses, 20, 27
Dressmaker's carbon paper, 55, 160,
161–62
Dressmaker's weights, 202
Dropped-shoulder sleeve pad, 404–5

Ease, 10–12, 62, 66, 98–100
Ease stitching, 245
Edge presser, 57
Elbow, 64, 68
Ensembles, 10, 44

Fabric
character of, 119–29
considerations before buying, 48–49
co-ordinated with pattern, 20–46
design built into, 32–46
and ease, 10
easy-to-handle, 15–16
folding for layout and cutting, 141
grain (*see* Grain)
hard-to-handle, 16
hard-to-stitch, 49
imperfections in, 125
layouts for special, 145–47
leftover, 156
markings on pattern transferred to,
159–66
muslin, 90
novelty, 16
one-way (directional), 33
pinning pattern to, 157–58
reaction to pressing, 264
shaping and foundation, 186–88
special, and special handling, 249–59
test, 90
two-way (nondirectional), 32–33
types, 13–15, 33, 34–35
ways to save if it runs short, 156
See also names and types of fabrics
Facing, 44, 71
added to front extension, 140
double thickness of cloth, 131, 217–19
flared, circular or shaped hems, 407–8
pressing, 265, 269, 270
that becomes a lapel, 133
Ultrasuede, 253–54
Fashion, shape of, 170–203
Feather stitch, 224

Figure
big-hipped, 80–81, 83
columnar, 22, 23
flat-chested, 77
hourglass, 22, 23
large-bosomed, 77
pattern corrections for, 73–88
slim-hipped, 81, 83
sway-backed, 81, 82
Filling knits, 38
Finger-pressing, 268, 272, 273
Fitting, 95–96, 103–5
coat or jacket, 96, 97
crotch, 448
pants, 98, 447–48, 449–50
pin, 355–56
second, 363
sequence, 97
skirt, 97, 447–48
sleeve, 97, 373, 393, 396–97
trial muslin (*see* Trial muslin)
waist-to-hip area, 447
Flap pocket, 330, 331, 341, 347–48
Flaps, 342–45, 348, 349
added to bound pocket, 349–50
double thickness of cloth, 131, 134,
217–19
fake, 350–51
interfacing, 182, 183, 191
one-piece construction, 343–44, 345
pressing, 261, 265, 282
two-piece construction, 344–45
underlining, 191
Flower motifs, matching, 42, 48
French belting, 192
French tack, 404
Furs, fake. *See* Phony furs

Garment
design, 10
and ease, 10–12
function, 10
Gathering, 21, 22, 246–48
pressing, 283
Glove stitch, 221
Grading, 222–24
pattern, 9 and n
Grain, 85, 86, 100–2, 119–25
cut off-grain, 120, 121–22
establishing, 120–21
extended line on pattern, 130, 131
finished off-grain, 120, 122–23
horizontal, 125
knit fabrics, 124–25
pattern layout, 137, 141
printed off-grain, 120, 123–24
vertical, 121
Gussets, 242

Hair canvas, 187–88, 191, 192
  armhole reinforcement, 196–97
  buttonhole and pocket reinforcement,
    357–58
  removing from construction seams,
    364–65, 372
Half backstitch, 292
Hem allowance, 134, 135
Hemlines, 109–11
  coat, 109, 110–11
  coat sleeve, 109
  jacket, 109, 110–11
  pants, 111
  plaids, 110–11
  skirt, 109, 110, 406
  taping, 369–70
Hemming stitches, 370, 388, 412
Hems, 105, 406–7
  attached, 422–24
  bias muslin interfacing, 192
  chain-weighted, 202, 413, 414, 415
  circular, 285, 407
  coats, 406
  dipping, 409
  facing, 407, 415
  gored or slightly flared, 406–7
  hair canvas interfacing, 192
  hang of, 409
  interfaced, 182, 183, 192, 202, 409–11
  jacket, 109, 110–11, 406, 408, 409
  lining, 422–24
  pleated, 285
  pressing, 261, 265, 269, 270, 284–85
  removing bulk after turning facing,
    415–16
  rounded, 408, 409
  sheer canvas interfacing, 192
  spot-weighted (dressmaker's weights),
    202, 413, 414, 415
  straight, 284–85
  straight skirt, 406
  tailor's, 411–12
  underlined garment, 413
  underlining, 192, 202
  very flared, circular or shaped, 407–8
Herringbone, 33
Hipline, 64, 108
  added width, 66, 67
  pattern adjustment, 68, 69, 70
Hips, measuring, 7, 8, 22, 64, 80, 81, 83
Hong Kong lining finish, 425
Hooks and eyes, 323, 324–26
  covered, 326, 327–29
*How to Make Clothes That Fit and
  Flatter* (Margolis), 9 n, 70 n, 74 n

Interfacing, 115, 171–84, 278
  coats, 172, 181–82, 184, 188
  darts, 228, 230–31

design details, 182–83
eliminating a dart, 434–35
fabric for, 186–88, 190
fusible (iron-on), 186, 187, 433–34
hard tailoring, 174–79
hems, 182, 183, 192, 202, 409–11
pocket, 171, 182, 183, 192, 330, 332
pressing, 261
seams, 228–30
soft tailoring, 171–74
tailor's linen, 190
and underlining, 185
unlined jacket, 184, 430, 431
vents, 182, 183
Interlining, 115, 192–95, 278
  darts, 228
  inserting into garment, 426–29
  pressing, 261
  seams, 228
Ironing board, 56, 57, 271
Ironing vs. pressing, 261–62, 264
Irons, 56, 57, 58, 266, 268, 271

Jacket, 10, 20, 27, 48, 66
  fitting, 95, 97
  hems, 109, 110–11, 406, 408, 409
  interfaced, 171, 173–74, 185, 188, 359
  interlined, 192, 193, 194
  pressing before stitching, 358
  shaped, 360–61
  unlined, 184, 236–37, 430–35
  woman's man-tailored, 174–79, 180–81
Jacquard weave, 35, 36
Jersey, 38, 39

Kimono sleeve, 48, 404–5, 424–25
Knits, 10, 35–40, 41, 249
  double, 38
  filling, 38
  for lining, 193
  grain, 124–25
  pattern selection, 40
  pressing, 262
  raschel, 39
  ribbed, 37
  sewing, 249–50
  sliver, 39
  tricot, 39
  warp, 38–39

Lamb's wool
  interlining, 192, 193
  underlining, 201
Lapels, 187, 188
  attaching facing, 385–86
  double thickness of cloth, 131, 217–19
  facing that becomes, 133–34
  pressing, 261, 265, 269, 280–81
  roll-line taping, 368–69

unit with collar, 373, 375
unlined garment, 435
Layout, 135–56
asymmetric designs, 143
bias designs, 143
combination folds, 144–45
crosswise fold, 142
design unit placement, 147
double fold, 144
economical, 140–41
lengthwise fold, 141
neck to hem direction, 137
one-way (directional) fabric, 34, 137, 141, 142
open single (full width), 143
pattern face up or face down, 138–39
possible seam and seam allowance elimination, 139–40
special, for special fabrics, 145–47
standard pattern arrangements, 141–45
stripes, plaids, and checks, 147–55
trial, 155–56
trial muslin (see Trial muslin)
ways to save material if it runs short, 156
Layout chart, 137–39
check after pinning pattern to fabric, 158
circled for later identification, 145
making your own, 136
trial, 155–56
Leg measurement, 8
Length measurements, 6–7, 8, 66–69, 71
Leno weave, 35, 36
Linen, 15, 16
preshrinking, 127–28
pressing, 264, 274
Lining, 17–19, 115, 193, 195
hem, 422–24
Hong Kong finish, 425
insertion by hand, 420–22
machine construction, 418–20
pile, 193
pocket, 330, 332
pressing, 261, 288
pressing garment before insertion, 287
quilted, 193
Long-float fabrics, 146
L square, 53

Marking materials, 55
Markings, 159–66
basting thread, 160, 163–64
dressmaker's carbon paper, 160, 161–62
notches, 165–66
not to be transferred to fabric, 159
right-side, 162–65
and stay stitching, 166–69

tailor's chalk, 160–61
tailor's tacks, 164
to be transferred to fabric, 159–66
wrong-side, 160–62
Measurements (measuring), 5–9
adjusting pattern to meet your measurements (see Pattern adjustment)
basic pattern, 70
circumference, 7
darts to control differences in, 22
length, 6–7, 8, 66–69, 71
seam line to seam line, 64, 69
Measuring tools, 53, 71
Melton cloth (interfacing), 190
Muslin fitting. See Trial muslin

Nap fabrics, 16, 33, 48
layout, 137, 141, 146
pressing, 58, 262, 271
Natural fabrics, 10, 13–15
Neck, 9, 74, 105
Neckline, 105–6, 108
added width, 66, 67
back, 74, 75
dropped, 66, 70
facing, 71
Needle board, 57, 58, 269
Needles, 55, 250, 252
Nondirectional (two-way) fabric, 32–33
matching, 44
yardage required, 41, 46
Notches, 165–66

Office of Commodity Standards, National
Bureau of Standards, 5, 11
Over-and-over stitch, 209
Overblouse, 48
Overcasting seam finish, 224, 225
Overhand stitch, 241

Pad stitch, 369
Pants, 7–8, 20, 27, 69, 131
construction hint, 450
crotch fitting, 448
dart control, 24, 25
ease, 98
fitting sequence, 98, 449–50
hemline, 111
matching blocks, 44
pattern adjustment, 68, 69, 70, 82–85
pressing, 288–89
seat, 81, 84
waistband, 436, 438–40, 442–45
waistline, 83
waist-to-hip fitting, 447
Patch pockets, 44, 330, 331, 332–38, 348–49, 430

attaching to garment, 333–34
interfaced, 332
lined, 332
rounded, 335
square, 335–36
topstitched, 336–38
underlined, 332
unlined, 334–35
Pattern, 3–12, 20, 53
  adjusting (see Pattern adjustment)
  considerations before buying, 47–48
  co-ordinated with fabric, 20–46
  corrected from trial muslin, 114–15
  design built into, 27–31
  and fabric design, 30–31
  grading, 9 and n
  hem allowance, 134, 135
  laying out on material (see Layout)
  markings transferred to fabric, 159–66
  pinning to fabric, 157–58
  seam allowance, 134–35
  size, 4–5, 8
  Standard Measurement Chart, 9
Pattern adjustment, 62–88
  abdomen, 81, 82
  arm, 79, 80
  armhole fullness, 76
  back, 78, 79
  back neckline, 74, 75
  basic pattern, 70
  distortion corrections, 85–88
  for figure needs, 73–88
  flat-chested figures, 77
  flat rear, 82
  hips, 80–81
  large-bosomed figure, 77
  length measurements, 66–69, 70
  making pattern larger, 73
  making pattern smaller, 73
  measuring pattern, 69–70
  meeting your own measurements,
    62–88
  neck, 74
  pants, 68, 69, 70, 82–85
  placement of pattern pieces, 63–64
  prominent seat, 81
  redrawing lines after adjustment,
    85–88
  right angle to grain, 71
  seam lines, 72
  seam line to seam line measurement,
    64, 69
  seat, 81, 84
  short upper back or front, 75
  shoulders, 75, 76, 77
  sleeve cap, 76
  sway-backed figure, 81, 82
  waist, 78
  width changes, 66

  within pattern, 72–73
Pattern companies, ease policy, 11
  Standard Measurement Chart, 9
Pattern preparation, 91, 130–35
Phony furs, 39, 146
  cutting and sewing instructions,
    251–52
  pressing, 272
Pile fabrics
  layout, 137, 141, 142, 146
  as lining, 193
  pressing, 58, 269–71
  sewing, 250–51
Pin fitting, 355–56
Pinking, seam finish, 225
Pinning, 210–11
  pattern to fabric, 157–58
Pins
  dressmakers', 53
  upholsterer's (T pins), 53
Plaids, 16, 89, 101, 131
  combined vertical/horizontal
    placement, 148–49
  crosswise dominant, 148, 149
  even (balanced), 150–51
  and hemlines, 110–11
  key pattern piece for, 155
  matching, 42, 43, 44, 48, 137, 141,
    150, 158, 213
  mirror image, 152, 153
  moving in same direction around
    body, 152, 153
  neck to hem direction, 152
  reversible fabric, 154
  right-and-left effect, 151, 152
  right and wrong side difference, 152,
    153
  style lines for, 47–48
  unbalanced, both directions, 152, 154
  uneven (unbalanced), 150–51
  up-and-down effect, 151, 152
  vertical dominant, center placement,
    147–48
  vertical dominant, side-seam
    placement, 148
  zipper installation, 304–5
Plain weave, 32
Pleats, 48, 160
  pressed, 20, 21, 265, 269
  unpressed, 21, 22, 48
Pockets, 20, 50, 131, 160, 162, 290, 291,
    329–51
  bound, 283, 330, 331, 341–42, 349–50
  construction seam, 330, 331, 338–41,
    348
  cutting duplicates, 137
  diagonal openings, 329
  flap, 330, 331, 341, 347–48
  hair canvas shaping, 357–58

horizontal openings, 329
interfacing, 171, 182, 183, 192, 330, 332
patch, 44, 330, 331, 332–38, 348–49, 430
pressing, 265, 269
stitched into slash, 330, 331, 341–51
underlining, 192, 330, 332, 357–58
unlined, 336–38
vertical openings, 329–30
welt, 330, 331, 341, 345–47
Point, stitching to, 239–40
Point presser, 57, 269, 272
Pounding block, 56, 57, 265, 267, 268–69, 272
Preshrinking, 125–28
cotton, 127–28
interfacings, 128
interlinings, 128
linen, 127–28
sponging, 125
underlinings, 128
woolens, 125–27
Press block, 56–57
Press boards, 269
Press cloths, 58, 264, 265, 266, 267, 268
Pressing, 20, 260–89
contour, 274–86
fabric reaction to, 264
final, 286
finger-, 268, 272, 273
general instructions, 262–63
individual garment problems, 263
right-side touch-up, 289
vs. ironing, 261–62, 264
Pressing equipment, 56–60, 260
Press mitt, 57, 265, 271
Press pads, 269
Pressure adjustment, 212
Prick stitch, 292
Prints, 33
matching, 137

Qiana, 49, 274
Quilted fabrics, 17
Quilted lining, 193

Raglan sleeve, 181–82, 404–5, 424–25
Ready-to-wear size, 5
Reversible fabrics, 35
Running hemming stitch, 412

Saddle stitch, 221
Satin, 17, 146
pressing, 273
Satin-backed crepe, 17
Satin weave, 32, 34
Scissors, 54
Seam allowance, commercial patterns, 134–35

extra, for zipper insertion, 134, 135
grading, 9 and n, 222–24
possible elimination in layout, 140
pressing, 261, 265, 270
Ultrasuede garments, 253, 254
Seam finishes, 224–25
Seam lines, 88
how to eliminate rippling, 244
how to release straining, 244
overlapping, 228, 230, 231
Seam line to seam line measurement, 64, 69
Seam roll, 131, 132, 269
Seams, 47
abutted, 229–30, 231
armhole, 106
circumference, 108
construction, 160, 363, 364–65, 372
corded, 214, 216
curved, 214, 216, 243
enclosed or encased, 217–19
fell, 214, 215, 236
in interfacing, 228–30
joining cross seams, 213
lap, 214, 215, 216
marking, 160
matching blocks, 44
notched to relieve strain, 244
piped, 216
plain, 213, 214
pocket in, 330, 331, 338–41, 348
possible elimination in layout, 139–40
pressing, 260, 261, 263, 275–76
removing hair canvas from, 364–65, 372
shaping (dart control), 20, 21, 22, 23–24, 25, 26
shoulder, 106, 107
side, 107–8
silhouette, 105–9
slot, 214, 215, 216
strap, 214, 216
taped, 365–68
topstitched, 214, 215
tucked, 214, 215
in Ultrasuede, 254–55
in unlined garment, 236–37, 433
variations, 213–16
welt, 214, 215, 216, 236
zipper installation, 293–94, 295–96, 298
Seed stitch, 221
Selvage, 121, 131, 142, 143, 146
Sewing, hand, 207. *See also* Stitches (hand)
machine. *See* Sewing machine; Stitches (machine); Stitching
shell, 355, 356–57
unit construction, 356

Sewing machine, 53, 207, 208, 210
    ball-point needle, 250
    ease stitching, 245
    even-feed attachment, 212
    pressure adjustment, 212
    taut-stitching techniques, 246
    two-needle, 219
Sewing materials, 47–52
Shape, shaping, 47, 62
    built into garment, 170
    contour pressing, 274–86
    dart control, 20–27, 47, 102–3
    interfacing, 171–84
    of fashion, 170–203
    tape reinforcement, 285–86
Shaping devices, 58–60, 269
Shears. See Scissors
Shell, pin-fitting, 355–56
    sewing, 355–72
Shirring, 246–47
    pressing, 283
Shoulder pads, 197–200
    attaching, 401–5
Shoulders, 9, 10, 75, 76, 77, 105
    added width, 66, 67
    seam, 106, 107
Shrinkage prevention. See Preshrinking
Signature, on garment, 451
Silhouette, of garment, 105
Silk, 15, 17, 123, 128
    pressing, 263, 264, 265, 269, 272–73
Size, 62, 95
    determining your own, 8, 9
    pattern, 4–5
    ready-to-wear, 5
    tailored garments, 9
Skirt, 27, 48, 69
    cupping under buttocks, 82
    fitting, 97, 447–48
    hemline, 109, 110, 406
    pattern adjustment, 68, 69, 70, 82
    pressing, 288
    shaping, 20, 21, 22, 24
    waistband (see Waistband)
Skirt marker, 53
Slacks. See Pants
Slant hemming stitch, 370
Slash
    pocket in, 330, 331, 341–51
    reinforcing, 242–43
    zipper in, 296–97
Sleeve band, 44
Sleeve board, 56, 57
Sleeve cap, 60
    and armhole, 393
    how to attach sleeve head, 400
    how to insert underlining, 400
    propping up, 201, 400
Sleeve head, 201, 400

Sleeve openings, 242
Sleeve press pad, 60
Sleeve roll, 56, 57
Sleeves, 17, 20, 50, 105
    and armholes, 393–95, 398–400
    closings and hems, interfaced, 182, 183
    cutting in pairs, 137
    dropped shoulder, 404–5
    fitting, 97, 373, 393, 396–97
    interlining, 193, 194, 195
    kimono, 48, 404–5, 424–25
    pattern adjustment, 68, 69, 70
    raglan, 181–82, 404–5, 424–25
    set, 373, 393, 396–97
    shoulder pads, 197–200, 401–5
    tailored suit, 109
Slip stitch, 333
Slubbed fabric, 34
Smocking, 22
    pressing, 283
Snap fastenings, 323, 324
    covered, 326–27
Sponging, 125, 126–27
Standard Measurement Chart, 9
Stay stitching, 166–69
Stitches (hand)
    backstitch, 209, 221, 292
    bar tack, 420
    basting, 208–10, 221, 223, 234–35
    blanket, 317–18
    bullion, 328
    buttonhole, 317–18
    catch, 223, 224, 228, 332, 412
    chain, 394, 395
    cross, 228
    feather, 224
    glove, 221
    half backstitch, 292
    hemming, 370, 388, 412
    over-and-over, 209
    overcasting, 224, 225
    overhand, 241
    pad, 369
    prick, 292
    running hemming, 412
    saddle, 221
    seed, 221
    slant hemming, 370
    slip, 333
    swing tack, 404
    vertical hemming, 388
Stitches (machine)
    overcasting, 224, 225
    straight, 249
    stretch, 249
    zigzag, 225, 249, 252
Stitching
    ease, 245
    flat (overlap), 253, 254–56

general directions, 211–12
stay, 166–69
taut-stitching techniques, 246
topstitching, 160, 214, 215, 219–21,
    334, 336–38, 444–45
understitching, 219, 221–24
Stitch ripper, 55–56
Stretch fabrics, stitching, 249–50
Stripes, 16, 89, 101
combined vertical/horizontal
    placement, 148, 149
crosswise dominant, 148, 149
dart control, 30, 31
dominant (darker bar), 148, 149
even (balanced), 150–51
key pattern piece for, 155
matching, 42, 43, 44, 48, 137, 141,
    150, 158, 213
mirror image, 152, 153
moving in same direction around
    body, 152, 153
neck to hem direction, 152
reversible fabric, 154
right-and-left effect, 151, 152
right and wrong side difference, 152,
    153
style lines for, 47–48
unbalanced, both directions, 152, 154
uneven (unbalanced), 150–51
up-and-down effect, 151, 152
vertical dominant, center placement,
    147–48
vertical dominant, side-seam
    placement, 148
zipper installation, 304–5
Style, 94–95
Style line, fitting, 111–12
that comes to a point or a corner,
    239–40
Suede, pseudo. See Ultrasuede
Suede cloth, 33, 251, 252
Suit material, 33
Swing tack, 404
Synthetic fabrics, 10, 15, 54
pressing, 264, 265, 274
pretreatment, 128

Tailoring, 9, 13–19, 90
classic (hard, structured), 49, 50–51,
    170, 171, 174–79, 418, 430–35
contemporary (soft, unstructured), 49,
    170, 171
hair-canvas interfacing for, 187–88
Tailoring techniques, 205, 207–47
Tailor's basting, 234–35
Tailor's board, 59
Tailor's buttonhole, 316, 318–19
Tailor's chalk, 55, 160–61
Tailor's ham, 58–59, 269, 275, 333

Tailor's hem, 411–12
Tailor's linen (interfacing), 190
Tailor's square (L square), 53, 71
Tailor's tacks, 164
Taping, 365, 371
armhole, 371, 394
hemline, 369–70
lapel roll line, 368–69
seams, 365–68
shape reinforcement, 285–86
vents, 369–70
Taut-stitching technique, 246
Thigh, measuring, 8
pattern adjustment, pants, 84
Thimbles, 55
Thread, 51, 219
basting, 55
for stretch fabrics, 250
tying ends, 226, 227
for Ultrasuede, 252
Thread loop, 328
Tools, 52–60
Topstitching, 160
hand, 221
machine, 219–21
pocket, 334, 336–38
seams, 214, 215
waistband, 444–45
Trial muslin, 67, 89–114
layout chart, 91
marking, 92–93
paper pattern corrected from, 114–15
pattern layout, 92
pattern preparation for, 91
putting together, 93–94
what to look for in muslin fitting,
    98–102
Tricot, 39
Tucks, 160
Tweed, 14, 33, 35
Twill weave, 14, 32, 33
Two-faced fabrics, 35, 256–59
separated for skirt/top contrast,
    258–59
sewing instructions, 256–58

Ultrasuede (pseudo suede), 251, 252–56
buttonholes, 319
pressing, 272
Underlining, 115, 184–88, 278
buttonholes, 357–58
darts and seams, 228, 232–35
fabrics for, 186–88
garment with fullness, 236
pockets, 192, 330, 332, 357–58
pressing, 261
Understitching, 219, 221–24
Unit construction method, 356
Unlined garment, 430–35

Velvet, 35, 39, 141, 146
  panne, 146
  pressing, 263, 271
Velveteen, 35, 49, 146
Vents
  interfacing, 182, 183
  taping, 369–70
Vertical hemming stitch, 388
Vest, cut-away hem, 408, 409

Waistband, 436, 438–42
  anatomy of, 436
  attaching to garment, 442–45
  bias, 440–41
  buttonhole fastening, 442
  inside, 446–47
  interfaced, 182, 183, 192, 441–42
  length determination, 440
  pants, 436, 438–40, 442–45
  placement, 437
  stiffened, 441–42
  topstitched, 444–45
  variations on straight, 442
  width determination, 439–40
  zippered closing, 440, 445–46
Waistline, 105, 108–9
  backward tilt, 437
  dart control, 30, 31, 227
  determining, 437–38
  forward tilt, 437
  pants, 83
  pattern adjustment, 66, 67–68, 83
  standard, 438
Waist measuring, 7, 8, 22, 64, 69
Weaves
  basic, 32–34
  complex, 35
  variations, 34–35
Welt pocket, 330, 331, 341, 345–47
Welts, 342–43
  double thickness of cloth, 131, 134,
    217–19
  fake, 350–51

interfacing, 182, 183, 191
  one-piece construction, 343–44, 345
  pressing, 261, 265, 269, 282
  two-piece construction, 344–45
Welt seam, 214, 215, 236
Width changes (in pattern adjustment),
  66, 67, 71
Woman's man-tailored jacket, 174–81
Wool Bureau, Inc., 127
Woolens, 13–14, 16, 48, 54
  preshrinking, 125–27
  pressing, 59, 263, 264, 266–69, 275
Worsted fabrics, 14, 34, 48
  pressing, 263, 268–69, 275
Woven fabrics, 10, 32–40, 42
  directional (one-way), 33, 41, 46, 48
  knits (see Knits)
  nondirectional (two-way), 32–33, 41,
    46
  pressing, 262
Woven sheer canvas, 188, 191, 192

X-Acto knife, 251

Yardage, 16, 41, 46, 48
Yarn, 32, 33, 34, 35
Yokes, interfaced, 182, 183

Zigzag stitch, 225, 249, 252
Zipper installation, 261, 291–305, 351
  exposed, 296–98
  extra seam allowance, 134, 135
  fly front, 302, 303–4
  hand-stitched, 291, 292, 296, 301–3
  in seam, 293–94, 295–96, 298
  in slash, 296–97
  invisible, 299–301, 301–3
  matching cross seams, plaids, stripes,
    304–5
  placket preparation, 261, 285, 294
  standard closing, 291, 292
  waistband closing, 440, 445–46